AN
EAST INDIA COMPANY
CEMETERY

AN
EAST INDIA COMPANY
CEMETERY

Protestant Burials in Macao

Lindsay and May Ride

*Abridged and edited from their manuscripts
with additional material*

by Bernard Mellor

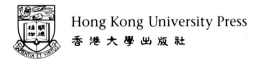

Hong Kong University Press
香港大學出版社

Hong Kong University Press
139 Pokfulam Road
Hong Kong

© Hong Kong University Press 1996

ISBN 962 209 384 1

Printed in Hong Kong by Nordica Printing Co. Ltd.

To the memory of the late
Sir Lindsay Ride

What though my body runne to dust?
Faith cleaves unto it, counting ev'ry grain
With an exact and most particular trust
Reserving all for flesh again.

— GEORGE HERBERT

The Contents

List of Illustrations

Section One

Section Two

Acknowledgments

꧁꧂

REPRODUCTION of *The Praya Grande, Macao* (about 1855) on page xii and *The Canton Factories* (early XIX century) on page 15, both by unknown Chinese artists, and of *Dent's House and Garden in Hong Kong* by Robert Fortune on page 51 is by courtesy of Martyn Gregory Gallery, London.

Reproduction of *Self-portrait* by George Chinnery (page 42), *The Red Rover* by W.J. Huggins (page 55) and *Dr and Mrs Colledge* by George Chinnery (page 175) is by courtesy of the Hongkong and Shanghai Banking Corporation Limited.

Reproduction of *The Whampoa Anchorage*, attrib. Youqua (about 1850) on page xviii, and *The Forts of Anunghoy Saluting the 'Lion' in the Bocca Tigris* by William Alexander on page 29 is by permission of the Urban Council of Hong Kong, from the collection of the Hong Kong Museum of Art.

Dr Colledge's Eye Hospital (1838) by George Chinnery (page 39): Medical History Library, Yale University.

Dr Morrison's Tomb at Macao (1838) by George Chinnery (cover and page 66): Private Collection; photograph Courtauld Institute of Art, London.

Self-portrait by George Chinnery (page 120): National Portrait Gallery, London.

Sir Andrew Ljungstedt by George Chinnery (page 143) and Captain Henry Bridges (page 191): Peabody Essex Museum, Salem, Mass.

Dr Robert Morrison by George Chinnery (page 231): Private Collection.

Copies of the portraits of Captain Christian Jpland (page 98), Captain Nathaniel Kinsman (page 195) and James Endicott (page 264) were obtained from their families by Lindsay and May Ride.

Photograph of Memorial 164 (page 261) by Solomon Bard. Photographs of Memorials 167–74 (page 266) 176–9 (page 267) and 184–8 (page 270) by S.E.T. Cusdin.

Foreword

⚜

IT IS now over 40 years since we were first introduced, independently so it happened, to a quiet corner of the Portuguese oriental city of Macao, where over 160 Protestant memorials of the last century stand screened by high walls from the gaze of all but specially interested or reverent eyes. In retrospect, we now realize what an impression these introductions must have made at the time: for in each of us, separately, they prompted a desire to learn something more than the brief stories the inscriptions told us of the men, women, and children whose frail bodies, unequal to the struggle for life in the Orient of their day, found their last resting place in this peaceful enclosure.

In 1954 it became possible for us to embark, under difficulties that challenged enthusiasm, on a series of joint studies, and transform an intermittent pastime first into a weekend hobby and then into the ambitious project of recording our findings in the form of a book, in which we might recreate the substance of the dead and the realities of the community in which they lived and died.

Here lies an infant child: what hopes of fond parents have thus been frustrated by unplanned fate? Here lies one struck low on the very threshold of expectation: what bonds have moved a friend to commemorate him so? Here is but a name: concealing what, revealing what? To decode their lithic epitaphs, to peer behind and between the lines, seeking their origins and their motives, tracing their interests and influence, logging their travels and exploits, and so to find the sum of their essence, absorbed all our free moments. They beckoned, they invited, so that as each successive inscription yielded its fuller meaning, the more we might share in their business and worries and pleasures. About many of them, of course, we found nothing to record, or far too little to slake our thirst.

For those to whom a cemetery is little more than an abode of the dead, so compelling an interest in tombs must be hard to comprehend, if not seem morbid. We were not, of course, the first, nor alone, in finding an inspiration in graveyards. Readers of Sir Walter Scott will recall how Old

Unknown Chinese artist: The Praya Grande, Macao (about 1855)

Mortality of the Waverley Novels forsook his wife and family in middle age, in order to spend the rest of his life mending gravestones in the Scottish lowlands. We and Old Mortality have much in common, except that our restorations were for the more general interest of readers; and we worked in consort and often under a tropical sun, with scrubbing brush and soap, Chinese brush and ink, beleaguered by mosquitoes and sandflies.

Cemeteries are often sited in areas of great beauty. This graveyard, together with the nearby Camoens grotto and gardens, is so pleasing a sanctuary so close to the heart of a crowded, noisy city, that its very serenity invites frequent visits. Moreover, it is small and self-contained, it spans a short period of time, and its tenants are all foreign settlers, many being associated in some respects. It thus offers a conspectus of an immigrant society living on the south China coast a century and a half ago. For anyone who still 'hath ears to hear', we wish to unravel their stories, understand their lives, break the bonds of their tombs, free them, and visit them while they live once again for us.

There are cemeteries famed for their beauty, or for artistic memorials, or for the distinction of their tenants. Some show how beauty can be created from a meagre setting, like many of those in the care of the War Graves Commission; the creators of some, helped by nature's hand and without loss of reverence, have left us places of great delight, as at Sai Wan and Stanley in Hong Kong. The days are gone when burial places were considered to be ill-omened, fit to be visited only by mourners and pilgrims; today is the day of the tourist and hiker – witness the daily stream of visitors to Westminster Abbey, St Paul's, Père La Chaise, the Campo Santo, Forest Hills, the Valley of the Kings, the Ming Tombs, Stoke Poges, Arlington, Bladon. As the

poet Edmund Blunden, himself once a member of the War Graves Commission, who came to know the Macao church and churchyard well, has written, somewhere, 'there are worse ways of occupying leisure than tours on foot through noteworthy cemeteries'.

We have no wish to give the impression that we started work with all this already formed in our minds. We had no planned object in view other than to please ourselves with a new interest. It was as we progressed that we saw we were also studying Hong Kong, as revealed in the lives and deaths of a few of the non-Portuguese foreigners who were working in Macao and in the 'factories' of Canton, in the special context of the founding of the colony. The rest of them lie interred in travellers' tombs along their trading routes, or were buried at sea, or were reunited with their families and laid to rest at home. Only in this cemetery is there, intact and accessible, a group of them large enough to be a cross-section of such a community. And this is our principal justification for publishing our findings. Memorial design, their originality, variety, inscription techniques, none of these is of an order high enough to merit that sort of preservation; so far, it has been the mixture of national sentiment, historical interest, and the sympathetic environment of a continuous community that has protected them, and even these have flagged at least twice in the last century. Even in such conditions, memorials cannot survive neglect over long periods, and so often succumb to times of racial, religious or political upheaval. The fate of all the other foreign cemeteries in China over the last half century is eloquent testimony to this.

Tombs provide material for many pages in the history of man. They are not just burial places: they and their memorials are evidence of the nature of man's progression through this world. As life passes from one generation to the next, each of them leaves its particular contribution to the records of its own transient civilization, be it in the most magnificent of mausoleums or in the humblest of graves. By forbidding oblivion to blot out our lives when we die – the dread attaching to us all – a memorial is one vehicle of our history, and to be effective it must be lasting, resist the ravages of time, be capable of relaying its message, and ensure that its subject will not fall 'to dumb forgetfulness a prey'. And so: brass and stone are preferred in the making of memorials; the secure enclosure of a church, a cemetery or a churchyard for the siting of

a tomb. There is even greater guarantee of survival in the written record, and it will be the printed page on which we shall need to rely if we are to conserve the story. It was not until we saw that it is in this burial ground that the story of Hong Kong's heritage really started, that our work broke away from the paths of chance, and we planned a line of progression and resolved to set down our findings, which we offer to all who may be interested in the people, the times, and the place.

Hong Kong 1968
L.T.R. and M.R.

EDITOR'S NOTE

I UNDERTOOK to edit the Ride manuscripts, which had assumed several shapes between 1958 and 1971, by reducing some 1,200 pages to a publishable size, a condition to which May Ride agreed with enough enthusiasm. In 1971 the Rides put most of these manuscripts to one side, the rest of them destined for a more general, introductory study of the whole range of Macao's historical monuments and buildings, which they decided should precede the completing of their account of the graveyard. This was in turn sadly interrupted, while at an early stage of its growth, by Sir Lindsay's last illness.

At the time the first version was completed, it was designed to fill two volumes. I first read it then, and urged greater brevity, hardly thinking that, after Sir Lindsay's death and three decades

later, I should myself be assisting his widow to prepare for publication an abridged fourth or fifth, but final, version.

The result, with its lighter armature and denser style, is a maquette in reverse, as it were, of their monumental sculptures, an attempt to abstract the essence, though at the expense of many of their particular sentiments.

Wherever it specially exemplifies events or personalities or enhances the general picture of life in the region, material from the original biographies has here been transferred into Section 1, and there may be a little duplication. Deleted from the manuscripts are the results of the Rides' painstaking searches into the histories of individual ships connected with the graveyard occupants and with their companies or relatives, and the still remoter results of their investigations of collateral families and ancestral links, and of the companies with which they in their turn were associated. The manuscript detail achieved in many of the paragraphs I have reluctantly had to excise is witness to their devoted labour in over 15 years' study, pursued not only in Macao and Hong Kong, but in Britain, New England, Holland, Denmark and Sweden. The result merits the perusal not only of interested readers, but of other writers engaged in other works. The Ride materials and a version of their full manuscript have been deposited in the archives of the English East India Company.

A remarkable number of those who were residing in Macao and Canton in the late 18th and the first half of the 19th centuries, or were serving afloat in trading or naval vessels in the Pearl River estuary, or were on visits to friends and relatives, recorded their own fascinated impressions of life and events in Macao and Canton. Upon their diaries, reminiscences and letters, some published, some still in manuscript and in the possession of their families or in collections, the Rides drew copiously in their drafts. Many of the writers were connected directly and indirectly with men and women buried in the Old Protestant Cemetery in Macao, and some lie buried there themselves. The second wife of Dr Robert Morrison (141), Eliza Morrison, who was in Macao from 1824 until his death in 1834, for example, has left us a lengthy compilation of his occasional writings and his life's work. Among other notable residents and visitors who left records were the Britishers William Hickey, who visited somewhat earlier than the main stream of reporters, George Bennett, a traveller, and James Molony, an East India Company supercargo.

But the most voluminous chroniclers of life in the settlements of the river estuary at the time were Americans. Robert Bennet Forbes, the brother of Thomas (163), visited Macao and Canton several times during the second and third decades of the century, and recorded some detail in his *Reminiscences*. The published journals and recollections of W.C. Hunter have offered rich pickings to historians. Popular and congenial, he was one of the few Americans to master Chinese and worked with William Henry Low, first as Chinese interpreter in Russell & Co, then as a partner from 1825 to 1844. W.H. Low was the uncle of the diarist Harriet Low, who spent four years in the middle of this period living in his Macao house, participating fully in a life of which she has left a lively record and a mass of personal detail. Gideon Nye, who Harriet Low says had a passion for curried chicken, was a business friend of Hunter and has also left interesting accounts of life among the foreigners in Canton from 1839 to 1878; he was the donor of the original stained glass – which was subsequently damaged and replaced by plain – for the east window of the church built on the burial property. The diaries of Rebecca Kinsman, in Macao with her husband Nathaniel (112) from 1839 until his death in 1847, have been preserved by her descendants. Another chronicler, Toogood Downing, was for a time a chaplain to the American East India Squadron. There is also the manuscript diary of the ship's master and merchant Sandwith Drinker (39), which covers a brief nine months after his first arrival in China in 1838, and is now in the possession of his family in Pennsylvania.

Some other material has been added that was not available to the Rides at the time they were preparing their manuscripts, chiefly from the scholarly biography of George Chinnery by Dr Patrick Conner (1993) and the diary of Lieutenant Edward Cree, R.N., who spent the years from 1840–50 in the Far East serving as ship's surgeon, reviewed his experiences in voluminous diaries, and illustrated them with some 1,700 lively aquarelles and sketches made on the spot.

I should not leave the manuscripts without also paying tribute, on behalf of the Rides, to the many correspondents who enjoyed access to unpublished material in Macao and Hong Kong, in America, Britain, Denmark, Holland, Sweden and Switzerland, and to the linguists versed in Armenian, Chinese, Dutch, Latin and Portuguese, all of them readily meeting the Rides' requests for help during the 1950s and 1960s. Reference to all these is made in Sources on page 276.

Lady Ride has asked that acknowledgement should be made of the following: Mr Y.C. Liang, whose hospitality over many years made it possible for the Rides to visit Macao whenever they wished, thus enabling them to decipher all the tomb inscriptions and bring about the restoring of the cemetery; Prof John K. Fairbank of Harvard for his encouragement and criticism; Mrs Isadore Smith of Ipswich, Mass., and Mr Francis B. Lothrop, Trustee of the Peabody Museum in Salem, Mass., who helped so much with their American researches.

The figures appearing in brackets throughout the text (and above) refer to the biographical entries in the second section, each entry there having its own serial number to accord with those in the plan of the graveyard itself on page 70.

On 28 October 1977, the late Sir Lindsay Ride's widow gathered with some relatives and a small group of friends from Macao and Hong Kong in the Old Cemetery, to witness his elder son, Dr David Ride, inter his ashes in the lower terrace, between the Hamilton tomb (72) and the commemorative tablet set into the wall. With them were Colonel Garcia Leandro, the Governor of Macao, and his wife. The Rev Cyril 'Henry' Clarke of the Hong Kong Methodist Church conducted the service, saying that the subject would surely 'rejoice to think of this link with history'. The Rt Rev Gilbert Baker, the Anglican Bishop, gave the Blessing. Lindsay Ride has his own entry (178), which gives further information on the tablet and its position on the graveyard wall.

In this study of that graveyard, the Rides identified, with Thomas Hardy,

The eternal thing in man
That heeds no call to die.

Abingdon
Oxfordshire 1994
B.M.

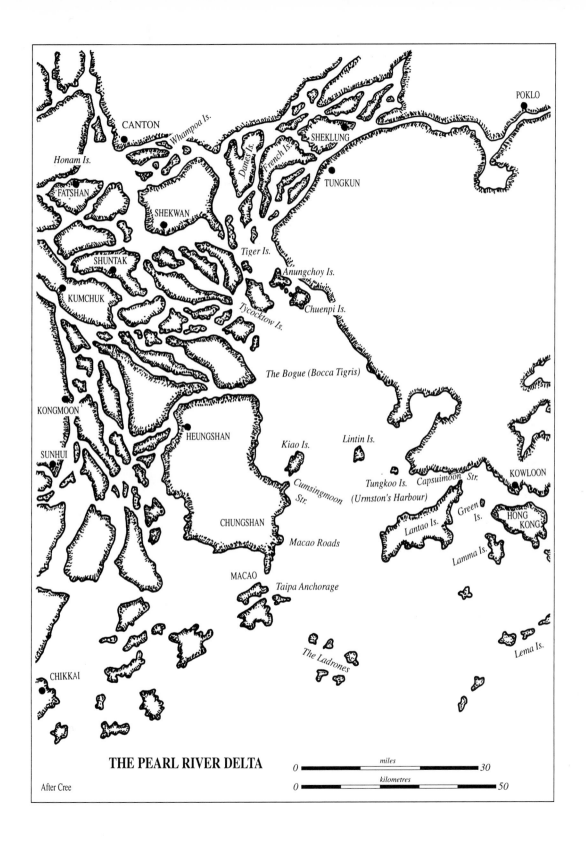

THE PEARL RIVER DELTA

After Cree

Youqua (attrib.): The Whampoa Anchorage (about 1850)

1

Macao and its Setting

MACAO

WHEN PORTUGAL'S CHINA SEA lane was established for trading in the 16th century, it terminated at Macao on the China coast to the east of the great Eurasian land mass, at the mouth of the Pearl River delta 110 kilometres downriver from Canton.

The territory is not more than 8 km square and consists of a peninsula and the two islands of Taipa and Coloane. About 5 km long and averaging 1.6 km broad, the peninsula, on which the city-proper stands, is part of the island of Heungshan, one of the large islands in the Pearl River estuary of which the principal town is Chungshan, birthplace of the revolutionary Dr Sun Yat-sen. 'The Taipa', the waters lying off the two islands and some 13 km out, offered an anchorage nearest to the city.

The name Macao derives from some obscure transliteration of Chinese characters; the name commonly given by the Cantonese, however, is O-Moon, the entrance to the cove; its official Portuguese name is Cidade do Nome de Deos na China, the City of the Name of God in China, as conferred by charter from Lisbon in 1586. The city bears witness to the blend of West with East. One accepts without surprise or demur the old-world cobbled streets, the southern European influence on its architecture, the façade of the 17th-century church of St Paul; but on the cobblestones, bare-bottomed Chinese children still play the ancient games of Cathay, behind the western walls stand ancestral tablets in a fashion ordained by custom before Europe awoke, and within a minute's walk of the church façade, a miniature Chinese village is set behind an earthen wall 1.5 metres thick, with its incense-permeated temple at the entrance gate, such as existed in China from the earliest times. In competition for the rich trade of the East, the merchants of other nations followed the Portuguese until in 1557 their favoured port of Macao ceased to be an intermittent trading post and became Europe's first permanent foothold in China. Anecdote has it that it was in recognition of the help of the Portuguese in suppressing the bands of pirates who infested the network of waterways and shores of the river delta, that the Chinese rewarded them with the territory.

POLITICS

THE PORTUGUESE RESIDENTS were permitted to set up their own political and religious institutions under the general authority of Goa, Portugal's principal settlement in India, so that Macao was able to develop its own local government, supported by its own legal system and a Portuguese governor, and in due course a bishop was appointed to meet the spiritual needs of the Portuguese residents. Being so far from both Peking and Lisbon, with little interest in them shown by the Viceroy at Goa, they were generally left in peace to pursue their lives – brief enough then and in that climate. Macao's relations with China were remarkable. By Imperial edict, all foreign trade with China was transacted through Canton; control of it was vested in the Chinese mandarins who resided at Macao, and they thus exercised great authority in the city. Until 1849, the city paid annual tribute to Peking from the customs revenues, which were collected by the local mandarins. These relations were greatly complicated with the arrival of the British, the Dutch, the French, the Danes, the Swedes, and later the Americans, all looking for a stake in the China trade. The political conditions for the Portuguese of Macao saw little fundamental change during the first three centuries of occupation: many gross changes, however, were experienced by the other nations that operated there. The East India Companies of Britain, the Netherlands, France and Sweden came and went; the territory withstood the threats of the Spanish and repulsed more than one attempt at invasion launched by the Dutch; the

British acquired Hong Kong as their entrepôt port; and the other Europeans and the Americans forsook Macao for more alluring prospects in China's coastal ports after 1842, when they were opened to foreigners through the Treaty of Nanking.

Political change came to Macao itself when in 1846 it ceased to be ruled from Goa and assumed colony status directly under Lisbon; and only three years later, when a Chinese assassinated its Governor, Lisbon refused any longer to be tied to China in mutual responsibility for the colony, compelled mandarins and other customs officials to leave, and stopped paying its tribute. In 1862, China confirmed the perpetuity of Portuguese occupation, and in 1928 revoked it, but at no time defined the border, which became an occasional matter of contention thereafter. Following the Tientsin Treaty of 1887, Macao was ceded to Portugal and became a province with an elected representative sitting in the Chamber of Deputies at Lisbon, a position never ratified by Peking. In the wake of the Portuguese Revolution of 1974, the province became in effect a Chinese territory administered by the Portuguese and, in the terms of the joint declaration of 1987, China will formally reassume sovereignty over the territory in 1999.

CLIMATE

MACAO IS JUST WITHIN the tropics and the typhoon zone, with a monsoon climate. 'Typhoon' is the term employed in the East for cyclonic storms which can reach great violence when over the sea. The southwest monsoon brings humidity and heat between May and October, when most of the annual rain falls; cool and dry conditions follow a steady northwest wind from October. The northeast monsoons are at their height around January, blowing down the China coast and making navigation in the China Seas difficult and perilous. The northwest monsoons are the major winds of July and tend to blow across the China Seas. The southeast trade winds blow in a constant course from the Dutch East Indies across the Indian Ocean towards the African coast. The trades blow seasonally and in a constant course, and are as often as not called monsoons. The term 'trade' ('trend') was perhaps more frequently applied to the winds in the Indian Ocean.

While the ships of Western traders were still under sail, the prevailing winds dominated the pattern of their sailings: in summer, out eastwards; in winter, off home. Incapable of beating up the South China Sea against a northeast monsoon, sailing ships that failed to arrive in China before the change of the monsoon in September-October were in trouble.

THE SEASON

THE CHINESE AUTHORITIES permitted foreign traders to stay in Canton only for the length of a defined trading 'season', while their ships were either loading or off-loading at Whampoa, its deepwater port. The season was a period defined by the monsoon months and by the times at which fresh tea crops arrived from the interior of China. For the rest of the year the merchants joined their families in Macao: the summers they spent together were invariably humid and baking hot. The season became fixed as the seven or so cooler months following September. As larger, swifter, and more powerful ships entered the trade, ships that could take greater risks and make some headway against monsoon winds, the pattern of movement slowly changed and the annual departure moved towards the end of winter, just before the wind turned; but the seasonal exclusion from Canton persisted, the Chinese officials assuming that all foreigners left for home as soon as the season was over. As trade burgeoned, the need became increasingly urgent for a permanent, all-year depôt.

WHAMPOA

THE FREIGHT ANCHORAGE was at Whampoa, an island some 19 km downriver east of Canton, lying in a branch of the river running north of Honam Island.

Its eastern end was the farthest point upstream which foreign sailing ships of the early 19th century could reach. Danes Island lay a little downstream to the east, French Island to the south. The part of the river adjacent to these islands formed the deepwater harbour of the Whampoa Anchorage, where merchantmen discharged cargoes into and loaded them from lighters, to be carried to and from the European factories at Canton. Once their ships had discharged and reloaded, merchants were no more welcome at Whampoa than they were at Canton.

At the island of Chuenpi, the estuary narrows from about 40 km to about 2.5 km, forming an inner entrance known as the Bogue, or Bocca Tigris; at Tiger Island the channel widens out to 5 or 6 km, 'but there are so many large islands that one cannot judge to a mile or two. The banks are low and muddy, intersected by streams and canals, planted with paddy, mountains in the distance. On two hills a pagoda. Numbers of fishing-boats and junks in the sluggish streams, the navigation impeded by numerous sandbanks, and the water very muddy',[1] so muddy as to form mud-banks, on which ships ran aground from time to time.

Though Macao was safer than Whampoa for the handling of opium, the Portuguese customs charged exceptionally high duty upon chests of opium as they entered. At Whampoa there was none, since after 1729 opium had become a contraband commodity. The 'country' traders arriving from India took their cargoes of opium direct to Lintin Island, where it was off-loaded and sent to Whampoa by river-boat to be stored, while awaiting buyers, in the dismasted ships' hulks that lay moored under heavy guard in midstream. In the wake of problems at Canton in 1821, all the chests of opium in Macao and at Whampoa, together with the storeships, were removed to Lintin Island and the outer anchorages. On occasion, there were opium storeships lying off Macao: one such, anchored in the Taipa, was the barque *Calcutta*, whose boats brought the opium from ships in the Macao Roads during the years from 1843–6, and which was under the command of Captain Thomas Osborne until he died in Macao, where he is buried in the cemetery (69) of which this book is a study.

In the height of the seasons of the 1820s and 1830s, there were often as many as 100 sailing vessels lying at Whampoa for three months or more, awaiting their cargoes of tea. As each ship would have between 50 and 150 people on board, together they formed a large concentration of souls and the death rate was high: scores of foreigners were laid to rest each year in hillside plots on Danes and French Islands, and some of their graves can be seen on the hillock in the left foreground of the painting of the anchorage on page xviii.

LINTIN AND THE OUTER ANCHORAGES

LINTIN ISLAND LIES ON THE eastern side of the Pearl River estuary about 32 km northeast of Macao and 32 km west-northwest of Hong Kong. The shipping which collectively gathered at Lintin was known to traders as the 'Lintin Fleet', and comprised the storeships owned by the opium-trading companies and anchored at one or other of the outer anchorages, including those at permanent anchor at Lintin; the ships of all nationalities bringing opium from Turkey and India; and the fast 'crabs' and schooners that distributed opium among the myriads of waterways between the river delta islands and to the smaller ports along the China coast.

From the later days of the Company to the ceding of Hong Kong, those engaged in the opium trade lived more or less permanently on board storeships, from which opium transactions took place after 1821. The lists of foreigners living at Lintin, in which sea-going commanders did not generally appear, show that Captain Crockett, who now lies buried in the cemetery (87), was then living aboard the opium storeship *Jane* in 1836, and that Captain Thomas Rees, whose wife (109) and brother (127) are also buried in Macao, was aboard the storeship *Austen* from 1836 to 1838.[2] In the estuary there were two alternative safe anchorages, and their names, Cumsingmoon and Capsuimoon, were often transfused. Cumsingmoon, the small strait (passage) due west from the Lintin anchorage, between Kiao Island and the large island of Heungshan, was within convenient distance of Macao for shipping both inward and outward bound, and was the choice of most of the ships in the fleet – those which were moveable and not just hulks – as shelter in which to ride out the stormy summer months of the southwest monsoons. When T.W. Riddles died in August 1856 – he too is buried in the Old Cemetery (63) – his death took place on board his ship, the *Cama Family*, while anchored at Cumsingmoon. Capsuimoon, the name of the strait between the northeast tip of Lantau Island and the small neighbouring island of Ma Wan, was the exit from Hong Kong harbour for shipping bound for Canton and other ports in the estuary. Due east of Lintin Island and off the mainland and the western limit of what is now known in Hong Kong as the New Territories, lies Tung Koo Island, which sheltered a small mainland bay, at that time known as 'Urmston's Harbour'.[3]

In summer, the waters of the estuary were often treacherous. One typhoon that hit the Pearl River delta area was so severe that the *Governor Findlay*, the British brig *Watkins*, the naval sloop *Raleigh* and the Portuguese brig *Santa Anna* were dismasted, and 11 other vessels, British, Danish, Portuguese, Spanish, American, barques, cargo, passenger boats, were all forced to cut away their masts or were driven ashore or foundered at anchor, with great loss of life and armament. Even in the best of weather, sudden squalls were the bane of the small boats that plied between anchorages. One claimed the lives of an entire crew of nine, as they were returning one February night in the ship's cutter, from Urmston's Harbour to the East India Company's ship *Atlas* riding at anchor off Lintin. The body of one was recovered and taken to Macao for burial (51); nothing else was found but 'a few hats of the crew, and the stretchers of the boat'.[4]

Despite the trials imposed by nature on the trading approaches to the Pearl River, and despite the spasmodic snags laid by the Canton mandarins for foreign traders, Canton was perhaps the most favoured of the world's trading locations. Though 160 km from the China Sea, it felt the pulse of the tides, as they flowed in and out around the maze of islands in the delta. There, the three-masters from Europe and America linked up with the coastal junks, with the sampans and other craft small enough to navigate the network of tributaries and narrow canals that wound their ways into the hinterland, and as ocean-borne freight collected the goods that had been born by man and pack-horse from fields and factories in the distant heart of China.

1 Cree p 75
2 ACK for 1836, 1837 and 1838
3 FC&HKG of 23/8/1856; Canton R of 15/7/1833. The harbour was named after J.B. Urmston, from 1819 to 1826 the Company's China chief: his infant son, George Urmston, is buried in Macao (115). It was in this harbour that the main body of the fleet assembled under Admiral Elliot, before sailing north to occupy Chusan in July 1840 and starting the series of actions that led to the cession of Hong Kong to Britain.
4 Canton R of 18/8/1835 and 3/2/1830

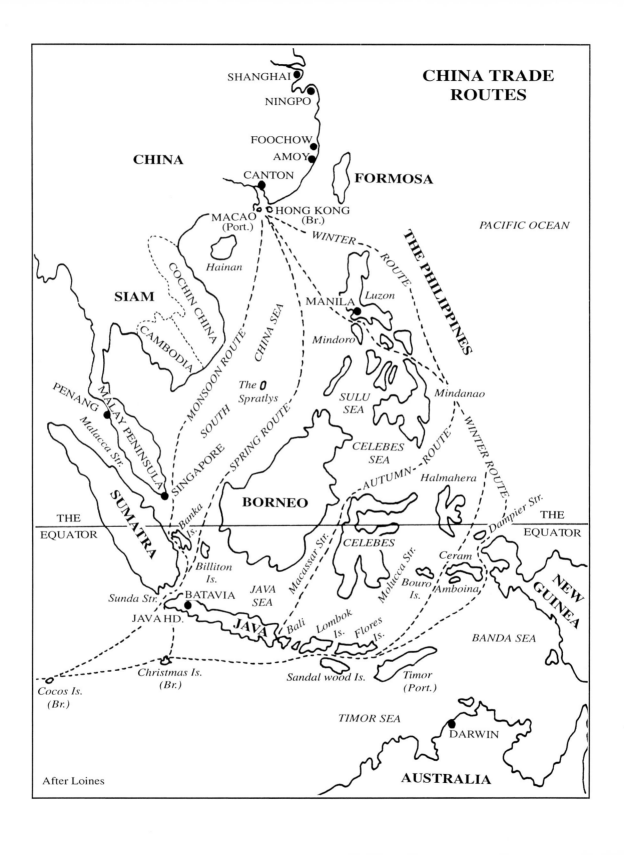

2
The Company and the China Trade

～❦～

THE COMPANY

ON THE LAST DAY OF December 1599, Queen Elizabeth I granted the Royal Charter that conferred on 'the Governor and Company of Merchants of London, trading to the East Indies' a monopoly of the English trade to the East for the next 15 years. Much the same provisions governed this trade until the Company's dissolution in 1874, as revised in their detail – to reflect changed conditions, improvements in commercial efficiency, nautical science and naval architecture – and renewed from time to time when the currency of each succeeding charter expired. In 1709, the Company amalgamated with a rival group, which had been chartered in 1698 by William III. This union took the title 'The Honourable East India Company', which was shortened for general use to 'the Honourable Company' and more often still to 'John Company', until it ceased its operations in 1834, after its monopoly of British trade with China was discontinued. Both the original company and its successor are now regularly referred to together as the 'English East India Company' (and in these pages simply as the Company).

The early interest of the joint Company was in the Indian Ocean, where it settled in its three 'Presidencies' of Bengal, Madras and Bombay. Later, its ships sailing east to compete with those of Portugal and the Netherlands, it opened new trading posts in the East Indies and Malaya, in Japan and China. During the Company's first forays in China, trading ports were founded in Amoy, Canton, Chusan, Macao, Formosa (Taiwan) and Tonkin; by the end of the 17th century, however, it had been forced to abandon all but those in Canton and Macao. The Company was thus governing vast areas of India, at the time when its trade with countries further east was profiting from a rapid growth. For their administration, it kept a civil service; for the protection of its trade and its shipping routes, it raised military forces and organized them into three armies, one in each of the presidencies. The infantry in each army comprised European infantry, local infantry battalions and native infantry. The officers of the native infantry were British – Captain Daniel Duff (138) was serving in the 37th Madras Regiment when it formed part of General Gough's expeditionary force sent to China in 1840, together with the 2nd, the 6th, the 14th, the 36th and the 41st; and Major Mark Cooper (22) was in the 12th Madras at Hong Kong in 1856. The Company also enjoyed the services of the Royal Navy. Without the dues that accrued to it from the China trade, it could not have kept its dominant status in India.

The Imperial reforms of 1760 embodied the Imperial desire to distance China's trade with Europe as far from the Throne as possible, by concentrating the whole of its maritime commerce in Canton, the most southerly of the Chinese ports and the furthest from the court. The European 'barbarians' would much have preferred to organize the trade through Ningpo and the Yangtzekiang, a clearer and speedier route to the middle of the 'Middle Kingdom'. As it was, the increasing wealth that flowed from the China trade flowed only through Canton, the market city, and Macao came to assume a commanding position as the out-station in China for Europe. For the next 80 years, all business was transacted in the Pearl River estuary between these two cities: it was not until a free trading port was established at Hong Kong that Macao moved into an inferior position.

The year in which America had embarked upon the Canton trade, Pitt's India Act formed a Commission for the Affairs of India, which was to take control of the Company's possessions there, on behalf of the Crown. The Company lacked a well-established base from which it might conduct its commercial ventures in safe, stable and reliable conditions, close to its export sources in China, and freed from the petty restrictions it met in Canton.

It was chiefly under the Company's pressure that in 1793 the British Government sent out the famous legation headed by Lord Macartney, in a fruitless attempt to secure such a base.

SUPERCARGOES
THE AFFAIRS OF THE COMPANY were controlled by a Court of Directors in India. In China they were controlled from 1773 by a 'Select Committee of Supercargoes', the 'Select' as it was then known, comprising a president or chairman – called the 'chief' by other members of the Company – and three or four other supercargoes, its official trading agents. Some other senior members of the staff who were also given the rank of supercargo but were not members of the Select, held a status defined as 'below the Select Committee'. The supercargoes were subtended by writers, translators, physicians and others with technical expertise. They all lived in Macao, moving to Canton for the trading season and leaving their families behind. Many Company officers and members of their families lie buried in the cemetery, some of them senior supercargoes: J.B. Urmston (father of the infant 115), W.H.C. Plowden (see 161), and Sir William Fraser (62) were all chiefs; Thomas Pattle (42) and James Robarts (157) were supercargoes second in seniority, as was James Daniell (see 97), who studied Chinese with Robert Morrison (141); he had just reached that position in 1834 when the Company's affairs were being closed down. Sir John Davis, who arrived back as Hong Kong's third governor in 1844, had been second supercargo in 1831, and was chief for a time the next year.

The supercargoes who were not appointed to the Select enjoyed some particular compensation, as they were permitted to engage in agency business on their own account, in a form of private trading as the agents of merchants in India exporting goods to China. The most lucrative commodity was opium, which the Company would not allow on its own ships. Pattle believed that any connection with the opium trade would bring 'discredit on the Company, which could not dis-sever itself from the actions of its own servants'. While he was still a junior supercargo in 1806, James Robarts (157) had set up Baring & Co, a private agency which dealt in cotton and opium. London withdrew permission in 1809, and there was much protest from such juniors, whose commission suffered badly.[1]

In addition to the Company's employees, there were those who were trading under Company licence, and the growing group of free-traders possessing neither licence nor position. Many had families at Macao and joined them there at the end of each trading season. Together, they formed a large British community.

EAST INDIAMEN
THE SHIPS EMPLOYED BY THE Company to operate the monopoly were known collectively as 'East Indiamen' or 'Indiamen'. Those few which were built for the Company according to its specifications sailed on trading voyages of which the number was carefully controlled, and bore names prefixed either by HEICS or by HCS; most were chartered voyage by voyage from the trade, and these bore a prefix either HEICCS or HCCS.

In the early 1700s, all East Indiamen were under 500 tons, some of them even below 200. To avoid a new requirement that vessels of 500 tons and over should carry a chaplain, all the ships built by the Company between 1748 and 1772 were registered as one ton less than this maximum. It was generally believed in England at the time that slack morals and irreligious practices were even more rife afloat than they were on shore, and a ship's chaplain would counteract these evil influences. Each of the smaller ships carried in its complement of seven, a captain, his four mates, a purser, and a surgeon, but no chaplain. When from 1772, the progress of trading demanded larger ships, the Company had larger ships designed and added chaplains to the crews.

Another, quite different, barrier to progress was the custom of building 'hereditary bottoms': the owner of a ship going out of service had the right to supply its replacement, which favoured shipowner and shipbuilder above trading needs. The amount of tea being consumed annually in Europe was rising rapidly, and larger ships were needed. An increase in the capacity of a trading ship by one half would double the load of tea it could carry, and larger ships could be designed for longer life and more trips. Rapid improvement and variations in design and size followed the introduction in 1796 of a rule requiring that tenders should be called when a Company ship was to be built. To be the speediest to arrive at Canton, to off-load and re-load, set sail again, and be first home with a cargo of tea was among the American captains in particular a much sought-after accolade. 'Instances occurred last season', reported one observer in 1800, of several of the American ships 'disposing of their imports, purchasing their export cargoes, and leaving the port in 20 and 25 days from the date of their arrival'. The Whampoa anchorage was already by 1787 host to 33 country and 29 Company ships, and when Jardine's fast clippers came into service the number of journeys from India with cargoes of opium doubled.

While in the early 1700s, the smaller ships

might undertake no more than four voyages to the Orient before being replaced, by the end of the century the number had increased to six, in 1803 to eight, and in 1810 the life of a ship would be extended for as long as it was judged still fit for service, by act of Parliament; the Company was building ships of up to 1,500 tons until the fleet was sold when the Company's operations were closed down after 1833.[2]

CARGOES AND SYCEE

REGULAR BRITISH TRADE WITH China started in 1700, silk being the principal export, with tea and porcelain as secondary goods. As European silks later replaced Chinese to some extent, and the European porcelain industry began supplanting imports from China, tea assumed by far the greatest importance. To satisfy what fast became a voracious demand for tea as its popularity grew in 18th-century Europe, and later in America, and because special climatic conditions were needed for the plant, the tea plantations of China kept expanding, and so often at the expense of the cotton fields that, by the 19th century, cotton was being imported from India.

The main licit import trade apart from that in Indian cotton was in sandalwood, pepper, tin, and increasingly woollen goods. Some imports were unusual – when in 1857 Captain William Sutherland sailed with his wife Mary Clark (15) from Calcutta on the *Hero*, it was with a load of Indian rice for consumption at Canton.

A consignment of goods was usually advertized as being available on application either to the consignee or to the captain of the ship, and when a consignment changed hands, uncoined silver was used as the instrument of exchange. It seemed extraordinary in the West that silver was preferred to gold; until the last decade of the 18th century gold was at such a discount against silver that a market in the exchange of the precious metals was bringing very high profits. Of the silver mined in America, a large part fuelled the China trade.

The silver was stored in the safe basements at Canton and in Macao, known in pidgin as 'godowns' from a Malay word: it took the form of bullion in ingots, called *sycee*, valued according to weight and purity. Exporting it to India as a trading commodity was itself a highly profitable business. Thomas Pattle (42) had a special responsibility in the Company for the trade, and his share of commissions for 1812, free of all deductions, was well over $7,124.[3] The sheer quantity of the *sycee* that flowed out of China as trade grew brought a severe imperial proscription against its export. The country trader was to some extent protected from the embargo, as he was able to obtain Company promissory notes for settlement in London. The embargo did not, of course, apply to Macao, from where Pattle worked almost exclusively and continued to draw his commissions throughout his last few years of service.

THE COUNTRY TRADE

ALMOST THE ENTIRE CHINA trade fell to the British during the 18th century, mostly in produce from India and the East Indies against the much-prized tea, which came to be the bulk of the Company's exports from China. The Select had devised a licensing system for trade in other goods, permitting private, non-Company ships – the 'countrymen' – to carry merchandise in pursuit of what was known as the 'country trade', but restricting them to trade between India and parts east, and to ships operated by British firms.

The Company exercised some further control over those holding its licences. A licence to trade was issued either at Canton by the Select or, on a higher level, by the Company from Calcutta. A licence issued at Calcutta could not be revoked at Canton. With this powerful tool at hand, the Select had the authority to issue orders to country traders in China and to discipline all British merchants – country traders as well as their own – when they failed to obey the regulations formulated by the Company in Calcutta. Its relations with the country trade were not without friction, and on occasion the Select had to threaten to refuse a licence, or to withdraw one already issued. On one such occasion, it revoked a licence issued at Canton to one of Jardine's ships; in the meantime the firm had secured three other licences, but direct from the Company in India. The barque *Lady Hayes* carried them from Calcutta, one licence for herself, and two for other vessels: one of them was for the ship whose licence had been revoked at Canton, which was thus able to continue trading in defiance of the Select. Captain Andrew Paterson was in command of the *Lady Hayes* when he died in 1842, and Andrew Forrest was its second officer when he died the following year: both lie buried in the Old Cemetery (82 and 123). Captain Donald Mackenzie, also buried there (86), was another commander of a licensed countryman.

The steady growth of British presence in India contributed to the rise in the numbers of an unlicensed group of private British traders operating under Portuguese company names and based in Portuguese India or Macao. The confusion of trading nationalities caused greater problems for the Canton mandarins than might have been expected, given a commercial scene so widely dominated by the country traders who flew the British flag.

PRIVILEGE TRADING

BY COMPANY RULE, SHIPS' personnel were allowed to carry some cargo for private and personal trade, limited by an agreed scale that reflected their status and rank. The allowance was known as 'privilege tonnage', which was rigidly controlled and might not be transferred, and the profit expected was in the region of 50 per cent.

The personnel of the other ships might sometimes be entrusted, by private persons at the port of departure, with sums of 'personal venture' money, with which to import produce from abroad. At the early age of 20, Nathaniel Kinsman (112) arranged this with an officer on a ship trading with the West Indies. At even earlier ages, the Forbes brothers (see 163) together invested a large cash gift as venture money, to be used in the export of silks from China. Mrs Kinsman was shown articles from Philadelphia by another American, Susanna Drinker (see 39), in her Macao house in 1845, with a view to selling them: there were 'some beautiful crewel socks – chair tidies, worsted lamp mats, etc. which she brought out as an adventure for an old lady who depends on her knitting for a livelihood'.[4]

OPIUM

INCLUDED IN THE COMPANY'S Indian revenues were the proceeds from auctioning the crop of Bengal opium, all of which it bought and disposed of in Calcutta. The country traders and the free-traders were major buyers, and Bengal opium quickly found a place in most of the cargoes being loaded in Calcutta and bound for Canton. In 1729 the Emperor Yung Cheng proscribed its import, but his mandarins failed to execute the order, and the trade continued as contraband. Opium soon became not only a major commodity on the illicit market but a contender against *sycee* as the main instrument of trading exchange. Despite the huge profits to be pocketed, the Company forbade its ships to carry the drug and forbore from trading in it; but it did little to discourage its officers from trading in it personally before 1809, when it issued express prohibitions. The Americans were not officially denied the trade in opium until 1858. Since ships with cargoes that included opium were denied anchorage at Whampoa, they could follow neither the normal procedure nor the normal route to Canton.

PROCEDURE

FOREIGNERS WERE PERMITTED to reside at Canton only during the season, approximately from October to March, between dates largely determined each year by the arrivals and departures of ships, and depending on the winds.

When a ship arrived in Macao from the high seas, its agent had to ask one of the Chinese 'Hong' merchants to apply to the Canton officials for permits, so that it might move up to the Whampoa anchorages, the only place on the Pearl River where the on-loading and off-loading of merchandise for and from Canton might take place. When in due course the Chinese customs officer at Macao was in possession of an authority from Canton, he was able to issue the first permit ('chop') and the ship could leave, but only for the first leg of the short journey, as far as the Bogue. Once there, a second permit ('grand chop') was issued allowing the vessel to proceed to Whampoa. To the British who had to deal with them, the Chinese customs posts in Macao and Canton and elsewhere were irreverently known as 'chophouses'. The officials of the Canton chophouse might refuse either of the permits or revoke one or other of them, with or without assigning a reason.

Once a cargo of legitimate merchandise had arrived at Whampoa, it was loaded into lighters and taken to Canton. When cargo destined for export had been purchased and cleared at Canton and freighted by lighter to Whampoa for the outward voyage, the ship left. There were other arrangements for the import of contraband, through transshipment made at Lintin Island, a remote enough excuse for any Chinese official who was prepared to close an eye to an illicit transaction.

TRADERS AND THE MANDARINS

THE CHINESE COMMISSIONER of customs at Canton (the 'Hoppo' to the foreigners) held his appointment direct from the Emperor. In 1720, for the closer control of his trading monopoly, he in his turn had appointed a small group of merchants, varied in size from time to time, as members of a body known as the Co-Hong (a 'Super-Company'). The wealthier of its members had the privilege of purchasing the right to wear the insignia of a mandarin, on a sliding scale of rank in the mandarinate. It was a group whose chief object was to compete with the foreign traders as a sort of 'Anti-Indies Company': some of them were business wizards, and the pickings for astute members could be enormous. Hunter states that Houqua (Wu Bingjian), its head member, whose family owned the Bohea (Wu-E) tea estates, and of whom there is a notable portrait said to be by Chinnery (40), assessed his wealth in 1834 as in the region of 26 million dollars, which must have gained him a place among the world's richest men. A ship named the *Houqua* was plying for the Shanghai arm of Wolcott, Bates & Co in 1840, and this is perhaps a measure of the regard in which he was held by traders. Almost all his income accrued from dealings with the Company, and to maintain the flow into his pocket, he employed foreigners whenever it fitted the situation. Forbes relates that at times when he failed to sell his tea or silk in Canton at the price he sought, he would charter a ship and send a cargo to Europe or America, commissioning a junior member of a foreign company to sign the invoices and other necessary papers, and otherwise complete the whole transaction for him. Not all the members of the Co-Hong were so capable, and some of the less astute piled up such massive debts that, under the pressure of their debtors, the country traders, the group was disbanded in 1771 and not revived until 22 years later, when its membership was increased to 13. Harriet Low said in 1829 that she had dined in Macao with two of its senior members, Mouqua and Tinqua.[5]

The Chinese merchants who were not members of the Co-Hong were officially excluded from all trading with foreigners. The exclusion was not wholly effective. Provided they succeeded in dodging the law preventing non-Portuguese from becoming owners of property in Macao, many canny Chinese dealers set up house and traded unlawfully – and successfully enough – from there.

It was not only the merchants who found a clandestine profit in foreign trade. Wherever they saw the opportunity, the officials sought to enrich themselves from the activities of the traders, including the shipping of opium and other contraband goods. Despite the prohibitions, smuggling between the ships anchored in Whampoa and the warehouses sited on the bank of the river opposite the foreign factories was rarely interrupted, on the general understanding that blind-eye fees changed hands.

It had also become a tradition that the mandarins, both the officials who played a part in the complicated control of foreign trade, and those who were privileged to wear mandarin insignia, were given Chinese Lunar New Year presents, with the simple object of easing the complications. The most acceptable of these gifts were the mechanical toys that played a tune, generally made in Switzerland and exported through a firm in England belonging to James Cox and his son John Henry. The son sailed to Canton in 1782 and formed a partnership with Daniel Beale (see 159 and 160), with the purpose of selling off accumulated stocks of toys. The five Bovet brothers, the wife of one of whom, Margaret (105), is also in the cemetery, were engaged in selling Swiss watches and musical boxes in China for some 40 years; Fritz, a fiddle-playing member of that family, studied Chinese popular music so that he might arrange for its melodies to be incorporated into musical boxes for export from Europe.

Whenever the mandarins faced a shortfall of these gifts, they were ready to reinstate rarely used trading regulations, at least until such time as the shortfall was in some way made good. Already in 1810, the Select considered that the importing of gifts for officials constituted a crippling drain on what they dubbed the 'consoo fund', a form of consolidated trading-profits reserve through which the mandarins could squeeze merchants without seeming to do so. By 1814 they were seeking means to put an end to the practice.[6]

THE FOREIGN FACTORIES AT CANTON

ALONG THE RIVER AND BEYOND the city walls was a range of buildings called the 'Factories'

('Hongs', the trading companies or their premises) controlled by the Super-Company, the Co-Hong. Each factory was leased to a trading nation, whose nationals might live and trade from there during the season. The factories were easily put to flame. There was a great conflagration in 1822; in the hostilities of May 1841, the Dutch and English hongs were looted and destroyed; later the Danish, French and Spanish factories were burnt to the ground; and Viceroy Yeh had all of them, including their replacements, fired in the Second Opium War, after which they were not rebuilt.

The factories were far better organized than were the independent traders, and some of them served also as consular posts. When one assumed the status of a consulate it offered, to those who were designated consular officials, the chance of continuing to trade from Canton throughout the off-season months, despite the Chinese prohibitions. In addition to the normal port and customs dues, the charge levied against the lease of a factory was a share of its trading profits, though it is unlikely that all the profit from consular off-season commerce, which often included trading in opium, figured in the calculation.

Hunter has left a detailed and interesting description of the accommodation in and around the row of hongs. There were no banks in Canton, and each factory contained a specially constructed treasury of massive granite entered through a heavy iron door; the rest of the ground floor was used for business and storage, and outside the treasury was a paved area with a table for weighing the money that changed hands in cash settlements. Rooms on the two upper floors mostly had deep verandahs; on the first floor were the dining and sitting rooms, on the top floor the bedrooms. Between the factories in the middle of the row and the river, a distance of about 90 metres, lay an open space – 'the Chinese were prohibited from loitering about this Square, as it was called.' At one corner stood a guardhouse with 10 or a dozen Chinese soldiers, acting as police to prevent disturbance or annoyance to the 'foreign devils'. On the edge of the river were chophouses, or branches of the Hoppo's department, whose duty it was to prevent smuggling, but whose interest it was to aid and facilitate the shipping off of silks (or the landing of cloths) at a considerable reduction from the Imperial tariff.[7]

That the Company itself was usually referred to as 'the Factory', much as if there were no others, was a measure of the Company's dominance of the Canton market.

It seemed not to matter much in which of the hongs a foreigner became a resident; for example, the address in Canton of the British Richard Turner (93) was No. 2, Spanish Hong, and the Dutch Factory was the address of the Swiss Bovet brothers.[8]

THE DUTCH

THE DUTCH FACTORY in Canton belonged to the Dutch East India Company, a company chartered in 1602 to recognize and establish officially the presence of Dutch trade in the Far East. The Dutch, successful in India and in what later became the Dutch East Indies, had found access to the China trade difficult. Despite the English Company's efforts to impede them at every possible turn, the first Dutch ships were allowed to trade from Canton in 1729, and by 1775 they were shifting the third largest share of the market, as calculated by the shipping then at anchor in the river, where there were 24 English, five French, four Dutch, three Danish and two Swedish ships.

Unknown Chinese artist: The Canton Factories (early 19th century)

Two of the officials from the Dutch factory lie in the Old Cemetery at Macao. J.H. Rabinel (43) was in 1787 a member of its trade council and promoted to the rank of supercargo five years later. He and Bernardus Zeeman (114), along with J.H. Bletterman, were responsible for organizing the visit of a Dutch embassy to the Imperial court in 1794–5. By the time Zeeman died, the picture was vastly altered: in 1821 when British trade was suspended, shipping off Canton was almost entirely either British (nearly 50,000 tons) or American (15,000 tons); only one Austrian ship and one Dutch came east, neither passing Macao.[9]

THE AMERICANS

THE AMERICAN DECLARATION of independence of 1776 brought changes to the mix in the foreign population of Macao. The immediate cause of the war that preceded it was a measure designed to provide relief for the Company. The government reduced the impost the Company paid on tea it imported into Britain, but offered no parallel relief on tea imported into the colonies. Once freed of imperial shackles, the Americans quickly found their own foothold in the tea trade, the first American trading ship, the *Empress of China*, reaching Macao by August 1784. The same reduction took the profit out of smuggling tea into Britain: the Swedes and the Danes, who were making a profitable trade by smuggling it into Britain, were confronted by so drastic a contraction of demand from their customers that they disbanded their national East India companies. As the Scandinavian tea trade petered out, the Americans came to outnumber all but the British in the China trade; this is reflected in the population of the Old Cemetery.

Much in the same way that centuries earlier the Pope had partitioned the world between the Spanish and the Portuguese missions, the Boston and Salem trading houses demarcated their overseas zones and trading routes, so that ships carrying Boston goods sailed in the wake of Magellan round The Horn, while those with Salem freight followed the route taken by Vasco da Gama round the Cape of Good Hope. For the China trade, the zones overlapped in the Pearl River delta, and to a lesser extent in the Manila and Java areas, where ships from both Boston and Salem mingled. As American traders appeared from other ports, from New York, Philadelphia, Baltimore, the zoning arrangement lost its purpose and fell into disuse.

American traders scoured the world seeking replacements for their dwindling supplies of furs, sealskins and ginseng, for the purchase of tea and silk at Canton, and finding them in the islands of the south Pacific, in the shape of sandalwood, béche-de-mer and rattan; Benjamin Leach of Salem, who lies buried in the Old Cemetery (52), served on the *Active*, the American ship that was the first to import sandalwood to Canton from the Fijis.[10]

To secure enough tea to meet the heavy demand, the Americans freighted American cotton and Turkish opium to China, in direct competition with the traders of other nations who were importing cotton and opium from other sources. To give their trad-ing procedures a measure of independence, they took over one of the vacated Canton factories; by 1807, little shipping could be seen on the Pearl River which was not British or American, and over the next decade the number of British and American sailors at Whampoa during the season increased to well over two thousand, with an annual death rate said to be near a hundred.

RESTRICTION AND EVASION

WESTERN TRADERS, OF whatever cast and despite the benefits that accrued to the Chinese from the industrious pursuit of trade, were not more than tolerated. Westerners generally were seen as a barbarous people, and the practice of commerce in particular carried scant esteem in China. It was to be expected that limits should be placed round their commercial activities. On trading from Canton the mandarins imposed eight or more conditions, frequently revised, which seemed designed specifically to discourage commerce. The city was placed out of bounds, all movement outside the factories was restricted and residence in them permitted only during the months when trading might take place; movement in the city was permitted on set days in each month of permitted residence, provided that the wanderer was accompanied by an approved interpreter, but on foot and never in a sedan chair. For each factory, a maximum number of Chinese servants was determined. Foreign women were denied access to the factory area and might not join their husbands. There were onerous rules that set out a lengthy and indirect manner of communicating with the local mandarins, and learning the Chinese language was forbidden. Foreign warships were prevented from sailing upriver beyond the Bogue. The procedure for other ships was arduous. The mandarins refused to treat with traders other than the members of the Co-Hong and the chairman of the Company's Select Committee. They regarded the chairman as officially responsible for the actions not only of the British, but of all foreigners while they were on Chinese territory and in Chinese waters: this was usually distasteful to other nationals and often embarrassing to the British. When the Company took a census of the foreign residents of Canton, such as that of 28 January 1831, it took it in order to have at hand some record of those – at least, those residing in the factories – for whom it was expected to assume responsibility.[11]

John Davis explained the nature of some of the restrictions to Harriet Low in 1831, 'of the absurd edicts' issued for the guidance of foreigners living in the factories, who were 'not permitted to go out, nor are they permitted to have Chinese servants, except one coolie at the gate, to see that no improper person goes in. They may have two coolies to work and one to bring water, but they must not be the companions of foreigners, who are crafty and deceitful, and not to be trusted, with many other like absurdities ... which it is quite impossible can ever be carried into effect'.[12] The conditions and edicts were neither always nor consistently enforced and the Company had devised its own systems, so that life in Canton might be regular and tolerable. But the Chinese and foreign merchants achieved a generally congenial working rapport, in spite of the problems, with profitable commerce their common aim.

The Chinese merchants were not alone in using tactics of evasion. The British were always under particular pressure from the Select Committee to abide by the rules, and to leave Canton for the off-season. But the severity and unpredictability of the restrictions encouraged some of them to take the risk of staying throughout the summer: the partners of some firms continued to deal – even in opium – under the cover of performing consular duties, to which they might succeed when taking over another company or when joined by someone already entrusted with them.

Some, of course, really were consular officials, such as M.J. Senn van Basel (see 99), who performed duties at Canton from 1830 to 1847. Others were not. In 1796 there were known to be five unofficial foreign residents in Canton, including the opium dealers Thomas Beale (159) and his elder brother, Daniel senior. Daniel was then consul for Prussia, and was succeeded in that office by Thomas from 1798 until about 1814; after he retired from his partnership in Beale, Magniac & Co., Thomas in his turn handed his Prussian duties over to Charles Magniac, still as cover for his other duties in connection with opium, and he relinquished the post when his business passed to Dr William Jardine in 1825. Jardine became Danish consul in succession to his junior, James Matheson, when their firms merged in 1827. To avoid the annual expulsion from Canton, the two British merchants Christopher Fearon, whose wife Elizabeth lies buried in the Old Cemetery (84), and J.W.H. Ilbery were both registered as consular agents of Hanover in 1828–9, while Hanover was still a domain of the King of England; later they worked from the Danish Hong. At the time of his death in 1829, Thomas Forbes (163) was engaged in opium deals while American consul at Canton.[13]

THE TOPAZE INCIDENT
SHOULD THE VICEROY DECIDE to order a suspension of British trading, as he did from time

to time, it would not be without good Chinese reason, and some reluctance. By far the greater proportion of foreign trade falling to the British, any such stoppage disrupted the livelihood of millions of Chinese workers and their families in the hinterland and along the coast, not only at Canton, the manufacturers of silk and porcelain, the producers of tea and other trading goods, the packers, the coolies and leaders of donkey-trains, the boatmen, the distributers and salesmen. Moreover, the tea estates and other production points were distant enough from Canton to give grounds for a whole series of tax-collection stations on the way, from which the revenue was a major contributor to the Imperial purse. The mandarins would risk Imperial displeasure should the flow diminish.

The famous affair of the frigate HMS *Topaze*, which ended in the temporary suspension of all British trade in Canton, took place during the Company presidency of J.B. Urmston, father of the infant buried in tomb 115. The incident illustrates the depth of the chasm dividing the axioms of the Viceroy from those of the Select when handling collisions of villagers with foreign seamen.

The vessel, with its 40 guns and a complement of about 300 men, arrived off Macao early in November 1821, at a time when the opium question was taxing official tempers, and the Chinese had entered an obstinately anti-foreign phase. On 15 December, a party from the ship landed on Lintin Island. Some of the villagers, having a ready eye for profit, had planted jars of liquor in the sand on the shore, to tempt the sailors to buy. Others stood around to watch the transaction. Unwilling to have to deal with drunken crewmen, the officer in charge of the landing party had ordered them to be smashed. Outraged, the whole crowd set on the group of foreigners: warning shots were fired and

the frigate sent armed parties to protect its men. In the skirmish, 14 seamen and several villagers were badly wounded and two Chinese killed. In quick response to protests lodged both by the village and by the captain of the frigate, the Viceroy suspended trading, and demanded the surrender of the 'foreign murderers' for trial and punishment on the 'eye for an eye' principle.

Fresh in Urmston's mind was the case of Francis Terranovia, seaman on the ship *Emily*, who it was alleged had knocked a Chinese woman overboard as she was offering him fruit for sale and who had promptly been surrendered by the American captain for trial: the Chinese court found him guilty and ordered his execution, which had been carried out by strangulation. Urmston refused to intervene in the matter of the *Topaze*, on the grounds that he had no jurisdiction over the Navy, a reason the Viceroy did not understand and refused to accept, at once suspending British trade. The Select Committee was at first divided in its reaction, two of its members wishing to take no action unless the Company was prepared, if necessary, to quit China; but the preference for an interim measure expressed by Urmston and Robarts (157) prevailed and, on 10 January 1822, the residents of the British factory were evacuated to their ships at Whampoa, the *Topaze* independently sailing further south to Chuenpi near the river mouth. This was enough to convince the Viceroy that Urmston had no real control over the Navy, and he annulled the trading veto, but without withdrawing his demand that the perpetrators should be handed over for trial. Urmston refused – his reason being that in British law there was a distinction between wilful murder and killing in self-defence – and requested safe passage for the factory personnel and ships through the Bogue. The Viceroy refused to withdraw his demand. The Select Committee then informed the Hong merchants of their decision that, should they reach a final impasse, they would retire from China altogether, a move which, had it been taken, would have either brought the Company humiliation or closed the China trade to it forever. As it was, the Viceroy – at risk of Imperial wrath – despatched an official to enquire fully into the episode. Urmston cancelled the exodus, feeling that this opened the door to further negotiation. The *Topaze* sailed from Chuenpi on 8 February and, after the usual face-saving parley, the factory personnel were allowed to return to Canton and resume trading.[14]

Trading had rarely continued for long periods without being interrupted by petty quarrels with the Canton mandarins: it was in some desperation, shortly after the *Topaze* incident, that the Select resolved secretly to try opening up the legitimate trade from other ports and outside Canton, sending a trial cargo of goods north in a sloop-of-war, but failing to establish alternative trading arrangements. The Select never abandoned its hope of discovering a satisfactory way of avoiding the suspensions.[15]

When at the close of 1833 the British Government abolished the Company's monopoly, many of its employees chose to remain and either join one or other of the independent trading companies or set up on their own. The abolition finally removed a kingpost from the crumbling edifice of commercial regulation. Company supercargoes were replaced with officials directly representing the British Government, and some of those Company employees who had not gone independent transferred directly into the service of a new 'Superintendent of British Trade with China'. There are memorials to some of these merchants and representatives, or to members of their families, in the Old Cemetery. James Daniell, for instance, was a Company supercargo at the time of the changeover, and then founded Daniell & Co with his brother Anthony, father of the infant Edmond Daniell buried in tomb 97. The Daniells, as we shall see, took up an unusual stance during the opium bond troubles of 1839. British merchants, no longer caught in the entanglements of local mandarins and the Select Committee, found they were rather at the distant mercy of representatives of governments in London and Peking. The story from then is of foreign and Chinese manoeuvres, mostly bloody, to secure the diplomatic high ground, and of British determination to secure a permanent place, where the consistencies of British law and a stabilized trade might prevail.

---

1 Morse iii p 79
2 Chatterton pp 177, 181; and Philips pp 80, 87
3 Morse iii p 176
4 Monroe lxxxvii p 148
5 Dermigny i p 77; Loines 115
6 Morse iii
7 Quoted by Loines pp 299–300
8 Dutch Archives 42, 317–21; Morse ii p 12, iv p 4
9 Morse iv p 128
10 Dermigny iii p 1194; Morse iii p 158
11 Morse iv p 254
12 Loines p 140
13 Morse iv pp 163 and 187; ACK for 1835
14 Morse iv pp 38, 40–1, and 87
15 Morse iv p 332

3
Trade after the Company

THE SUPERINTENDENT OF TRADE
DURING THE TIME OF ITS operations, the Select Committee developed into the instrument of
discipline for all British traders and the only effective channel of communication with the Canton
authorities. British merchants, chafing under Company rules, had been successful lobbying for the
abolition of its monopoly, now saw the opportunities of unlicensed trade opening before them, and
had hopes of shaking off most of the fetters on
commerce, unaware of the Company's failure of
1832 to open trading in other ports. Lord Napier
(164) was sent out by the British Government to
take over its functions as Superintendent of Trade;
he arrived at Macao in July 1834 with his family,
and as the opening move of an attempt to demonstrate his status, he moved to Canton, without
waiting for the customary 'chops', to announce his
appointment as head of a new commission, whose
other members were two of the previous supercargoes, John Davis and Sir George Robinson. Among
his retinue were Dr Colledge (see 94–6) as the

commission's physician, and for the briefest period
Dr Morrison (141) – who soon succumbed to ill-
health and pain and died at the start of August – as
its Chinese interpreter.

The disappearance of the Company from the
scene and the sale of its trading ships heralded a
dramatic increase in the body of country traders,
including those illicitly importing opium, and few
were amenable to regulation. The established chain
of command was broken. Among the traders, the
commission could not attract the same general
respect as the Company had, as it was not itself
engaged in trading. There were no courts for the
enforcement of its restrictions. There was a vacuum
in discipline and communication, which hostile
Chinese authorities filled as sole arbiters and
enforcers. Inspired by common interest, the traders
founded a British Chamber of Commerce in an
attempt to present a united front at Canton, electing
James Matheson as its chairman and, until his
death in March 1839, Richard Turner (93) as his
deputy.

Napier believed that the Viceroy would refuse to support the drafting of a commercial treaty unless persuaded by the threat of force, and that the long-term answer to trading problems was to occupy Hong Kong, to set up British courts of law, and from there to engage in protected trading with rules that could be applied with consistency. London had warned him not to get embroiled in activities that 'might needlessly excite jealousy or distrust', and to ensure that the merchants obeyed both Chinese regulation and Chinese custom. These warnings conflicted with the further instruction that when he arrived in Canton, he was to write direct to the Viceroy announcing his arrival, which he did. Napier immediately found his mission at risk: he had arrived without seeking permission, and the regulations forbade foreigners from entering into direct correspondence with the Viceroy; the mandarins refused to recognize his position and froze British trade. Napier ordered two warships to force entry past the Bogue forts and sail to Canton, then was forced to leave for Macao, laid low with a raging fever, only to die there on 11 October. Davis, a later governor of Hong Kong (1844–8), removed the Commission to Macao and, disappointed by the months of inactivity that followed and considering that he would better serve the cause by pleading it in London, left for England. Captain Charles Elliot succeeded him as superintendent in December 1836. Matheson sailed home to lobby the politicians on behalf of his colleagues at Canton, taking the rest of the Napier family with him. The debate on the need for a permanent British trading base opened in London in earnest.

British trading dipped sharply after 1834: the rapid increase of opium imports – almost doubling by 1838–9 – and the intolerable drain on China's reserves of silver to pay for them being the principal cause of decline. In the immediate run-up to the first Opium War, the deterioration of relations between the mandarins and the traders is well exemplified by incidents in the lives of merchants and others who themselves, or members of whose families, lie in the Old Cemetery: James Innes (137), Robert Forbes (see 163), Sandwith Drinker (39), Senn van Basel (99), H.G.J. Reynvaan (see 106), Nathaniel Kinsman (112), Henry Bridges (108), James Daniell (see 97) and Vincent Stanton.

THE INNES INCIDENT

R.B. FORBES, YOUNGER BROTHER of Thomas Forbes (163), has left a detailed record of one incident in Canton which grew into one of international extent before the problem could be resolved. In December 1938, James Innes (137) employed coolies to unload boxes consigned to him as 'specie'. As they were carrying them from the quayside, customs officials noticed how, on the journeys from boat to wharf, each coolie shouldered two boxes of what it stated in the documents was a commodity far heavier than that. On investigation they were found to contain not silver, but opium. When arrested and interrogated, the coolies were commendably unwilling to implicate their employer, even under torture, and stated that the boxes came from the ship *Thomas Perkins*, commanded by Captain Talbot. Russell & Co, the American firm with which Forbes was connected, was the ship's consignee. The ship was detained, several merchants and compradors were arrested, all manner of cargo boats prevented from running, and unjust accusations made against many of the American and other foreign traders. In due course, the investigations narrowed down to Innes, and he was ordered to leave Canton. This order Innes ignored. The mandarins immediately stopped foreign trading, made a number of arrests, and threatened the Hong merchants with the *k'ang* (a wooden collar, akin to the stocks). The newspapers carried the story. In the foreign community feeling ran high against Innes; Captain Elliot was so soured by the incident that he wrote, as Superintendent of Trade, to Lord Palmerston, who was then Colonial Secretary, promising that if the only way to solve the problem was for him to arrest Innes himself, that he would have to do. Innes gave in, however; he and the freighter were released, he applied for the 'chop' that would permit him to leave Canton for Macao, and from that safe haven wrote a letter vindicating all the accused. In the meantime, the authorities discovered that other boats in the river were employed in smuggling and refused to reopen trade.[1]

When on 19 December Captain Drinker (39) made for Whampoa, he arrived to find trade at a complete standstill, and when trade was reopened 12 days later while he was still loading his cargo of tea, it was only to face a further decline of a situation that now saw all foreigners put under house arrest, in 'detested prison' in the factories, where they remained for four more months until the authorities saw fit to release them.[2]

BRITONS AND DUTCH EXCLUDED
TO HALT THE FLOW OF SILVER out of China the Emperor appointed a mandarin of the highest rank as Imperial High Commissioner with a mandate to scupper all trading in opium from then on. Commissioner Lin Tse-hsü arrived at Canton in March 1839 and ordered that all foreigners must yield up their stocks to be destroyed, and when the British refused to comply, laid siege to all 13 of the factories, from which the traders were denied egress until all stocks were surrendered. When the British stocks of nearly 20,300 chests had been handed over, Elliot was free to withdraw the British nationals to Macao, hoping to make common cause with the government there. Lin then issued such strong inducements to the Macao authorities that Elliot had little recourse but to evacuate the British and their families to anchorages near Hong Kong Island. In full pursuit of his aim, Lin countered by threatening an attack, issuing a warning that he would also besiege the houses of any who returned to or remained in Macao and refuse to readmit them until they had signed a bond. The bond would consist of an undertaking never again to carry opium into the 'inner seas' in any of their ships, and an understanding that if the signatory did so, the guilty ship and all its cargo would be confiscated, and someone surrendered for death by strangling. Some American captains signed, but Elliot forbade British captains and traders to sign before he had secured guidance from London.

Lin believed that the Dutch possessed opium stocks of about 20,000 chests. Their consul, Senn van Basel (99), had persuaded the merchants to hand over all they had, which was in fact much less. Lin was far from satisfied, assuming that they were still withholding a quantity in stock. When Senn van Basel left for Batavia in November, before the affair could be settled, it was his business associate Reynvaan (see 106) who, as Netherlands commercial agent in China, then faced the task of convincing Lin, and the complication of the bonds. Lin held the Dutch merchants in detention in the factory until in April 1840 Reynvaan gave him an assurance firm enough for him to accept. Long delays preceded their release and consent for them to retire to Macao.[3]

AMERICAN WINDFALL

MANY OF THE MERCHANTS WHO were not British took advantage of the extra opportunities offered by the vacuum and continued to trade. Some British ships were sold to Americans; a small clandestine trade was organized, with British firms chartering ships flying other flags and foreign ships taking British goods on board. Cotton was piling up at Hong Kong, tea and silk at Whampoa. Everyone was working feverishly to reap the freight harvest before a British blockading force arrived. In the midst of the proscription, on 23 October 1839, Nathaniel Kinsman (112) arrived at Hong Kong from Salem in command of the *Zenobia* and in a letter described how 60 large British ships were lying at anchor there, unable to get upriver to Whampoa, while American vessels were hurrying back and forth between the two anchorages, carrying cotton up and tea down, both for themselves and for the British. Kinsman engaged himself in this oblique trade, loading the *Zenobia* with cotton on behalf of Jardine, Matheson & Co and moving to Whampoa. There he waited for six weeks until the price of tea had dropped far enough for a profitable buy. 'My intention,' he said, 'is to remain perfectly quiet and watch the moving of the waters and when I see a chance, walk into the tea market, load my ship, and be off and leave the belligerents to fight out their differences, in their own way, wishing success to the English ...' When the British enforced their blockade in January 1840, down came the price of tea, and Kinsman sailed for New York with 1,400 tons in the holds, expecting to make a level of profit never realized before, and scarcely believing his luck.[4]

Robert Forbes was in Hong Kong when Captain Henry Bridges (108) arrived in the *Navigator* carrying freight consigned to Russell & Co. Taking his 'fast boat' to the ship, he found that its lower hold was full of betel nut and its between-decks nearly full of rattan, and told Bridges that 'rattan did not count under the present circumstances; that he must pile them on deck, up to the cat harpins if necessary, and fill up the between-decks with cotton. He seemed to consider me out of my mind; but when he came to learn that seven dollars a bale could be had, and to realize that by getting down all his upper sticks he would not turn over, he came to believe I was sane, and I think took in six or seven hundred bales. I mention this as a mere sample of the way we managed. Coming down with teas, dunnage was laid on deck, tea piled up under mat-houses eight or 10 feet high.'[5]

THE DANIELL INCIDENT

IN OCTOBER 1839, SHORTLY after the British merchants had bowed to Captain Elliot's demand to surrender their stocks of opium to the Commissioner, James Daniell (see 97) arrived in Macao by way of Calcutta, as a passenger on the ship *Thomas Coutts*. A cargo of cotton, rattan and pepper had been taken on board at Bombay consigned to the firm belonging to the brothers Daniell, but no opium. Its master, Captain Warner, had already taken advice on the legality of Elliot's order before he left. By the time they anchored off Macao, they had decided to take all the steps necessary to acquire permits to proceed upriver for trade: they defied Elliot by signing the bond required by Lin, secured the 'chops' – without encountering any kind of problem – and sailed up the river. Once at Whampoa, they were able to dispose of the cargo profitably, and were rewarded by Lin with presents of livestock in the hope that others would follow suit. Lin badly needed the reopening of trade to sustain Imperial revenues and asked Captain Warner, who was planning an immediate return to London with a shipload of tea, to deliver a letter to that effect to Queen Victoria. Other ships whose captains signed the guarantees were the *Royal Saxon* and the American ship *Mermaid*.[6]

THE STANTON INCIDENT

THE WIFE OF RICHARD TURNER (93) had arrived at Macao about six months before his death, accompanied by two of their sons and their tutor, Vincent Stanton, a divinity student of St John's College, Cambridge. When the chaplain, Rev G.H. Vachell, returned to England, young Stanton undertook to preside over the services in the British chapel at Macao until a successor was appointed, and decided to stay on after the family left again for England. He was one of the handful who refused to leave when Commissioner Lin ordered the British out of Macao in 1839, an exodus which Lin had encouraged by offering a large reward to anyone who managed to kidnap any of those who had remained.

Early on the morning of 6 August 1840, Stanton had left his lodgings to join two friends in a swim from Casilha Bay. They arrived and, apparently ahead of him, waited for some hours before organizing a search for him throughout the peninsula. He could not be found, and the mystery of his disappearance continued to perturb them until news of him came from Canton, revealing that he had arrived at the rendezvous before his friends: being by himself, the crew of a junk lying close inshore had attacked him with ferocity and

taken him off as a prisoner to Canton, in high hopes of Lin's commendation and the promised reward. During four months' confinement in a Canton prison, his arms and legs in chains, Stanton was subjected to a process of humiliation and interrogation. The authorities believed, not without some justification, that the British were every one of them dealers in opium – Stanton had after all been living in the Turners' house and must, surely, after his employer died, have taken over his business in opium. The purpose of prolonged months of questioning and ill-treatment was to wring from him the confession that would certainly lead him to execution, and when it became clear that he had no confession to make, he was finally released.[7]

THE FIRST OPIUM WAR

WHEN JAMES MATHESON HAD returned to Canton, William Jardine retired to Britain and in his turn took up with Lord Palmerston the cause of foundering British business in China and the pressing need to secure its proper defence against sabotage. The Prime Minister appointed the Elliot cousins, Rear-Admiral George and Captain Charles, as joint emissaries, with full powers to negotiate, charged with delivering to Peking Britain's demands for the recognition of Charles Elliot as Superintendent of Trade, the opening of ports to foreigners, an indemnity for the surrendered opium and other losses suffered by British traders, and the ceding of a suitable territory to the British crown. To accompany them and add persuasion to these demands, he commissioned an expeditionary force under the command of Commodore Sir James John Gordon Bremer, consisting of a force of some 4,000 British and Indian troops, protected by three battleships and 14 frigates and sloops of the Royal

Navy, and four armed steamers which had once been the Company's.

As the expeditionary fleet assembling off Hong Kong was in the last stage of its preparations to head north to Chusan, the Chinese made a surprise attempt at a final defeat of the British, obliging Bremer to detach four naval vessels for a blockade of Canton. The blockade was enforced and the main fleet sailed north in May, making rendezvous south of Chusan early the next month. The demands were delivered to Tientsin, for the Manchu Kishen, Governor of Chihli, to transmit to Peking.

When agreement came for talks to start, it was not without great difficulty, and on condition that they took place in the south. The expedition withdrew to the Pearl River, leaving a force behind in occupation of Chusan as a guarantee of Chinese assent to the process.[8] Kishen, transferred to Canton to represent the Emperor at the talks, was there joined by Lin, relieved of his status as High Commissioner, and Teng Ting-chen, his predecessor at Canton, as his advisers. The two sides faced one another in the Pearl River in November 1840, the point at which young Stanton was given over into the custody of Rear-Admiral Elliot on board his flagship *Melville*. The next month, the Admiral fell sick and returned home, leaving cousin Charles in sole control.

HONG KONG

CHARLES ELLIOT'S PRINCIPAL requirement was that the Chinese should cede an island from which the British might prosecute their trade untrammeled. To prevent negotiations from drawing out, he imposed a deadline for agreement and, when it had passed, mounted so devastating an attack on the Bogue forts that Kishen offered Hong Kong and an indemnity of $6 million for the seized opium. Elliot ordered the evacuation of Chusan, and Bremer formally took possession of Hong Kong. The Emperor dismissed Kishen and repudiated his offers, whereupon the British force captured the Bogue forts and Whampoa, invested the factories, and made to attack the city of Canton itself. Cree noted that 'a treaty of peace was said to be concluded with China, after the children of the Flowery Empire had got a severe drubbing and about 600 of them killed, and the forts in the Canton River knocked about their ears'. Elliot's failure to complete the actions at Canton was believed to have broken the heart of Sir Humphrey Senhouse (136), and it was a particularly emotive moment as Captain Daniel Duff (138), who had himself taken a leading part, watched the coffin being lowered into the grave in the Old Cemetery.

The prices that were placed on the heads of the leaders of the expedition had by March 1841 reached unprecedented levels for the capture of British ships and persons. Elliot and Bremer were each valued at $50,000 captured alive, $30,000 dead. The Chinese set J.R. Morrison's (143) price at the same level as these two most senior British commanders, a measure of the respect with which they viewed his abilities.

Cree's ship anchored in Hong Kong harbour early that April, and he and some others had a look round. As they were walking back along the shore 'through a valley, through which ran a stream of sparkling water, we met Sir Fleming Senhouse and Sir Hugh Gough and A.D.C. with a guard of marines. They stopped to have a talk about the place.' Senhouse had little faith in the permanence of the new colony and expressed his preference, should he chance to die in the region, to be buried rather in Macao than in Hong Kong. While at

Canton only two months after meeting Cree, he succumbed to the 'Hong Kong fever' (a form of malaria), died at Hong Kong and, his body transported to Macao, was buried in the Old Cemetery (136) in accordance with his wish.

Having forced a truce, Elliot transferred his headquarters from Macao to the Canton factories, taking his wife with him. 'We hear shocking accounts of the cruelty of the Chinese Government,' records Cree, 'which appears mad with rage at their defeat, five mandarin officers who commanded at the Bogue forts being burnt alive in boats.' A further defiant attempt to defeat the British failed in May: when the British forces prepared to invest the city of Canton itself, negotiations reopened, Elliot drafted the conditions on which the Treaty of Canton was based, and returned to Macao, while the forces withdrew to Hong Kong. Appointing the first magistrate and the first head of government of a free port of Hong Kong, with J.R. Morrison (143) as Chinese secretary, Elliot moved his headquarters to a tent there on the beach, and prepared for the first sale of land.[9]

The auction took place in June, with successful sales. Little significant building followed, however, the main deterrent being the island's insalubrity and a high death-rate from the Hong Kong fever. The cause of the fever was said to be the first-time exposure of tracts of earth to sun and rain during the preparation of sites for building. Such building as there was suffered extensive storm damage in the typhoon of 21 July. In the same typhoon, Elliot and Bremer were shipwrecked on one of the Ladrones south of Lantau Island, as they were on their way from Macao. On 10 August 1841 Sir Henry Pottinger arrived to take over from Elliot, and after a fortnight of handover formalities, both Elliot and Bremer departed from the scene.

Hostilities were not over, however. To secure a firmer basis for completing the agreement, Pottinger sailed north with the fleet and occupied Chinha and Ningpo close to the mouth of the Yangtzekiang, and the island of Chusan. Pottinger himself returned and in February 1842 transferred the Superintendency of Trade from Macao to Hong Kong. The Chinese made their preparations to retaliate, intending to regain their territory, seize Hong Kong and murder the barbarians settled there; and in March, as a preliminary, made their attempt to reinvest Chusan and the occupied cities on the coast. But, put to flight, they were pursued by Pottinger's forces up the Yangtzekiang as far as Nanking, where they sued for peace. The Treaty of Nanking was concluded on 29 August, providing for an indemnity at the much larger sum of $21 million, the opening of the ports of Canton, Amoy, Foochow, Ningpo and Shanghai to foreign trade, with permission for the British to reside in them and be subject only to British laws, and ceding Hong Kong to Britain for all time. In June the next year, the Emperor's representative entered Hong Kong to exchange treaty ratifications, and Pottinger was duly sworn in as the first governor of the new colony of Hong Kong.

That July, Hong Kong fever struck with increased power, one regiment alone losing a hundred of its men in six weeks. The exodus to the less insalubrious Macao the following month included the governor himself. Among the summer deaths was J.R. Morrison, whose body was transported to Macao for burial next to the graves of his parents (141, 142, 143). Many of the merchants shifted their offices to Hong Kong, while keeping their houses in Macao for holidays and for occasional escape from the – only slightly – higher humidity and heat of Hong Kong; some opened branch offices in the Treaty Ports; but in Canton itself the activities of the foreign traders were still confined to the national factories.

---

1 Canton P of 8, 15, and 22/12/1838 and 31/10/1840

2 Forbes p 346; Canton P of 8/12/1838; JASHK iv (1964) pp 9ff; Nye Morning

3 Canton R of 2/4/1839 and 6/10/40; Canton P of 6/4/1839

4 Monroe lxxxv

5 Forbes p 152

6 Blake p 36; Forbes p 152; Canton P of 12 and 19/10/1839; Waley p 93

7 Canton P of 13/10/1838, 13/11/1839, and 8/8, 15/8, and 19/12/1840; FC&HKG of 1/12/1847; Endacott and She pp 9–14. On his release, Stanton was taken to Macao and thence took passage back to England to be ordained. He returned in January 1843 as the first Colonial Chaplain in Hong Kong, and was to preside there over the marriage in November 1847 of Dr James Young and Margaret Hutchison (150), and where it was largely through his care that the Cathedral Church of Victoria was opened two years later.

8 Cree (pp 55–8) presents a vivid account of the attack on Chusan, in which he took part.

9 Cree pp 72 and 78

4
At Sea

A PRETTY SIGHT

THE MOST ROMANTIC OF ALL spectacles was a tea clipper under full sail. When under the command of Captain Shamgar Slate (13) in 1857, the celebrated clipper *Wizard* was hailed enthusiastically as of the most noble 'appearance, 'alow and aloft'. An extreme clipper of 1,600 tons, she had been built at a cost of $95,000 for his firm, Slate & Co of New York, by the master Boston shipbuilder Samuel Hall. Her stern was round and richly gilt, and her figurehead a splendid oriental magician, one arm clasping his book of spells. The fastest trader seen in the China Sea, she completed her voyage from New York to Hong Kong in 44 days, and arrived back at San Francisco in 45, 'ahead of some six vessels which sailed before her'. The poster issued for one of her voyages described her as 'unsurpassed by any Clipper afloat, for model, speed, ventilation and the excellent manner in which she has invariably delivered her cargoes'.[1]

A warship of the Royal Navy, sails bellying in the wind, was a sight even handsomer than that of many of the Western trading ships. To look out on a naval force at sea bound for the China station must especially have made the heart swell – a truly 'pretty sight, so many transports and men-of-war ... all with their white sails spread to the breeze' – at least it was so until Singapore hove into view, where it might be joined by a mismatched following of Chinese junks, the oddest-looking craft Surgeon Cree confessed he had ever seen.

NAVAL SHIPS

VESSELS OF THE ROYAL NAVY patrolled the China seas and the Pearl River estuary as protection for British trading interests, and as a show of strength in times of tension. They rarely put to sea carrying only the crew: there was usually a contingent of marines on board, and the larger ships might be called upon to act as troop transports, often with a force of the Company's Indian troops, and not infrequently at odds with the weather, sickness and pirates. From time to time until the

Alexander: The Forts of Anunghoy Saluting the 'Lion' in the Bocca Tigris

Company was deprived of its monopoly, naval ships were employed to carry Company merchandise, a service for which the Select Committee determined the charges it should pay.[2]

Sometimes there were families on board in addition to the men, and of course a load of provisions – when Cree's ship stopped at Trincomalee on its journey out to the China station, it took on a new batch of troops, but 'this time without the women and children but with a supply of ducks, fowl, and sheep for a six weeks' voyage to Singapore'.

Naval and marine officers fed in separate messes, and were generally on good terms. Breakfasts for the officers might comprise such delicacies as 'fowl pie and claret'. Because treating the sick did not usually fill his time, the ship's surgeon often performed the duties of mess-caterer. Cree was responsible for replenishing his ship's stocks of food and drink, and paid local purveyors 'a fair price for everything' he bought, while in harbour as they drew alongside in boats, or from villagers on foraging trips to farms ashore. When ashore for the purpose, he was usually accompanied by sailors and marines, since it was 'not safe to go far from the ships unarmed in foraging parties'. The food they took with them on these shore trips included 'cold meat, bologna sausage, hard-boiled eggs and bis-cuits', all washed down with brandy and water. Their searches brought pineapples, bananas, mangosteens, eggs, fish, sweet potato, pig, goat, duck, chicken, pork chops; on one foray, Cree shot swan; on another, even 'a pied and a green wood-pecker' which, in an access of surgical skill when back in the galley, he skinned.

As a dainty for his menu, he fished the depths for shark, patiently but not always effectively: two large ones once 'followed the ship for a couple of hours this morning but refused to take a bait of a 4-pound piece of pork'. On the other hand, the shark's own patience brought him a sailor from time to time. Cree tells of a young marine who fell over-board in the China Sea: the cutter failed to reach him before 'he disappeared to rise no more. They tried to reach him with the boat-hook; as the water was clear, they saw an enormous shark had got hold of his white jumper in the middle, gradually going down deeper and deeper till they disappeared ... This makes the third Marine we have lost out of six with which we left England'.

Performing similar duties to those of the Royal Navy, ships of the American Navy were increasingly in evidence. Among the most important official American visitors to Macao in the period were Edmund Roberts, special envoy to Muscat, Cochin-China and Siam between 1832 and 1836, who journeyed for the purpose in American warships until he died at Macao (88). Caleb Cushing was in the region from 1843 to 1845 as first Envoy Extraordinary and Minister Plenipotentiary to China, charged with securing for America the same most-favoured-nation status as that accorded to the British in the 1842 Treaty of Nanking; as was Commodore Matthew C. Perry, whose object during 1853–54 was to secure a similar most-favoured-

nation treaty with Japan. The missions of both Cushing and Perry were protected by the warships of the American East India and Japan Squadron.

Caleb Cushing sailed east on the US frigate *Brandywine*, flagship of the squadron's commander, Commodore F.A. Parker, which anchored off Macao in February 1844. Ashore he was referred to by the Americans as the 'Plenipo', and accommodated in apartments on the Praya Grande, where he waited while the *Brandywine* took on stores. When frus-trated in his intention to sail to the mouth of the Peiho, he had first put in at Manila, and then spent the eight months to December 1844 cruising in Hong Kong-Whampoa-Macao waters. He secured the Treaty of Wanghsia, which is reputed to have been signed on a table still in the Kun Yam Tem-ple in Macao, commemorated there by a tablet.[3] Two of the frigate's crew were buried at Macao (76 and 77).

Commodore Perry was the most distinguished and efficient officer of his day in the US Navy, and in the Mexican war had commanded the largest naval force ever assembled in American history up to that time. Appointed to head the Japan mission, he assumed overall command of the American East India Squadron. The squadron was enlarged for his purpose to 12 ships. Six were serving vessels: the sloop-of-war *Saratoga* (see 5), the steam frigate *Susquehanna* (see 7), the storeships *Lexington* and *Southampton*, the *Supply*, and the sloop-of-war *Plymouth* (see 64, 65, 68, 134 and 147), which was in Shanghai when she was detailed to join his expedition. The other six were sent out from America to join the expedition: the steamers *Mississippi*, which had been his flagship in the Mexican war, *Princeton*, *Alleghany* and *Vermont*, and the sloops-of-war *Vandalia* and *Macedonian*. The *Princeton*'s trials proving unsatisfactory, Perry replaced her with the steam frigate *Powhatan* (see 18 and 38), which was able to follow him some weeks after his own departure for the Far East, arriving off Hong Kong in July 1853, and leaving immediately for Japan. The *Susquehanna*, under the command of Captain Buchanan, figures in all the reports on the subsequent diplomatic moves and countermoves of the Americans with the Japanese and, at the end of the first stage of negotiations in August, she returned to Hong Kong with Perry on board.

As gifts for the Emperor of Japan, Perry had brought a number of agricultural implements, a lifeboat, a miniature steam railway and a new electro-magnetic telegraphing system. A member of the expedition was John Williams (23), a merchant captain from Utah whose special task was to show the Japanese how to work the telegraph, in the setting up and operating of which he was expert; for this he was permitted to accept from the Japanese Commissioners the gift of a piece of patterned red crepe and some lacquerware.

Perry's plan was not to return to Japan until the spring of 1854 but, becoming suspicious of French and Russian movements, he sailed north in January, transferring his flag to the *Powhatan*, which from then and throughout the treaty negotiations, lasting until mid-July, became the centre of American activities, social as well as diplomatic. He was accompanied from Hong Kong by the *Lexington* and the *Southampton*; the *Macedonian* and the *Supply* had already gone north; the *Plymouth* and the *Saratoga* had had orders to rendezvous at the Lew Chews. The squadron was a mixture of sail and steam; but if the greatest impression was to be made on the Japanese, it was essential that its ships should all arrive in Tokyo Bay together, and this demanded a uniform speed and a common course

from the Okinawa base. The steamers took the sailing ships in tow, the *Mississippi* towing the *Plymouth* and the *Susquehanna* taking care of the *Saratoga*, so that the 12 ships assembled outside the Bay at the same time and, dropping the tow-ropes, all were able to make impressive entrances independently. As soon as the terms of a draft of the Treaty of Kanagawa was agreed, the *Saratoga* carried Perry's despatches and the signed agreement as far as Honolulu. There it was transferred to the *Susquehanna*, which arrived at Hong Kong in April, 'bringing the gratifying news that Commodore Perry had succeeded in the objects of his mission in a manner that will confer honour on his country and enduring fame to himself'.

The *Powhatan* left Japan to tour the China coast ports and the Pearl River delta until January 1855, when the ratified draft was returned to Hong Kong for transportation back to Japan. Her return from Japan was delayed by the rehabilitation help she rendered at Shimoda, which had been destroyed in the 1854 earthquake. Back in Hong Kong by May 1855, she immediately prepared for another tour of south China ports, and it was during her visit to Macao that June that Seaman Hickman (18) died and was buried in the Old Cemetery.[4]

THE LINTIN FLEET

THE INTERMEDIATE ANCHORAGES at Lintin Island were organized for the receipt and distribution of opium. At anchor were ships engaged in activities of three different ranges, together referred to as the 'Lintin Fleet'. One group stayed at the outer anchorages for prolonged periods, each belonging to a company and used as temporary storage for opium whenever cargoes containing it hove to; schooners and other small craft received opium from these storeships and set off to one of the many illegal receiving stations scattered through the myriad veins of the estuary, or to the ports along the China coast; and in the third group were the merchant ships bringing opium from India and Turkey for discharge into store. Those ships which were also carrying non-contraband items in their cargo might then, provided they had first secured their 'chops' in Macao, sail innocently on to join the others at the Whampoa anchorage.

When he took passage from the Capsuimoon anchorage in 1837 on the Boston clipper *Rose*, W.C. Hunter was able to see for himself the coastal operations of the opium trade. On its way from Lintin to the distributing station on the island of Namoa near Amoy, the schooner was carrying a dangerously full cargo of opium, 'her scuppers within two feet of the water'. The *Harriet* – a 'small fore and aft craft' originating from the Macao shipyard of the American carpenter Lewis Hamilton (72) – called at Namoa on her way south with a cargo of gold bars and *sycee* (silver) worth $430,000, which the captain had collected from the opium storeships stationed along the coast: unwilling to await the off-loading of the *Rose*'s opium, Hunter took passage in the *Harriet* for his return journey.[5]

Several inhabitants of the Old Cemetery were actively engaged in the moving and the storing of the chests of opium. By the time of Hunter's overloaded trip, there were as many as 25 opium storeships securely anchored off Lintin. Among them were the *Lord Amherst*, whose master was Captain Thomas Rees (the husband of 109) and the *Jane*. Captain John Crockett (87) had abandoned a life afloat in the 1830s for the command of the *Jane*, which he found much pleasanter and much more profitable, as it gave him many occasions to

supplement his salary, such as in 1835 when he advertised for sale the large quantity of opium salvaged from the *Sylph*.[6] He could still have been aboard when he died at 'Capsingmoon' the next year. Captain Charles Woodberry (19) was living on board the barque *Hygeia*, another opium storeship. Lintin continued in use for the purpose even after Hong Kong had been seceded – Woodberry was also master of the Peruvian schooner *Rosita*, an opium storeship anchored there in the early 1850s.

PIRACY

VALUABLE CARGOES OF SILVER and opium were magnets for pirates. British and American ships, forming by far the largest contingent of foreign trade shipping, were the most susceptible to their onslaughts. Several of the occupants of the graveyard had tangled with them. In October 1844 Captain R.V. Warren (74) briefly left his ship the *Fair Barbadian* lying in the Macao Roads, to take a trip to Hong Kong on the schooner *Kappa*, which was carrying opium. Nearing Kowloon, she was attacked by pirates who had followed her from Taipa and were apparently very well aware both of the nature of her cargo and of the small number of her crew. In the ensuing struggle, her captain was so severely wounded that he did not live long, and Warren himself was killed. Warren's body was found and returned to his brother, with whom he appears to have been engaged on the coastal opium run, for burial in Macao. After the piracy, the *Kappa*'s name was changed to *Dido*, perhaps in the hope of avoiding a repeat experience.[7]

In 1840 the *Lady Hayes*, probably by then having been taken into the command of Captain Andrew Paterson (82), was sailing in line with the schooner

Sylph and the trader *Cowasjee Family* on the run between Calcutta and Canton, when they were attacked. The captains of the two last had already suffered pirate raids: their cargo on this occasion was particularly valuable – probably silver bullion – and they had taken extra guns aboard. Unaware of the strengthened armament ranged against them, the pirates suffered heavy losses and fled in disarray.

Shortly after the death of Seaman Hickman (18) on board the *Powhatan* in Macao, she was forced to undergo repairs in the Hong Kong shipyard and, while thus incapacitated, lent her equipment and crew to HMS *Rattler* for an operation on 4 August 1855 against a strong band of marauders then threatening the trade routes. The force, comprising a pinnace and cutters from the *Rattler* and two launches and a cutter belonging to the *Powhatan*, engaged a fleet of some 30 armed pirate junks near Kuhlan in a desperate battle, causing the destruction of 10 of them and the 'liberation' of seven prizes; 15 of the smaller vessels were able to escape unharmed into shallow water. The American and British vessels together lost nine men, and 15 more were wounded or suffered burns. The marauding fleet was on this occasion so disorganized and dispersed that it long ceased to menace Hong Kong waters.[8]

Piracy was even more frequent in the estuary and in the innumerable inlets of the Pearl River delta. In the hot August of 1805, two Americans, a Mr Dobell and a Mr Biddle (probably 58), were pirated in the river while they were approaching Macao in the 'chop boat' from Canton, and lost all their possessions. At Hong Kong, Cree heard tales 'of pirates in the neighbourhood getting very bold and attacking small vessels between this and Macao'. On a June evening in 1843, while returning from the Macao Roads to the barque *Calcutta*, lying in the Taipa under the command of Thomas Osborne (69), the Chinese crew of one of its boats murdered the second mate and a head Lascar, tossed their bodies overboard, and made off with a load of 14 chests of opium. The Dutchman Reynvaan had moved his company from Macao to Canton, following the death of his wife (106) in 1846; and as he had not infrequently done before, one night in the humid heat of the following summer joined the Swiss merchant Vaucher, to take passage on a fast night-boat to Hong Kong; bad weather delayed their sailing beyond the Dutch and French Forts, where they anchored and retired for the night. In the dark, armed robbers boarded the boat. Disturbed by the noise, the two friends rushed on deck, where Vaucher fell or was pushed into the sea and drowned; Reynvaan suffered two spear wounds in his neck and extensive bruises. The pirates made off with all their luggage, including $4,000-worth of specie and Swiss watches, and with all the valuables of the Chinese passengers. By the time the remaining passengers were picked up by another fast boat returning from Whampoa, the captain had disappeared. Reynvaan was taken back to Canton; and Vaucher's body, discovered after the sun had risen, was buried at Whampoa.[9]

Cree gives a vivid account of a pirate-hunting expedition that took up most of October 1849 in the river and around the Hong Kong and Tonkin coast, ending with a complete rout of the pirate fleet, 1,700 pirates killed, 58 junks destroyed, 1,000 pirates and only six junks escaping, illustrated with a lurid sketch of the main encounter in the Tonkin River, and another of a 'boatload of piratical rascals' escaping, only to be speared by Cochins waiting for them on shore.[10]

SOME OTHER HAZARDS

THE HAZARDS OF SERVICE at sea in the East claimed the lives of large numbers of servicemen. They were assailed by a wide miscellany of sicknesses, they drank contaminated water, they were fed victuals to which they were unaccustomed and which had often gone bad, they fell from the rigging and were swept overboard in weather to which they were ill acclimatized, suffered ship-wreck in heavy seas or wounding or death at the hands of pirates; and wounds received during naval engagements were not infrequently infected with tetanus. And ashore, they were at the constant mercy of malarial mosquitoes.

When General Bremer's expeditionary force sailed north in the midsummer of 1840 from its assembly point in a Hong Kong anchorage, the humidity of the heat was as stifling as in a sauna bathhouse, the temperature reaching over 32 deg. C in the shade. By the time they had arrived at Chusan almost one in five of the servicemen had gone down with dysentery and coughs, brought on by 'bad water and bad provisions and a damp climate'. Death claimed a large body of them; no wonder, Surgeon Cree wrote, 'considering the water we are drinking, stagnant from the paddy-fields, all well mixed with liquid manure. It stinks and is white and flatulent, but there is no other to be got in the neighbourhood'. From Hong Kong in the summer of 1850 it was reported that the men of the 59th Regiment were panic-stricken at the mounting toll ashore from epidemics of malaria and dysentery, and the food with which they were nourished was 'stuff unfit for a dog to eat'.[11] When such disasters struck, naval surgeons were overwhelmed with problems.

Danger was everywhere, for merchants as well as naval officers and men, and not only out at sea. Of the hazards of life in the region at the time, many are the reminders laid to final rest in the Old Cemetery. The adventures that befell the Beale family (159 and 160), Thomas Pattle (42), George Kennedy (83); the misfortunes suffered by members of the crew of the American ship *Plymouth*, by its seamen Griffin (64), Smith (147) and Swearlin (65), and by its Surgeon Brooke (68); the assaults of pirates on Captains Warren (74), Paterson (82) and Thomas Osborne (69), on the boat of Seaman Hickman (18), on the husband of Clazina Reynvaan (106), and probably on George Biddle (58): any one of these would have narrated a vivid saga of personal risk and peril.

The Beales were among the early independent British traders in China. In 1789 there were no more than two such traders: one was Daniel Beale senior, his resident status at Canton protected by his position as Prussian Consul and effectively taking him out of the risk of expulsion by the Chinese, and the other a Mr McIntyre, who was a permanent resident of Macao.[12] Daniel's partner was John Henry Cox, who had sailed to China in 1781 for reasons of health and had contrived in some manner to elude the expulsion orders. The ship Cox bought a decade after arrival, carrying its first cargo for him of some 8,000 sealskins, to be imported into China, was denied permission, as a British vessel, to enter the Whampoa anchorage; in a quick partnership cobbled together with Daniel, they frustrated the risk of confiscation by putting her in with his Prussian flag hoisted. By 1796, the number of unofficial Canton residents had increased only to five: one of the additional four being Daniel's brother Thomas Beale; and when in due time Daniel left for India, he was succeeded as consul by his brother. It was through Charles Magniac, who became Thomas's vice-consul in 1802, that the consulship later fell to Jardine, Matheson & Co, which continued to make profitable use of its protection against risk.

Daniel's son Daniel junior, and his nephew Thomas Chaye Beale (T.C.), were both members of the firm of Magniac & Co in 1826, the year before Daniel junior died, and T.C. had quit his interest in it by 1833, when he bought a part-ownership of the Portuguese barque *Susana*. He was aboard the *Susana* when, in April 1835 she took on the survivors from the ship *Eliza*, lying wrecked in the Paracels. The *Eliza* had left China with a load of tea on 21 March, and two days later she struck the Crescent Reef in a fresh wind, stove in her counters, and within two hours had become a total wreck. Taking to the ship's boats, some of its crew succeeded in landing on Robert's Island the next morning and, after a few days when the winds had abated, returned to salvage tea, charts, clothing, and chronometers. A junk with 10 men on board picked up the captain and two of his crew and at first treated them well: but when for this he rewarded them with 70 of the chests of tea he had taken with him, they in their turn rewarded him and his two men, by throwing them overboard and taking the rest of the tea. Swimming ashore, all three were able to join their mates on Robert's Island, and together they gave chase to the junk in a pinnace and a jollyboat. The pinnace was swept out to sea, the jollyboat returned to the wreckage with its 10 crew, and during the next six days they were plundered twice by junks. Only six of the crew remained to accompany the captain when he finally embarked in the jollyboat, in a valiant attempt to reach Singapore. After two full days at sea, they were picked up by the *Susana*.

In June 1836 the same ship, this time with Thomas Chaye Beale himself on board, sailed from Bombay bound for China, with a valuable cargo comprising 1,383 chests of Demaun opium, supplemented in the Straits with 200 bales of cotton and other goods, only to be caught in a storm when within sight of the China coast; the storm raged for three days, during which they had had to cut away the masts, and his ship went aground off a beach. As soon as the storm allowed, some villagers threw them ropes so that the crew might come ashore, then seized those who had ventured ashore, let go of the ropes, and robbed their captives. Ten of the crew were drowned in the incident; the rest, including T.C. Beale, were befriended by a Chinese and taken safely by lorcha to Macao.

The first Chinese trial at which Europeans were officially allowed to be present exemplifies the risks facing sailors when they were on shore leave. Among those present at the trial was the Company's second supercargo, Thomas Pattle (42). The trouble started when a party from the *Marquis of Ely* were enticed into Chinese boats, stupefied with bad liquor, robbed, stripped, and thrown into the river. Next day, the crew of the British ship *Neptune* staged a retaliation in which it was alleged that one Chinese life had been lost. The Chinese demanded the surrender of one of the sailors, and all 52 who had taken part in the fighting were handed over for trial. To satisfy the twisted brand of Chinese justice then in vogue, it was mandatory that one of them should be found guilty: guilt fell to the unhappy lot of Seaman Edward Sheen, who was perversely adjudged to be the most likely to have delivered the fatal blow, since it was he who had suffered most injury in the fighting. He was duly found guilty: and had not the charge been altered to one for which the penalty could be met with a fine, before sentence was actually passed, he would have been publicly executed.[13]

The seamen Griffin (64) and Smith (147) both

plunged to their deaths from the rigging of the American warship *Plymouth* while it was close to land in the Macao Roads, perhaps dropping asleep aloft in the heavy summer of 1849, or simply slipping in a heaving swell. The *Plymouth* seemed destined to suffer such losses, for Swearlin (65), one of the marines on board, died the same day as Griffin, and Surgeon Brooke (68), who died at Macao the following autumn, was either from the *Plymouth* or from the brig *Dolphin*, at the time the only two American naval vessels in the Canton waters.

With the presence of large numbers of all sorts of foreign ships plying the China Sea, the local Chinese traders and fisherfolk had much greater hope of succour in times of danger, though there is no evidence that they realized, let alone valued it. Jardine's brig the *Governor Findlay*, for instance, when under the command of Captain George Kennedy (83), sighted the hull of a capsized passage-boat, which had been blown over by a strong gale on 'a sharp, cold day' in April 1835, while running from Namoa Island (some 320 km up the coast from Hong Kong) to Tatoo. As it turned turtle, 19 of the 68 on board had succeeded in clinging to the hull and in remaining there for several hours. Hauling them aboard, members of the brig's crew had 'stripped off their own clothes for the purpose of clothing these poor unfortunates'.

The human devotion of the brig's crew, however, brought no sign of official recognition from the Chinese government, though their efforts at rescue, and the *Governor Findlay*'s progress through the Straits carrying the rescued passengers, had all the time been under the watchful but unhelpful eyes of an official fleet of two mandarin boats and two war junks.[14]

For the merchant and naval officers who survived the hazards of life at sea, if not for the lower orders of seamen, there was the occasional compensation of music or dancing on board and of picnics, conversation, and flirtation with local residents ashore.

---

1 Dixson HKG for 1854; Cutler p 341

2 Charges were calculated on the value of the goods being carried. In 1807, we find the naval sloop *Modeste* under the command of Captain the Hon George Elliot figuring in a dispute with the Select Committee about the charge. The shipment at issue was a cargo of silver bound for India: since the Chinese would not allow a foreign man-of-war to pass the Bogue, the bullion had to be moved in Indiamen boats, first from Canton to Whampoa and then from Whampoa to Chuenpi in the *Albion*, a 'country' ship. Whether by design or by ill fortune, the *Albion* caught fire and sank, but its silver cargo was saved. Elliot demanded a 2 per cent freight charge for moving it on to Calcutta, which the Committee refused to pay. The Governor-in-Council in India finally had to settle the dispute, concluding that the maximum to be charged to naval vessels would be 1 per cent.

3 Canton P of 2/3/1844; FC&HKG of 5 and 9/3 and 20/4 and 22/5/1844; Monroe lxxxvi p 142

4 FC&HKG of 27/9/1853 and various issues between May and July 1855; CM of 16/4/1854; Hawks Wallach p 4

5 Hunter 1911 pp 71–2

6 ACK for 1836–8; Canton R of 28/4/35

7 FC&HKG of 19/3/1845

8 A memorial bearing the names of the dead in this joint action stands at the junction of Morrison Hill Road and Leighton Hill Road in Happy Valley, Hong Kong.

9 Morse iii p 8; Cree p 78; Canton P of 24/6/1843; CM of 17/1/1847

10 Cree pp 194–202

11 Cree, pp 48, 51–2, 60, 61–3, 65–6, 84, and 123; FC&HKG of 3/8/1850

12 Morse ii p 175

13 Morse iii pp 36 ff

14 Canton R of 28/3 and 9/6/1835

5
Ashore – The Context

SPIRITUAL ARRANGEMENTS

MACAO WAS THE HAVEN not only for the British, but for all the other foreigners who had to make their exodus from Canton at the end of each trading season: the members of the Danish, Dutch, French, and Swedish East India Companies, and for the independent American, Baltic States, Indian, Parsee and Spanish merchants. This community of foreign merchants and their families – despite the privations of a life far from home, the irregularity and staleness of the news from abroad, martyr to disease, hopes too often dashed by the high mortality rate, daily activities hazed and confused by restriction and delay – was at least able to endow its small world with ampler consolation, the more it expanded to meet the increasing rewards and prospects of trade.

Most of them were Protestants and had been left to cater for their own spiritual needs and the performance of religious rites. The Company chief usually conducted services for the marriages, births and deaths of Company personnel in Macao and in Canton, and of some others closely connected with it, and until 1820, when its growth made the appointment of resident chaplains expedient, considered it to be among his duties. For example, George Urmston (115), one of the infants buried in the Old Cemetery, was baptized before his death by the chief. Dr Robert Morrison (141) several times asked a later chief, Sir William Fraser (62), for leave to preach in the British factory at Canton in his place but, in spite of their growing friendship, was always rebuffed.

THE CHAPLAINS

WHEN REV GEORGE H. VACHELL was appointed as resident chaplain to the Company to succeed the Rev Henry Harding, his service was to extend over some 10 years with only one short break in 1833, when the Rev Charles Wimberley officiated for him; and he would become the religious link between its last chief and his successor, the Superintendent of British Trade. During the period 1829–38, he conducted the burial services of 19 of those who lie in the cemetery, having also baptized five of them. Macao 'is a dreadful place to get married in,' complained Harriet Low in 1836 as she cut out the wedding dress for her friend Caroline Shillaber, who was preparing to be married to Dr Thomas Colledge. 'No shops to go to.' Vachell seems to have been on duty at Canton for the ceremony, over which Wimberley presided, but he did perform both baptismal and burial services for each of her infant sons Lancelot, Thomas and William between 1837 and 1838 (94, 95 and 96). He was a popular choice for weddings, in 1835 even sailing to Manila to perform the marriage ceremony for Dr Colledge's sister Matilda.[1]

After the Company had relinquished its China monopoly in 1834 and Vachell had finally left, the religious needs of Macao and Canton were met by missionaries who, in addition to preaching and conducting services for Anglican baptisms, weddings and funerals, had other duties to perform. Protestant missionaries appeared in Macao from time to time in quite large numbers. On one such occasion, as many as eight of them hired a lorcha there in which to sail on an exploration of the countryside of the new colony of Hong Kong, taking advantage of the cool weather of February 1841; one of that group was Rev W.H. Medhurst, whose wedding 13 years later took place in the house of Gideon Nye in Macao under the direction of the Rev M.C. Odell, and whose baby girl born of the union is buried at Macao (35). The young Rev Charles Barton was brought out from England in 1851 as the first full-time chaplain to serve the combined Anglican community of Macao and Canton, but survived less than four months and himself lies in the Old Cemetery (11).

LEARNING CHINESE

AMONG THE MORE RESOLUTELY applied of the regulations with which Chinese authority had early burdened foreigners was the prohibition against learning the Chinese language. Its effectiveness was reinforced by the stiff penalties imposed upon any Chinese found teaching it, and by the condition, rarely observed, that on the few days a foreigner might have permission to stroll the streets of Canton, it must always be in the company of an approved interpreter. Anyone who wished to learn Chinese had to learn it in Macao and his tutor had to move from Canton to teach him. Whenever the Company contrived, after much furtive enquiry, to find a tutor willing to damn the consequences and move to Macao, his pupils had to cross the city in secret and seek him out in his private quarters in order to attend his tutorials. The teacher engaged in 1793 to impart Cantonese to Thomas Pattle (42) and two other members of its staff was even afraid to accept his fee, which had to be paid to his father at Canton, lest the local mandarins tumble to his wickedness. The arrival of George Staunton early in the century as the Company's Chinese interpreter heralded a change, since he was already versed in the language.

A HEALTH RESORT

MACAO WAS A RESORT where sufferers went to recover their health, though many that did go did not survive. Christian Boeck (46) died two days after arriving in Macao from Calcutta on a health visit. Mark Cooper (22) was in Macao on sick leave from his regiment in Hong Kong when he died, probably from malaria. Rebecca Kinsman was moved to reflect on the numbers of forlorn people who went to Macao as invalids – 'from H. Kong,

Chinnery: Dr Colledge's Eye Hospital

Canton &c, our pretty Protestant burial place here, has received many accessions to its members, from the victims of that fearful H. Kong fever, who finding they could not recover, come here to – die … The fever is not nearly as prevalent as last year, and it is thought will be still less so, another, as the new houses become more thoroughly seasoned.'[2] J.R. Morrison (143), sent over from Hong Kong for a change of air and a rest, died in Macao a few days later. Charles Barton (11) and Frank Bacon (59) were in Macao to recover from a bout of ill-health when they died, as was Justices' Clerk William Leggett (70).

CLINICS

CLINICS WERE HELD IN Macao and in Canton from time to time, and sometimes they were referred to as hospitals. Dr John Livingstone, a Company surgeon and father of an infant girl buried in the cemetery (Charlotte, 41), opened a clinic for the Chinese at Macao in 1820, with the help of Dr Robert Morrison (141). Another Company surgeon, Dr Thomas Colledge (see 94, 95, and 96), was a specialist in diseases of the eye and opened a free ophthalmic hospital financed wholly by himself in the late 1820s, and this became the model for a similar institution set up a few years later in Canton by the famed American missionary Dr Peter Parker. They were the first two charity hospitals to be set up in China, and the first to undertake the training of young locals in paramedical duties. When trading was suspended in 1829 and the British withdrew from Canton to Macao, the surgeon of the Company's ship *General Kyd*, Dr Frederick Alleyn (55), stayed on to man a temporary clinic so that members of the foreign community who remained would not be cut off from medical advice and help. Richard Turner (93) was actively concerned in the setting up of a British floating hospital for seamen anchored at Whampoa, following a public meeting called at Canton for the purpose in 1835 by Dr William Jardine.[3]

In some entries in Section II of this study, there is mention of 'hospitals' in Macao of which there is no record: in an inscription of 1850 appears a 'US Naval Hospital' (1); a 'Hospital, Macao' (3) in the log of the American ship *Marion*, a 'Portuguese Hospital, Macao' (4), and an 'American Naval Hospital' (6), all in 1851; newspaper reports of 1840 and 1841 refer to a naval hospital in Macao (131 and 132); and Cree held a consultation in a 'Macao Hospital' on 11 June 1841. The eye hospital organized in February 1838 by Colledge and Parker, acting for the Medical Missionary Society, was the only institution that corresponded with these titles, though it appears that a temporary American 'naval hospital' offered treatment 'under the superintendence of the fleet surgeon'.[4]

NEWS

DR ROBERT MORRISON (141) and the American missionary Dr Elijah Bridgman founded *The Chinese Repository* in 1832, offering readers English commentaries on the political and mercantile situation, as well as items on Chinese customs and history. Prior to this, the community in Canton and Macao had had access to trading news only in the *Canton Register*, the first English-language periodical in the area, started in 1827 and edited by an American, which included currently quoted prices for the sale of opium. *The Anglo-Chinese Kalendar* was published annually from 1835; the *Canton Press* appeared in September 1838, financed by Jardine, Matheson & Co and containing some items of news; and in Hong Kong the *China Mail* first appeared in 1845, the *Hong Kong Adviser and Directory* the following year, the *Friend of China* and *Hong Kong Gazette*, and from 1850 Dixson's regular trade and shipping publications.

PERSONAL MAIL

BEFORE THE ROYAL MAIL started delivering personal mail overseas, it was carried in packets from Britain and India in the charge of ship's captains. It was the custom for the captain of a ship which made Macao its first port of call in south China to hand letters over to the addressee in Macao if possible, or if not, to a representative of his firm or even to his friends before he moved on to Whampoa or other ports, where the procedure was repeated. In the case of a ship belonging to or chartered by the Company, its captain handed over mail not addressed to the ship's consignees to the steward and butler of the factory, who then took it either to the president's house or to the factory office; from there, letters were delivered to the individuals addressed. Mail carried on opium clippers was on some occasions taken first to Lintin. Thomas Forbes (163) and Samuel Monson (56) tried to anticipate a mail delivery by sailing from Macao to Lintin in Forbes' yacht but, overtaken by a typhoon, they failed to contact the clipper carrying it and were wrecked and both drowned.

Hong Kong became the terminus for British shipping after it was ceded, though many continued to call first at Macao: but captains refused to break open letter packages before they reached Hong Kong. As there was no regular mail boat between Hong Kong and Macao, the delivery of letters for Britishers in Macao after that was often delayed for an extra week or more, even when a ship known to have letters aboard could be seen riding at anchor in the Macao Roads. Mail carried from Calcutta in December 1829 on board the Portuguese ship *Temerario* was evidence of the need to adhere to a strict routine: it had arrived with a mail bag addressed to the Company chief, which disappeared. It was discovered lying in the

Portuguese Customs House, but not until more than three years after its despatch. When in November 1841 the British living at Macao were notified that Patrick Stewart (44) had been authorized to open and distribute ships' packets in Macao, it was to their great relief.

Letters from England took as much as six months to arrive, and sometimes much longer when addressed to a serviceman who was at sea. Off Chusan in 1841, Surgeon Cree was brought a letter that 'was thirteen months old and had postmarks on it Colombo, Trincomalee, Calcutta, Singapore, &c., and smudged all over'. Mail was frequently lost on its way: Cree received news brought to Chusan by an opium clipper from Hong Kong, that the steamer *Madagascar* had been 'burnt at sea between Hong Kong and Amoy … as she was bringing up the mail I fear I have lost my letters'.

Among the occasional clashes that occurred between the free-traders and the Company that licensed them, particularly in the period when its authority was waning, one was sparked by an irregularity in the delivery of letters. On 19 June 1833, the factory steward was waiting for a bag of mail from the Company's ship *Red Rover* (see illustration, page 55). While conveying it to the factory, the coolie had been stopped by Captain Grant of Jardine's ship *Hercules*, an opium receiving ship, who took it to Markwick's Tavern and opened it in the presence of James Innes (137) and Richard Markwick (104), spreading the letters and parcels over the table in view of some members of the public. The Company took a serious view of it and revoked the ship's licence to trade in China.[5]

MOVEMENT

HARRIET DUDDELL (21) OFFERED phaetons and horses for hire from her husband's hotel, the Oriental, for short journeys. For journeys to Canton, Markwick operated, in addition to his Tavern and his shop in New China Street, the small river schooner *Sylph* – one of 14 steamers taking freight and passengers up and down the Pearl River between Macao and Canton in the middle of the century; some were offered for chartering on special occasions. $30 was the return passenger fare in 1830, or $5 more by way of Lintin. On its way to Lintin from Macao during one trip in July 1833, the *Sylph* was caught carrying 14 cases of silk goods and four of miscellaneous items, contraband in all worth $5,000: the cargo was confiscated and the boat broken up. Twenty-six years later the fares had descended steeply, when one-way fares were $8 from Macao or Hong Kong to Canton, and $5 from Macao to Hong Kong – press advertisements in Hong Kong warned passengers to pay for freight or passage in Spanish dollars, and advised them 'to bring their own wine and spirits'. Charles Woodberry (19) and J.B. Endicott (166) ran a fleet which steamed between Macao and Hong Kong under the agency of Sandwith Drinker (39), and Canton where W.C. Hunter was agent: among them was the *Spark*, commanded first by Charles Woodberry (19) and then, on Woodberry's death, by John Williams (23). The next year Williams took command of a new river steamer, the *Lily*. As a quicker means of moving between Canton and Macao, fast 'chop boats' could be hired.[6]

---

1 Marriage R 11,218 p 329
2 Monroe, August 1844
3 Canton R of 16/6/1835 and 10/10/1837
4 Morison, p 348; Hawks, p 338
5 Loines p 30; Morse iii pp 356–61; Cree pp 72, 77 and 95
6 CM of 11/8/1853; Dixson HKSL for 1855 and 1856 and Dixson HKG of 22/10/56; FC&HKG of 9/8/1856

6
Life Ashore

EASE

THE PROFITS OF PRIVATE TRADE could be large, and the wealth of successful merchants supported a lifestyle of great ease. Most diarists have passed some comment on the opulence of life. Harriet Low frequently mentions a cohort of butlers and maids and other servants charged with making life easier. Up to 20 servants was not unusual for a Macao house kept by single men, a degree of aid offering the chance of entertainment on a generally noble enough scale. Residents dressed generally in fashion and in apparel fitting all occasions. Carriages were a rare sight in so confined a territory, most foreign residents riding the streets on horseback. The salaries of Company men did not reach the same heights, but were more than ample for a good life while it lasted. George Chinnery (40) characterized them as spending 'six months in Macao, having nothing to do, and the other six months in Canton ... doing nothing'.[1] Foreign living was little different in Canton, from where Morrison (141) reported to the London Mission: 'It would be impossible for me to dwell amidst the princely grandeur of the English who reside here.'

Chinnery: Self-portrait

CHINNERY AND PORTRAITURE

GEORGE CHINNERY, ONE OF a family of artists, was the most highly reputed of the local portraitists of the time. He made paintings of many of the foreign residents' children, a difficult task and perhaps as much of an occupational hazard for him as it was a welcome preoccupation, between trading seasons, for their mothers. He had a special eye for handsome women and was thought to have drawn and painted Elizabeth Fearon, in whose house he lived for a time as lodger, several times. Harriet Low, who sat for him over six days for what became one of his better-known pictures, took sketching lessons from him. She said her aunt and uncle also sat for him. He painted several of the notables later buried in the Old Cemetery, and members of their families: of the Colledges a year after they married (the parents of the infants 94, 95 and 96) and of Dr Thomas Colledge showing him standing with his servant and three of his Chinese patients; of George Cruttenden (151) and Sir Andrew Ljungstedt (60); and of Dr Robert Morrison (141), his first wife Mary (142), their son John Robert (143), and his son Robert by his second wife Eliza. He left eight known self-portraits, four in oil and four sketches.[2]

Rebecca Kinsman (see 112) had the portrait of her second child 'Ecca', then aged four, painted by Lamqua (Kwan Kiu-chin), who painted fine portraits in oils in the Western style and was Chinnery's pupil and Canton rival. Her sittings were in Macao during the cool days of December 1843, and sometimes stretched to two unnatural hours, the child meantime finding it scarcely tolerable to be sitting still for so long, even under the reprimands of her mother, and losing her usual 'bright expression' in the process. Lamqua, her mother said, was 'very fat and no one could imagine on looking at him, that he possessed a spark of genius, though he has in reality a great deal, and is considered a great portrait painter among the Chinese. He has painted Sir Henry Pottinger, Admiral Parker, and various other distinguished men. As a very great favour and it certainly was one, he came here to paint Ecca, as it would have been very inconvenient for so many of us, to have gone to his room, and Ecca beside would not have felt so much at home or looked so natural'. Ecca's father (112) thought he 'did not do justice to Ecca, for she was more beautiful than her picture; no artist can copy her soft brilliant eyes'.[3]

OTHER PERSONAGES
SEVERAL OF THE OTHERS connected with the Old Cemetery were of some consequence in Macao and Canton, or were colourful eccentrics or have since become famous or, like Chinnery himself, met all these criteria.

Thomas Beale (159), whom Hunter recalls as living in 'one of the finest of the old Portuguese houses ... on a narrow street known as Beale's Lane', was a naturalist, opium speculator, shady bankrupt, and finally a suicide. The Company's chaplain, the Reverend George Vachell, was a gambler and the local flirt. There were also Dr Frederick Alleyn (55), freelance smuggler and a tea-taster; James Innes (137), puffed-up cad; Gideon Nye, rich ship-salesman, popular host, and voluminously boring writer, in due course being the oldest of the foreign merchants resident at Canton; Richard Markwick (104), man of many hats as shopkeeper, river-boat owner, taverner and general dealer in contraband; and other characters whose doings made the tongues wag.

Some have since become noteworthy, largely because of their personal connections with the illustrious and powerful which have since been recognized. Captain Isaac Cotgrave (the father of Louisa Stewart, 44), for instance, had commanded a division under Nelson in 1801. The father of George Washington Biddle (58) was commissary-general to George Washington, the first American president (1789–97), and so close a friend that the president became his son's godfather. Lieutenant Joseph Adams (38) was closely related to two American presidents, having John Adams, the second president (1797–1801), as his grandfather, and John Quincy Adams, the sixth (1825–29), as an uncle. Lord Henry John Spencer Churchill (133), son of the spendthrift regency buck the fifth Duke of Marlborough, was a well-known freemason in England when he left to join the East India Squadron in the Pearl River as captain of the warship *Druid*:

Chinnery: Dr Robert Morrison translating the Bible

his tomb in Macao is visited, not so much for these reasons, as for his family connection with his great-grandnephew, Sir Winston Churchill. Frank Scott (50) was not only a first cousin once removed of the novelist Sir Walter Scott, then at the height of his fame, but the son of James Scott, partner and friend of Sir Stamford Raffles, the founder of Singapore.

Some became as famed abroad as they were in the cities of the estuary. When he returned to Linköping, his home town in Sweden, Sir Andrew Ljungstedt (60), leader of the Swedish community, added to the respect in which he had been held throughout his unusually long life in south China

as philosopher-historian, carrying his wealth back with him to endow educational institutions.

Dr Robert Morrison, the scholar based at Canton and Macao all his working life, was the first of the Protestant missionaries to move to China and is widest known for being the earliest translator of the New Testament into Chinese, compiler of a Chinese dictionary and a Chinese grammar, and founder of an Anglo-Chinese school in Malacca. The money for his Christian mission was sent from England through Beale & Magniac – in company, as Austin Coates reminds us, with remittances for the support of the women kept by merchants, while they were absent at Canton for the season. Neither that, if he had realized it, nor his audacious evasion both of the Company's rules and the official restrictions imposed at Canton – by the subterfuge of accepting employment in the Company, technically as a merchant but in fact as an interpreter – nor his disregard of the regulations by continuing his Chinese studies, none of these seemed to him to clash one whit with the narrow principles he professed, as he pursued the unswerving way of his vocation. He taught the Chinese language to his friend and colleague Rev Samuel Dyer (146), to James Daniell, uncle of the infant Edmond (97), and to Thomas Smith, the brother-in-law of Miss Wedderburn (145), among others. Coates offers a picture that cannot be bettered, in sentiment and briefness, of the regard in which he was held: 'for all his peculiarities – irritating, narrow-minded, scornful, and completely humourless – the man who by his endurance, his achievement, and his moral bravery stands out inescapably as the most considerable European in China in the early nineteenth century ... honoured by universities, received by the King on a visit in 1825, welcomed by the leading orientalists of Europe, and the mere mention of whose name in the House of Commons produced cheers'.

The Rev George Vachell lived far lower on the intellectual but far higher on the congenial scale, popular as a preacher and effective in his pastoral duties as the Company's chaplain. Its chaplains who remained in Macao during the season were usually drawn into the social whirl. Vachell was always willing to show visitors round the settlement; he was equally ready to take the women for walks and partner them in waltzes and at cards, and turned up to call on them as frequently as he could, without regard for the dictates of propriety, dis-

playing 'little of the gravity of the clergyman' expected by a Christian community. He seems to have been criticized for the unremitting attentions he lavished on Harriet Low in particular; and attended the local horse-races, cheering on whichever of the horses he had backed to win.[4]

The social round was also enlivened from time to time by the port activities of officers on shore-leave from visiting British and American warships, and by the occasional visit of a man of distinction, like the American special agent Edmond Roberts (88), the US 'Plenipo' Caleb Cushing and Commodore Matthew C. Perry, round whose presence dinner parties and dances might be organized. There were the well-known who were at Macao too briefly to play much part in the community life of Macao, but chanced to die or were brought to be buried there: Lord Napier (164), the British envoy to China; Sir William Fraser (62), the chieftain of a Scots clan; Sir Humphrey Senhouse (136), the ageing commander of the British East India Squadron, who had taken Nelson's personal surrender as flag captain of the *Superb*; Eliza Wedderburn (145), descended from the Earls of Dundee and the family that bore the hereditary office of Standard Bearer of Scotland; and Samuel Dyer (146), who introduced metal-cast type into the Chinese printing process.

As the foreign community was doubtless basking in the light shed by its more illustrious members, it was at the same time taking much of its entertainment from the improprieties of the more newsworthy, such as Thomas Beale, the litigious James Innes and philanderer George Vachell.

WOMEN AND CHILDREN

FOREIGN WOMEN HAD BEEN forbidden to

enter China and, to avoid any unnecessary problems with the officials, were denied berths in Company ships sailing from India, even as far as Macao, lest the mandarins took to annexing that territory to their prohibitions. Not until the final years of the 18th century did English women reach Macao; within the first decade of the next they had become an established element in the society there and the Company was closing its eyes to the arrival of the wives and daughters of its officers. Until then, Company officers had little recourse but to enter into the sorts of arrangements with local women which, at the insistence of the Company, must exclude marriage if they were not prepared to risk at the very least a scandalized ostracism from polite society, and at the worst the sack. In Canton, which the women did not penetrate until 1830, the officers liaisons were usually more casual.

The wife of William Baynes, then the Company chief, was determined to see for herself the 'princely grandeur' in which her husband lived while he was in Canton and which so appalled Morrison, and in April 1830 persuaded him to take her to Canton for a visit, with Elizabeth Fearon (84) and the wife of another supercargo, Mrs Robinson. They became the first to defy the Chinese ban on foreign women, and their arrival brought threats from a nonplussed Viceroy that he would stop all trade in the factories and send in soldiers to remove them. Baynes's answer was to position Company cannon at the factory gate and order in a hundred armed men from Company ships, enough to prevent the Viceroy from matching words with action. The women had announced they would attend service in the Company chapel while there, to hear the Reverend Vachell preach; the apparition was witnessed, that morning of Sunday the 8th of May, by the largest congregation ever. They created a great stir, Mrs Baynes by wearing a dress 'in true London style, which, much admired by us, is considered frightful by the Chinese', and Mrs Fearon by her arresting beauty. To placate the Viceroy, the ladies were persuaded to leave after a few days of mounting pressure.

November the following season saw a wave of American women visitors determined to follow Mrs Baynes's example, but this time to stay for three weeks. For part of the journey they were on the fast clipper, the *Sylph*, which was to capture the record for a trip from Calcutta during the summer next year with an opium run of only 17 days. Among the group of tourists on board for the excitement of a visit to Canton was another of Macao's beauties, Harriet Low, who left a detailed account of the adventure. The men were better prepared for this visit, and 'the second day after they arrived several old codgers were seen in immense coats, which had been stowed away in camphor trunks for ten or fifteen years, and with huge cravats on, and with what once were gloves'. After attending a service one Sunday evening, the women were shown round the factory area, with all lights lit so that the Chinese residents might 'behold our fair faces, and we had quite a rabble round us ... though they were all perfectly civil'; in Old China Street by the side of the American factory, however, 'Foreign devil women!' was shouted at them as they passed. Their paramount impression was of the great luxury of it all: 'You have no idea how elegantly these bachelors live here. I don't wonder they like it.'[5]

Captains engaged in the country trade first started bringing their wives out with them; mostly they settled them in Macao, though some continued to take them on trading voyages. Some came to have connections with the Old Cemetery: Captain

47

Duncan (48) brought his wife out in in 1833, shortly before he died; Captain Drinker (39) brought his in about 1842; Captain Sutherland (see 15) arrived at Macao with his wife on his ship the *Hero* from Calcutta early in January 1858, only six days before her death. Captain N. Durant's wife Euphemia (111) was in the habit of travelling with him to and from the Indian ports on his ship the *Good Success*: on one such occasion in 1833, when they attempted to board the boat that was to convey them from Macao to the anchorage in the Macao Roads, the Chinese customs officers at the landing stage on the Praya Grande demanded 'squeeze' in the form of embarkation fees from them both, which he refused to pay. A fight ensued, in which he and his comprador were badly injured before they were rescued by foreign residents.

Traders who remained in Macao during the trading season and were available to entertain the women were few and far between, though there were frequent visits of officers off naval vessels when they visited. Even then, the services of a suitable companion for a spinster could not always be found. Walks on Lappa or other parts of the countryside near Macao were not safe without an escort. The shortage was a burden to Miss Low: 'Oh, hard is the lot of spinsters in Macao!'[6]

Some 40 infants were baptized between 1820 and 1833, most of them the children of Macao residents, a few of ships' masters calling for the purpose. Children occupied much of the leisure time of the women during the trading season; Jane Daniell, later to become aunt of the infant Edmond Daniell (97), had six, all born in Macao between 1825 and 1835, but in the off-season months their demands did nothing to inhibit her and her husband James from being the centre of a social whirl. Harriet Low recounts her pleasure at several of the Daniells' parties during this period – 'a sweet woman, and she has a husband as pleasant'. One took place on 11 March 1833 – 'everything very elegant' – only six weeks after her fourth child was born, no doubt joining the others in the capable care of a Chinese 'amah'. For another, when Jane was blessed with but three of them, Harriet pictures herself 'sitting ascribbling here, waiting for the hour to arrive when I may dress for Mrs Daniell's, for at half-past eight we are to go. Is it not absurd to introduce London hours into Macao?'

FOOD AND DRINK

MACAO PRODUCED NO FOOD of any kind, no eggs, no meat, no vegetables: all essential to sustain life but water was imported from China. The Kinsmans (112) kept three cows for a supply of fresh milk for the family until 1845 when the last of them died. Mrs Ritchie (mother of John Ritchie, 61), the doyenne of the American ladies in Macao, sent over a temporary supply of goat's milk twice daily until Mrs Kinsman could make other arrangements. By the next year, their loss was made good with the purchase of two more cows, and they had enough milk to make icecream daily for the family. Rebecca Kinsman tells us that the local icehouse supplied ice at 6 cents a pound, a cent cheaper than ice bought in Hong Kong, of which the weight reduced by 'one half in coming over'.

Cutting blocks of natural ice from the rivers in winter and storing them for use during the rest of the year was a northern Chinese custom which had long attracted the attention of European visitors. Early in the 19th century, a Boston shipowner, Frederic Tudor, was exporting to the West Indies ice cut from Wenham Lake in Massachusetts so profitably that by 1835 he was trading to the Far

East, in ships with holds specially insulated for the long voyage. After Hong Kong was founded, Samuel Drinker (39) became his agent and sold ice to casual buyers for 4 cents a pound, on seasonal contract for 3 cents, and was able to arrange daily deliveries from his icehouse.[7]

In 1846, 'an abundant supply to last through cold weather' arrived at Macao aboard the ice-ship *Helen Augustus*; the consignee, 'fearing combustion', left his icehouse doors open: 'when alas – the moment the air entered, the ice disappeared like vapour and was not. Was it not singular?'; and no more was expected before the following April. The Canton supply had petered out by the end of September; and when the Ritchies threw a dinner party a week later, their icecream was made with the very last of the ice to be had in the region. Among the guests on that occasion were Mary Rawle (wife of Samuel Rawle, 134), tastefully clad in white muslin, and an elegant Mrs Forbes, the wife of P.S. Forbes, a merchant with Russell & Co and American Consul at Canton; but the Parkers had not been asked, as there was 'a difficulty between them and the Ritchies'.[8]

The sprightly Miss Low describes a Christmas Day (1829) dinner with the Company 'at half-past six, where we shall be as stiff as stakes, and, I suppose, shall not enjoy ourselves at all. These dinners are amazing stiff, but I shall rig myself in a white satin under-dress, with a wrought muslin petticoat, and a pink satin bodice to set neatly to my neat little form, and made by my own neat little hands. I shall then jump into my neat little chair, and proceed to the scene of action. I shall say all the neat little things I can, and discuss the merits of the several dishes in my own way. Later – at half-past six we jumped into our chairs, and were the first to arrive, which did not exactly suit our feelings. However, we were soon followed by all the ladies and whole squads of gentlemen. After conversing awhile, I was led to an elegant table, and seated between the elegant Mr Daniell [James], and Mr Vachell, the chaplain. Everything on the table was splendid, – a whole service of massive plate. There were about sixty at table ... Everyone brings their own servant to wait upon them at table. When the first course is cleared away, these extra servants all fall back to the wall, and the regular servants carry out the dishes, handed to them by the butlers ...there was nothing stiff about it. Everybody appeared perfectly easy and at home'.[9] John Leathley (78) was the importer of champagne and hock.

LEISURE IN HONG KONG

HONG KONG WAS, the unmarried Cree thought when he had been ashore a few times, 'a good place for marriageable girls' despite their paucity – 'ladies are so scarce and doctors so plentiful, that each lady has her own doctor exclusively'; and it is of some point, when considering what amusements diverted the foreign population of Macao, to take a peep at those that filled Cree's spare time when anchored at Hong Kong. His service in the China seas opened when he was a man of 26 and ended at 35. When ashore, he enjoyed with unfailing relish the round of 'visiting friends, flirting with the girls, country rambles and picnics', attended the races and dinners, and at one of the many dances engaged himself in a new one, the Polka, 'lately arrived from civilization'.

Dinner-dances there were a-plenty: Cree writes an inviting account of one at which there were 'about forty ladies and four times as many men', following a naval regatta in the harbour. After the show, 'at 6 dinner, but only half, about 140, could sit down at one time, although the table extended the whole length of the main deck. After dinner dancing commenced on the quarterdeck, which was prettily decorated with the flags of all nations, chandeliers of bayonets, variegated lamps, transparencies, and flowers. On the poop were cardtables, &c. About 11 supper was served; afterwards dancing was kept up till 2 in the morning'.

During the last two weeks of March 1845, he attended three dances on shore: a ball given by the 18th Regiment, a dance at the McKnights' house at West Point, and a dance organized by the officers of the 4th Madras Native Infantry, which was 'plenty of fun, but so much dissipation with the thermometer at 80 rather takes it out of me. This party was not large, eighteen ladies and twenty-four gentlemen, but kept it up till 3 in the morning. Last night we took our musicians to McKnight's and afterwards gave our friends in town a benefit.' For the next month of April, there was 'little else to record but dinners, dances, and flirtations', including yet another evening for 'a little music and a dance' with the McKnights, who rejoiced in 'three pretty stepdaughters, a pleasant addition to Hong Kong society', and another dinner party on board his ship also followed by a dance on its quarterdeck. On a Sunday after church service the same month, he picked up the girls on their way home for a sail across the bay in the ship's cutter and sketched a charming picture of them as they scrambled over rocks and through brambles, on which the girls had torn their Sunday dresses and an officer 'split his continuations', all to great hilarity. For a picnic at Lyemun, Cree and his shipmates hired a lorcha, on board which they had hoisted a piano to accompany singing and dancing on the beach; for yet another at Shekpikwan they borrowed the ship's cutter again.

And so the round went on through May. A 4th Madras dinner followed by a visit to the girls; a 'poor dinner' at Government House, where 'the Governor [J.F. Davis] is said to be stingy'; a musical party at the house of William Caine, chief magistrate of Hong Kong – 'some famous German performers there ... there was a large party and some good music, champagne iced, and a capital supper, dancing and green-tea punch to finish ... home about 2 o'clock'. And before embarking for home and repairs to his ship, he spent a regretful last evening at Hong Kong listening to the music and songs of the girls and gazing out on the harbour from the verandah.

On his second tour of duty in Chinese waters, Cree took up where he had left off – 'whist, &c' after dinner once with Chief Justice John Walter Hulme, a man who had problems with drink; over lunch at the bungalow of J.M. Dent the merchant, a talk about the prospects of cultivating tea in the Himalayas with the botanist Robert Fortune, who had been 'sent out by the Government to get tea plants to take to India'; a pleasant chat with 'old Chinnery, the artist', who on another occasion was staying there; and so on.

When exhibitions of amity were called for, Chinese officials could be persuaded into a Western dance. During a ceremonial visit of the High Imperial Commissioner Keying and his vast entourage, the Manchu Tung spoiled a quadrille by doing a hornpipe with the Chief Justice – 'a laughable exhibition; Tung fat, and enveloped in his silk coats, cap and peacock's feather and satin boots, with soles 2 inches thick, and capering about like an elephant, and the Judge anything but grave, flinging his long skinny legs, encased in breeches and black silk stockings, in all directions, his long visage and protuberant nose, his bushy

Robert Fortune: Dent's house and garden in Hong Kong

head and broad grin, having anything but a judge-like appearance. Keying asked if we had many more judges on the island'. The round of British and Americans in Macao differed only in degree, not in kind.[10]

TALK AND HORSES

CONVERSATION STIMULATED many leisure moments of Macao life. Thomas Pattle (42) was regarded as 'a man of remarkably convivial Habits and of great Conversational Powers which rendered him very popular with some of the young men' – he was then about 35 years old, and able to enjoy the good things of life.[11] Now and again the talk was of horses, the seasonal excitement of the races antici-pated by the stimulation of watching them exercise and discussing form and the betting odds. Chap-lain Vachell placed careful bets and adored the action. The Maiden Sweepstakes at Macao was won in April 1829 by a mare running for James Innes (137) in an amateur race. Ridden by J.H. Astell, who was later the deputy Superintendent of British Trade, it won easily enough – 'all the other horses in the race having bolted'.[12]

MUSIC, THEATRE, AND DANCING

SOME RESIDENTS HAD THEIR OWN musical instruments, several military and naval bands were in the region, and sometimes professional entertainers visited. The Daniells owned a piano, which appears to have been moved from one house to another to accompany singing at parties, including one thrown by Harriet Low, where there was also a guitarist 'and four Portuguese musicians, to the grinding of whose fiddles we danced'. When Nathaniel Kinsman (112) arrived to settle in Macao with his family in 1843, they were accommodated on the Praya Grande in the house of William Lejee of Philadelphia, a member of his firm, Wetmore & Co. A niece, Mary Ann Southwick, was with them, devoted to dancing and music, and her aunt records that Lejee had 'appropriated to her use a very fine harmonicon – presented to him by Mrs Coolidge [Mrs Colledge] (my old school mate Caroline Shillaber)' (see 94).[13]

Captain Drinker (39) took his wife Susanna with him on short voyages, and persuaded Rebecca Kinsman to accompany them in 1845 on what turned out to be, in part, a very rough voyage to Manila and back in the American ship *Geneva*. Mrs Drinker had put her piano on board and one of the passengers, a Mr de Silver, played the flute and sang; whenever the gales subsided, there were musical evenings. With them were her little daughter, who had been ordered a change of climate after a long sickness, and the 17-year-old Mary Ann, whose choice of partner for the first cotillon of a dance in Manila caused such a clash with the Drinkers that the Kinsmans returned to Hong Kong on a different ship.[14]

The members of ships' bands, most of them foreign-born, were enlisted men who performed in the band in addition to their normal duties. They played at concerts and receptions aboard or ashore, piped the men when manning the capstan, and piped flag officers when leaving or boarding. Troops being transported took their regimental bands with them. Occasionally, when it was calm enough, the band could play at sea: on such an occasion Cree's ship was 'running for the Straits of Malacca. In the afternoon the band of the 18th [Regiment] gave us a little music on the quarterdeck'. Harriet Low was in a party paying a three-week visit to Lintin, anchoring in the midst of 23 other ships, and one evening on board the Jardine, Matheson ship *Red Rover*, they 'danced a quadrille upon the deck and the gentlemen waltzed'.[15] The *Red Rover* was the first and fastest of the British opium clippers to be launched, and it is probable that during her 30-year commission she carried more opium than any other ship.

In June 1844, Commodore F.A. Parker's flagship, the US frigate *Brandywine*, put into harbour with Plenipotentiary Caleb Cushing on board. Rebecca Kinsman has left a description of a long anticipated dinner-dance, at which the ship's band would play – Charles Ganger (77) was one of the musicians. During dinner 'the band played some lively airs ... after dinner, some of the guests, as well as the gallant officers, danced cotillons on the spacious quarter deck'. At dinner she sat next to 'the Plenipo'. This was repeated a week later, but ashore on Coloane, then an island off Macao and now connected by a causeway, where Gideon Nye offered a picnic of chowder, cold meats and fruit to much the same company, including the 'Plenipo' and the Commodore, and after a ramble over the island a merry dance accompanied by the band, all ending with 'a pleasant sail home, under the light of a bright moon'.[16]

The US steam frigate *Susquehanna* – which had

lost its quartermaster, Daniel Cushman (7), the previous year – boasted a very good band, mentioned several times in the reports on Commodore Perry's negotiations with the Japanese. It gave a grand concert in Macao one evening in September 1853, to which a special boat, the *Sir Charles Forbes*, made the trip from Hong Kong, taking people who wished to attend. At a subscription ball held that year in Hong Kong's Victoria Theatre on the night of Boxing Day, its 'enlivening strains' accompanied dancing until daylight.[17]

George Duddell, the brother of Frederick (27), was the builder of the Victoria Theatre in Queen's Road, Hong Kong's first theatre, opening it in November 1848, a venue presumably intended for theatricals staged in English and musical concerts produced by local amateur and by visiting artistes. Chinese theatre in Hong Kong was at that time, when the number of Chinese in the community was small, represented by spectacles of a kind at which they were singularly cunning and which would be more readily understood by foreigners. At Chusan, certainly, while ashore one Saturday afternoon, Surgeon Cree had been 'amused by watching a Chinese puppet show, very cleverly managed'.[18]

The Corps d'Opera Ambulant was in Macao for six months from April to October 1833, playing mainly comic opera on a stage far too small at 'ten feet high, sixteen wide, and twenty deep'. The Corps had only five singers – three men and two women contraltos, one of the women 'invariably taking gentlemen's parts'. The orchestra was directed by a local Portuguese, Mr Paiva, and led by an American chorus-master, without a chorus. In spite of its lack of even one soprano among the soloists, the company contrived to perform, in addition to individual appearances at soirees, some 11

operas during the season, including seven by Rossini – the *Barber of Seville* (its most successful, though requiring a tenor and two sopranos), *Tancredi*, *La Gazza Ladra*, *Othello*, *The Italian in Algiers*, *L'Inganno Felice*, *Elisa e Claudio*, and the patchwork *Eduardo e Christina*. Harriet Low seems to have attended them all, the *Italian* as a treat for her 24th birthday. Encouraged by the reception, Paiva successfully directed a Spanish version of *Cinderella* after the Corps had left, drawing most of the singers from the local Portuguese community.[19]

A form of drama that engaged Chinese talent for show to the full was the firework display, and it was used to spectacular effect in 1845 by the French opium-shipper J.A. Durran, when he marked the anniversary of the American Declaration of Independence by laying on a gorgeously noisy show of pyrotechnics from the deck of his clipper *Sylph*, watched from nearby ships and the shore by an awestruck population.

The 'droll genius' Chinnery (40) appeared in several of the amateur (and much less meretricious) theatrical productions, in roles for which he had been chosen chiefly because he was so ugly. Harriet Low recalls a production in November 1829 of *The Poor Gentleman*, a play by George Colman the Younger (1802),[20] as 'one of the drollest things you ever saw ... the most amusing were the female characters. Mr Chinnery was one, and they could not have chosen anybody less fit to perform a female part [that of Lucretia Mactab]; but, however, his ridiculous appearance made such sport ... she was supposed to be breaking the hearts of all the young beaux, and you have no idea how ugly she was!'. Chinnery had also painted the scenery. As reported by the press in 1837, the members of the British community gave a performance of *Sheridan's Rivals*, attended by the Governor and practically all the foreigners in Macao, including Captain Charles Elliot and members of his trade commission. Mrs Malaprop was played by Chinnery, whose 'well known traits of humour for wit and glee and his inimitable acting of this first rate character drew forth reiterated cheers; and really I do not believe it possible to match his performance throughout this play, in the wide extended range of English amateurs'. So great was the impression that, when Toogood Downing visited Canton several months later, its fame still 'resounded among the foreigners in China at this time'.

SICKNESS

THE STRAINS OF TEDIOUS voyages, exposure in ports to sicknesses that rarely afflicted the West, and the climatic rigour of summers on the south China coast suffered by travellers and settlers, weakened their resistance to cholera, dysentery, malaria and the new 'Hong Kong fever' attributed variously to the preparation of building sites, disintegrating granite, and damp houses. A hard life at sea, the dangers that attended encounters with pirates and sharks, falls from the rigging and all sorts of accidents accounted for many other deaths.

Provisions and the water supply obtained from shore in the estuary and on the China coast were rarely of a quality to help unaccustomed men recover from sickness, even when serving ashore, and foods quickly went rotten in summer. When a combined epidemic of malaria and dysentery struck Hong Kong and was decimating the 59th Infantry Regiment then stationed there, the men grew panic-stricken and a local newspaper was moved to a round condemnation of their diet, as 'stuff unfit for a dog to eat'.[21]

Before Hong Kong was founded, the ships' of-ficers might be brought sick from anchorages in the estuary to recover in Macao, then die and be buried there. The men, on the other hand, were usually buried ashore close to wherever they died. They mostly died young. The large-scale death toll among the officers and men from sickness and battle wounds depressed Surgeon Cree: 'many a gallant fellow who escaped in the field has succumbed to disease'.

In the temperate climates of the West, life expectancy in the 1840s was 40 years. A great deal less was the general age at death of the foreigners buried in Macao. The average age of those who were buried in the cemetery during the same decade and whose age when they died is known, was no more than 35, in a wide range of ages, from 5 months to 76 years.

Dr Alleyn (55) suffered from hypochondria, and both he and Louisa Ilbery (57) from continual constipation, a condition which introduced them to their graves in Macao. Others in the Old Cemetery who did not meet an end in battle or an accident, were taken off in attacks diagnosed as diarrhoea, dysentery, cholera, a miscellany of fevers, pulmonary tuberculosis, sunstroke, delirium tremens, poison, and other causes of sickness not always recorded.

The troops and trading ships may often have caused the spread of a disease by bringing it with them from other parts of the world. From Trincomalee, Surgeon Cree writes that there was 'a great deal of sickness amongst the troops – choleric diarrhoea'. Cholera had broken out in the 18th Regiment, the headquarters company of which his ship was transporting to China: those who did not succumb on the voyage were bound for a service which was unsparingly plagued by sickness and infected wounds.[22]

W.J. Huggins: The Red Rover

When a ship carrying provisions for the US Navy arrived at Hong Kong in the summer of 1844, Commodore Parker decided it was preferable to store them in Macao; they were sent over in the keeping of the American Consul and of Thomas Waldron (75), the government store keeper at Hong Kong, who was attacked by severe pains one evening during his visit and, despite the ministrations of Dr Anderson who 'found him in the "collapsed state" of Asiatic cholera', he had succumbed by the following afternoon. Mary Kinsman Monroe re-corded: 'This is the first instance of Asiatic cholera, which our physicians have ever known in China.' Cholera of a type not diagnosed as being specially of 'Asiatic' origin was probably known earlier: the American trader B.R. Leach (52) suffered from 'diarrhoea contracted by his exertions and exposure' in Canton in 1838, Maria Orton (85) of 'relapsed dysentery' the following year.

The cholera epidemic that raged in 1850 killed off large numbers of Chinese and many of the Portuguese resident in Macao, including its Governor; Seaman Oliver Mitchell (1) is likely to have expired from the dysentery induced by cholera that July. While in command of the *Wizard*, at anchor off Hong Kong, Captain Slate (13) was a victim of dysentery for several weeks before he died in Macao. When disembarking his detachment of troops on the south coast of Hong Kong, Major Cooper (22) had been overcome by a sickness, probably malaria, was given sick leave to shake off his fever by resting in Macao at Shaw's Hotel.

Fevers were known by many names – they were diagnosed, perhaps randomly, as nervous fever, remittent fever, intermittent fever, and choleric fever, and there was the fever given by a severely septic wound. Isaac Engle (73) died of nervous fever. While the ships anchored at Hong Kong were flying their flags at half-mast following the death of Captain Sir Humphrey Senhouse (136) in June 1841 from fever – though it was widely held that he died from a broken heart at what he thought was a craven decision to withdraw from actions in the Pearl River – Surgeon Cree himself was among 'half the ship's company on the sick list with fever (intermittent)'. He writes from Hong Kong in the same month, of 'a great deal of sickness: remittent and intermittent fevers and diarrhoea very prevalent. The line-of-battle ships have each 100 sick. The former disease is carrying off three men a day from the 55th Regiment at West Point Barracks. The sickness is attributed to turning up the new soil for building and road making and the quantity of disintegrating granite. There are no efficient drains yet. ... The nights are very hot and sultry, bad for the sick.'[23] James Endicott (166) succumbed to typhoid.

Tetanus in wounds was a sure killer. Cree has many reports of tetanus infection: he tells us, for instance, that men of the 18th Regiment wounded in the engagements of June 1841 had succumbed to it, even from 'a trifling wound'. He was called on one occasion to a consultation in Macao about the inflamed knee-joint of Lieutenant Edward Fitzgerald (132), from which a shot had been removed. The leg should have been amputated, but Fitzgerald refused.[24]

Admiral George Elliot had a heart attack when sailing south from Chusan bound for Hong Kong; the trader J.H. Larkins (122) caught smallpox. At least one of those at rest in the Old Cemetery died from pulmonary tuberculosis, Walther Schaeffer (24), brother of a local merchant, in 1857.

POISON
THERE WERE ALSO PROBLEMS of poisoning after consuming alcohol and bread. The former ship's master Henry Warren – probably the H.V. Warren who had interred in the Old Cemetery the body of his murdered brother, R.V. Warren (74) – had to such effect indulged his longstanding 'habit of indulging in ardent spirits' that it finished in a dreadful death at Hong Kong from delirium tremens.[25]

The American merchant captains, Sandwith Drinker (39) and John P. Williams (23), were among the many victims of the notorious bread episode which occurred in January 1857, also at Hong Kong. It was 'poison administered in the bread ... by the Esing [Esang] Bakery' that killed them. The story handed down in the Drinker family is that he 'gave a dinner to some English officers for which the Chinese cook, who hated the English, put arsenic (or ground glass) in the bread. Finding this out after his guests had gone home, Captain Drinker went round with a bucket of mustard and water and they all got rid of the poison in time. He forgot that he had eaten a small piece and died of dysentery as a result of the poisoning'. The victims, however, were not all at the Drinker dinner party, and quite a different cause emerged. In the wake of a British assault on Canton in October 1856, the Viceroy had ordered that no Chinese might co-operate in any way with the British, and that the factories in Canton should be burned down and the British wharves at Whampoa destroyed. It was believed that the large quantity of arsenic which was found to have been baked into the bread delivered to the foreign residents of Hong Kong early on the morning of the 15th, had been inserted into the dough by his specific order. After settling his outstanding debts, Cheong Ah Lum the baker had made arrangements to quit Hong Kong for Macao with his family early on the morning of delivery, before breakfast. Seized and extradited to Hong Kong, he and nine others were committed for trial on the charge of 'administering poison with intent to kill and murder James Carroll Dempster, Colonial Surgeon'. Though the evidence against the staff of the bakery proved inconclusive, there was no doubt about the effect on many of the 400 foreign customers who suffered great impairment of health. They included the wife of Hong Kong's Governor, Lady Bowring, who never wholly recovered from its effects, and probably Susan Drinker, both of whom died the following year.[26]

The Western obsequies of the stricken illustrious, particularly of senior servicemen, were grand enough spectacles, to watch the eccentricities of which the Macao population turned out in force, marvelling at the precision of drill displayed by the naval and army corteges, at the rich pomp of uniforms, sometimes at the Governor and other Portuguese officials in ceremonial dress, as they traversed the city to the cemetery in sad procession, slow-marching with other public figures, and the well-known foreign residents. The individual entries in Section II recount several such funerals.

---

1 Cunynghame ii p 238

2 Loines pp 181–6; Conner plates 69, 91, 95–6, 98–9, 100–2, 146–7, 150–1, 154, and 156–62

3 Monroe lxxxvi pp 38–95

4 Loines pp 139 et al

5 Loines pp 132–4 and 304

6 Loines p 193

7 Morison pp 280 ff, and FC&HKG of April–June 1848

8 Monroe lxxxvii p 127 and lxxxviii pp 50–2

9 Loines pp 118–9; James Daniell was promoted to the Select Committee a few weeks later.

10 Cree pp 69, 142–8, 173, 175, 178 and 190–1

11 Molony; JAS 10/1922

12 FC&HKG of 21/4/1829

13 Monroe lxxxvi. The harmonicon was a new form of keyboard instrument operated by bellows blowing across a system of brass tongues, a domestic organ but without pipes. Many instruments like the harmonicon were devised during the 1830s in Paris and Munich; each was a stage in the development of the version in England known as the harmonium, a portable instrument which soon came into general use to accompany hymns at evangelical services of the simple kind, being much more robust than any of the earlier versions of the piano.

14 Loines pp 178-81

15 Cree p 48; Loines pp 163–5

16 Monroe lxxxvi pp 110n, 128 and 131

17 CM of 16/9/1853

18 Cree p 69

19 FC&HKG of 3/10, 5/11 and 6/12/1845; Monroe lxxxvii pp 148–9, 269–70 and 281–3

20 CM of 2/11/1848; Monroe lxxxvii p 140

21 FC&HKG of 3/8/1850

22 Cree pp 46–7, 49 and 121

23 Monroe lxxxvi p 280; Cree p 121

24 Canton P of 26/6/41; Cree pp 87–9

25 CM of 8/6/1848

26 FC&HKG of 9 and 20/1/1858; Wood p 75; Kyshe i pp 414ff

7
Death

꧁ꕥ꧂

THE 1813 REVIEW OF THE COMPANY'S CHARTER

AMONG THE MANY REVIEWS of the Company's charters between its founding in 1600 and its dissolution in 1874, the review of 1813 was of particular significance to events in Macao. Apart from renewing the charter, the review extended the sovereignty of the British crown to include the Company's East Indian territories, abolished the Company's monopoly of trade with India, but not yet, for another 20 years, of its trade with China, and redefined the status and range of the churches it had established.

Under the provisions of the 1698 charter, the Company was required to found and maintain ecclesiastical establishments; chaplains had accordingly been appointed by its Court of Directors to the three Presidencies in India, as also to the Canton Factory in China. Until the 1813 review, however, English missions were prohibited from evangelizing in the Company's territories. The revised charter provided for the appointment of a

bishop and three archdeacons to superintend the activities and property of the church, for their direct subordination to the See of Canterbury, and for the revenues of India to be the source of their funds. These provisions effectively opened the door to the English missions. At the same time, Parliament considered the needs of members of the Scots Church, and approved the revisions only on being assured that 'every disposition would be shown by the East India Company to support the Scotch Church in India'. The letters-patent issued in May 1814 constituted the British territories and a Bishopric of Calcutta, and it was from these that the Company derived its authority to acquire and maintain from its Indian revenues, the church property in Macao with which this study is concerned.

The Company's presence in Macao was already large by 1787. In addition to four houses on the Praya Grande, it had purchased a large house as its chief's residence, pride of the Portuguese community with its garden that contained the outcrop of rocks known as the 'rocks of Camoens'. Services for Company marriages, births and deaths often fell to the Company chief in person to perform before 1820, when resident chaplains were appointed; and until a site was identified and purchased for the purpose, the garden was used as a place of burial for the Company's dead and for some others.

FOREIGN BURIAL IN CHINA

GRAVES IN CHINA WERE mostly sited separately or in family groups, always on a hill, and either in family fields or in places chosen for the relicts by geomancers. Filial piety demanded that both choice of site and its upkeep should be a family responsibility. The European custom is to inter the dead in community ground particularly set aside, or in holy ground such as a church or a churchyard, and as its title of ownership is vested either in the community or in a church body, family responsibility is limited to the upkeep of the grave itself. The placing of individual memorials in public burial grounds not then being a Chinese practice, it became the duty of foreigners, or of foreign organizations, to ensure the conservation of their cemeteries and memorials in China: when they moved elsewhere, these were left without caretakers.

Not that Chinese communities always ignored the funerals of foreigners far from home. A moving account of the burial ashore of a young sailor from the HMS *Alceste* in 1816 was given by the ship's surgeon. Seaman William Hares died on one of the Lew Chew Islands at night, 'whereupon a coffin was made by our own carpenters, whilst the natives dug a grave, in the English manner, in a small burial-ground under some trees near the landing-place. Next morning we were astonished to find a number of the principal inhabitants clad in deep mourning (white robes with black or blue sashes), waiting to attend the funeral. The Captain came on shore with the division of the ship's company to which the man belonged, and proceeded to the garden where the body lay ... The natives, who had been watching attentively this arrangement, and observing the order of precedence to be inverted, without the least hint being given, but with the unassuming modesty and delicacy which characterize them, when the procession began to move placed themselves in front of the coffin, and in this order marched slowly to the grave. The utmost decorum and silence prevailed whilst the funeral service was performing by the chaplain, although there was a considerable concourse of people; and afterwards they marched back, in different order, to the garden. Here they took directions for the shape of a stone to be placed at the head of a tomb, which, as a mark of respect, they had already begun to erect over the grave. This was soon finished ... The day after the interment they appeared at the tomb, with their priests, and performed the funeral service according to the rite of their own religion'.[1]

Not until the Chinese authorities had confined foreign shipping to the single locality of the Whampoa anchorage, did the burial of foreigners assume a community importance in any one place. For three months or more at a time at the height of each trading season in the early 1800s, there might have been as many as 100 sailing vessels lying at anchor there, the complement of each ship varying from 50 to 150. The death rate was high: scores of foreigners were laid to rest each year in hillside plots on the islands nearby, of which no trace remains. An account of a burial at Whampoa early in the century – a luxury compared with 'being launched headlong into the abyss of the ocean' –

describes the river procession from ship to burial place: 'The body is borne up the side of the hill on the shoulders of four of the shipmates of the departed, the grave is found after a little search and enquiries among the Chinamen who may happen to be present: a short service is then read and quickly the ground is smooth and even over the mortal remains of a fellow creature. When the little tumulus is raised, a messmate tears a branch from a neighbouring bush and plants it upright on the grave, leaving this frail, leafy memorial to wither and decay.'[2]

Foreign cemeteries began appearing elsewhere in China only after the Treaty Ports opened. An exception was that designed and built at Peking to receive the body of the Italian Jesuit, Matteo Ricci, founder of the first Christian mission in China, and later those of other members of the mission: the Emperor had elevated Father Ricci to the highest rank of mandarin, and for his burial gave a plot of land at Chala, just beyond the city walls. Previously, the remains of members of the mission had to be transported from Peking to Macao for burial in the grounds of the Jesuit College. The Chala cemetery was demolished to make room for city expansion, but details of its memorials have been preserved.[3]

The remains interred in a British cemetery, opened in Peking in 1861 shortly after the first British standing legation to the Imperial Court, were dug up in the Boxer rising of 1900, all except for four. The remains of all foreign victims who fell in the plenipotentiary massacre of 1860 had been buried in a Russian cemetery; the four had been later re-interred in the new British cemetery, and under a memorial so heavy that it could not be overturned and survived the Boxer shambles. A later description was accompanied with biographi-cal references to no more than a selected few of its occupants.[4] By way of reparation, the Chinese government built a mortuary chapel on the site in 1903, but this and all its memorials have since been effaced. No records appear to have survived of foreign cemeteries in Tsingtao, Tientsin, Shanghai or the other cities where there were foreign settlements.

Those who died at Whampoa were buried on the hillsides near the anchorage, even after the opening of the Macao cemetery. River transport for a coffin was not always permitted or available: when it was, the distance made it costly. Land at Whampoa was more easily procured than in Macao, and prices were lower and less liable to fluctuate: in the 1830s, a plot two metres by one on Danes Island cost but $12. For more than a century, the hillsides around the Whampoa anchorage were the main foreign burial area in China.

PROBLEMS OF FORMALITY AND THE LAW

REMAINS FOR BURIAL WERE transported to Macao only from the outer anchorages such as Lintin and Cumsingmoon: 87, 98, 100 and 155 are examples. One body in the Old Cemetery (58) was removed there from a hillside plot by a visiting member of his family; another (90) had first been buried on Tung Koo Island.

A Chinese Customs importation permit was required for each such re-interment in Macao and trouble ensued if the requirement was not complied with. If a burial was to take place within the city walls, permission was also needed from the Governor of Macao; the Company's garden was just within this restriction. Burial on the hillside outside the walls might be made without permission.

When in September 1817 the body of Lieuten-ant Wintle, a Royal Navy officer serving in a Company ship, was brought from Lintin to Macao to be buried 'in the place set aside for dead Protest-ants' on a hillside, it was with the Governor's permission, but failure to seek an importation per-mit from the Chinese Customs in Macao to import his body from China was seized upon as a pretext for confrontation – and might have become ugly but for the intervention of Robert Morrison (141). The whole of the staff of the British factory was lined up on the Praya, waiting at 'the landing place outside the Chop House' for the remains to arrive. H.B. Morse was with them, and his account has it that when the coffin was ready to be lifted up to shore, the crew were threatened by a group of Customs employees lined up outside their office, 'armed with swords, spears, etc., violently desiring the Officer and Boat's Crew not to approach up the steps at the landing place with the Body ... by the most insulting gestures and menaces, and did all but proceed to blows, leavelling the points of their Weapons at us, making a considerable noise, and in short seemed determined not to allow the Corpse to be landed at that place. The Englishmen showed great forbearance, but they held their own in face of the threatening mob: but, while the two parties were thus at a deadlock, Mr Morrison took the boat a few feet to one side and caused the coffin to be raised directly on to the quay; the funeral proces-sion was then formed and proceeded to the burial place without further molestation'.[5] After the Com-pany ceased operating in Macao and its property had passed into other hands, Wintle's headstone was shifted to the Old Cemetery (155).

Dr Robert Morrison of the London Missionary Society came to occupy a unique and powerful position in the Macao foreign community of 1841.

Arriving in China in 1807, he had found himself forthwith subject to Chinese expulsion orders, and it was only the action of the Company in appoint-ing him to be its official translator and interpreter that saved him from the ignominy. As his wife Mary Morrison (142) lay dying of cholera, to which she succumbed on 10 June 1821, he promised her that she would be buried in the same grave as James, their first-born child. Following his death 10 years earlier, the infant had been interred out-side the city walls and on the slopes of the Meesenberg Hill.

Negotiation to buy and use a burial plot was always difficult and tedious, fraught with unpre-dictable complication and delay: the problem of settling ownership was often aggravated by intran-sigent bureaucracy. In Macao, the traditions of the Chinese assumed the force of law whenever the Chinese so decided. In this case, not only was the apparent owner Chinese, complication enough, but the plot was already occupied by the infant's grave. To disturb a grave – unless the coffin had first been exposed by the elements – constituted a crime for which the punishment in the Chinese penal code was a hundred strokes and banishment for life; for uncovering a corpse, the penalty was death by strangulation.[6] The presence of a body in the plot discouraged the coolies from disturbing the grave – an attitude that persists to this day, but now assumes more of the character of superstition – and Morrison, presumably not having the means of outweighing their understandable reluctance, was faced with dishonouring his promise to Mary.

In Portuguese law, moreover, neither foreigner nor foreign organization might own land in a Portuguese colony – a rule readily ignored when expediency demanded. The Company was pursuing a policy of open denial that Macao enjoyed colony status, which accorded with the general stand taken by Chinese officials, but not in all circumstances held to, that the Portuguese had no right to sell land to foreigners. The Company's very presence in Macao had at the time become an embarrassment to the Portuguese. Its attempts since the issue of new letters-patent in 1814, to acquire land from the Macao Government suitable for a Protestant burial ground, had been of no avail. One attempt in 1815–6 to negotiate with one Baron d'Almeida the purchase of land and a house entered off the Praia Luis de Camoens, had been blocked by his son-in-law, who was the Chief Justice.

The immediacy of Morrison's predicament in 1821 renewed the Company's attention to the lack of a burial site, and was the motive for a further attempt to purchase land from the Baron, but a different plot of ground: and by then, jointly and heavily enmeshed in opium speculations, both the Chief Justice and his father-in-law were in such urgent need of ready cash that the former was as prompt to approve the second sale – of a property worth between $3,000 and $4,000 – as he had been to veto the first.[7] The headlong speed with which the transfer was hustled through was perhaps, in the circumstances, not surprising, and the new cemetery was ready to receive Mary's body by June.[8] In order 'to place the subject beyond the reach of litigation, should the validity of the grant be hereafter called into question', the deed of transfer was confirmed under Royal Seal of Portugal on 20 July.

After Mary Morrison's interment, permission was given to re-inter in the new burial ground the remains of some of those already at rest in hillside graves outside the city walls, and this accounts for those who lie there but had already died before it opened. The earliest is the American George Biddle (58), who died in 1811; the headstone of Lieutenant Wintle (155 – see above) was another. Others in this group were Thomas Pattle (42), John Rabinel (43) and the infant children of Dr John Livingstone (41) and James Urmston (115).

What precisely the qualifications were for burial there, however, remained a puzzle. During the fine, quiet Sunday night of 7 July 1833, for instance, a boat from the ship *Guardian* turned turtle while plying through the Macao Roads, due it was said to careless handling by its crew of six. The crew included a lad who did not know how to swim, Charles Orgai, whom one of his mates tried to save by swimming with him straddling his shoulders, until exhaustion forced him to release the boy into the sea, where he drowned. After swimming for several hundred metres, the rest of the crew were found by three Tanka Chinese boats and put ashore. They were taken in by Mr Lindsay, the Company secretary. Young Orgai's body was recovered the next day and taken to the 'Chinese Tavern', whose owners refused it shelter and threatened to kick it out on to the open beach. It was also believed that the Company had refused it burial in the cemetery, and the body was interred, with due ceremony, on the hillside outside the city wall. A news report of the Company's refusal gave rise to much ill feeling in Macao, and was vigorously denied by the ship's master, Captain Sinclair, and by Mr Lindsay, as being 'wholly and entirely false': their denial produced two abject apologies from the weekly paper that had made such a 'malicious accusation'.[9]

Though the cemetery was officially for its employees and their dependants, the Company opened the amenities to Protestants of all nations and of all professions, without either Chinese or Portuguese demur, and this arrangement continued after the Company had ceased its China operations and after the British Government had assumed responsibility for it in 1834. In the spirit of 1386 and what is the most longstanding formal treaty of friendship in the world – that between the Portuguese and English nations – the existence, until its formal closure in 1857, of a burial ground provided by the English for Protestant foreigners, was ensured only through the ready co-operation of the Roman Catholic Portuguese officials of Macao.

Not included in the site when it was acquired in 1821 was the courtyard where the present church stands, which the Company later contrived to rent, also from the Baron. It contained a building, to which the Company moved its printing press. What was called a 'mercantile failure' finally broke the Baron and when he died in 1829, his goods and property were sequestered for public auction to meet the demands of his creditors, including the rented courtyard. The Company could not bid for it except by openly flaunting both Portuguese and Chinese authority and thus facing quite unforeseeable consequences; and so, following the usual procedure, it engaged a middleman. By good fortune the middleman chanced to be a nephew of the Baron, 'a Married Citizen and Merchant of Macao', one Antonio Pereira. Buying the site for $875 at the auction, Pereira made the Company a present of it by simple deed of transfer dated 5 July 1830, for a suitable, but unrecorded, cash reward, 'in order to its being used as a place of reception for the funerals of deceased foreigners, on account of its contiguity to their place of interment'.

THE CHAPEL AND THE OLD CEMETERY

WHEN THE COURTYARD WAS transferred to Company ownership, the Company removed the printing presses and put the building to use simply as a mortuary chapel: devotional services continued to be held in the large room of a Company house on the Praya Grande, which served as what the English press referred to as 'the chapel of the British Factory, Macao'.

After the Superintendent of Trade had moved to the new Colony of Hong Kong in 1843, the mortuary chapel became also the place of worship, for up to 40 members of a reduced Protestant community, and continued in its double function until the cemetery was closed in 1858, after which it was simply the 'Protestant Church'.

As the Protestant community dwindled further, the building fell into disrepair from disuse and neglect: when Archdeacon Barnett visited from Hong Kong after the First World War, he found a ruined structure being used as a firecracker factory. The two memorial tablets that are still seen on its walls (165 and 166) had miraculously survived its ruination.[9] A successful appeal for restoration funds was launched in the European communities of South China; when in due course the new building rose on the site, the partners in the Hong Kong firm of Leigh and Orange waived their architects' fees.[10]

Through the personal interest of the Braga family and of John Reeves, then the British Vice-Consul at Macao, the building was secured during the Second World War from complete disintegration through neglect. The Protestant Missions hold special services in the chapel, such as that for the centenary of Dr Morrison's death in 1934, when the Chinese memorial set into the south wall of the lower section of the burial ground near his tomb was unveiled, and for the service of thanksgiving at the end of European hostilities in 1944. Regular Church of England services have taken place in it. In 1948, a second appeal in Hong Kong raised funds for its repair, and since then, an active Board of Trustees has conserved both chapel and burial ground.

The cemetery has been reopened only twice for use since its closure, once in 1971 for the resiting of 18th- and 19th-century memorials, and once in 1977 for the scattering of ashes (167–189).

THE NEW PROTESTANT CEMETERY

TO ANNOUNCE THE CLOSING of the cemetery, the British Crown Agent issued a notice to the Protestant residents of Macao dated 16 October 1857, in which he said that he had 'received a communication from the Hon'ble the Municipal Chamber of this City directing that as it is no longer deemed advisable to continue the practice of burying the dead within the walls of the City, no interment can take place in the British Cemetery after the 1st of December of the present year. Having [no] instructions from HBM's Government to provide another Cemetery, the undersigned begs hereby to notify the Protestant Community ... of these facts, in order that they may take such steps as may seem to them most advisable for the sepulture of the dead'.

Sensing the urgency of the situation, the local press followed up with a notice, issued with the owner's permission and for the attention of the British Government, stating that Father Almeida's Garden might be bought by foreigners at an asking price of $8,000 and an annual ground rent of $8. Eminently suitable, the notice indicated, the garden boasted 'a rich collection of beautiful and rare flowers of almost every kind and country, [was] ornamented by buildings and balustrades, and in the centre ... [stood] a small cupola-shaped edifice,

supported by 16 pillars, with a fountain inside'.

The Protestants called a meeting and elected a committee of the consuls for Britain, America, Prussia and Saxony, and the Netherlands, which succeeded in reducing the estimate to $5,000, a figure that included much of the work needed for its conversion, and launched an appeal for subscriptions. Their failure to reach the target, and the prompt purchase of Father Almeida's property by the Macao Government to be set aside for its Governor's summer residence, forced the committee to turn its attention to the less costly site of Carneiro's Garden, which it purchased on 12 July 1858 for a New Protestant Cemetery, and which remains in use. Its earliest memorials pre-date the oldest in the Old Cemetery by some 30 years, since remains were disinterred, from time to time, from various hillside burial sites in and around Macao and resited within its protected and more sacred confines. The most recent of these resitings took place when the remains of 11 graves were removed from the Meesenberg Hill, which became scheduled in 1834 for demolition to provide reclamation fill.[11]

In 1942 and again in 1954 the Trustees sold parcels of land to the Macao Government for use respectively as a Municipal Cemetery and as a Roman Catholic Mortuary Chapel, and so it is that these two cemeteries in present use lie adjacent. The title deeds to the Old Cemetery had disappeared by 1870, and the British Minister at Peking was instructed to arrange for its transfer to the Trustees of the New Cemetery: the indenture is so worded that, were the deeds ever found, their provisions could have no effect on the transfer terms.

THE SITE

THE PRAIA ON WHICH THE Old Cemetery is

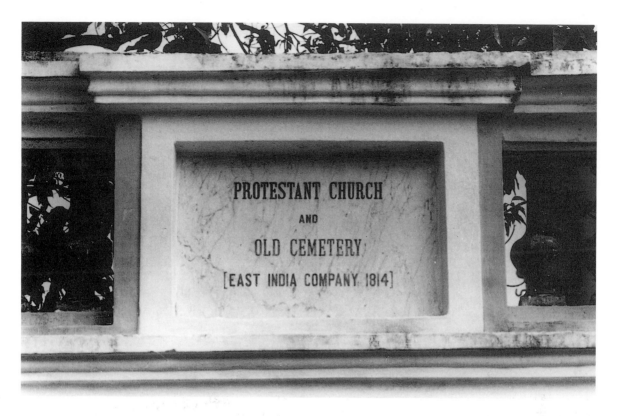

sited is dominated to its west by a high hill crowned by the Monte Fort; to its northeast, one of the gently wooded, low-lying hills characteristic of the Macao peninsula displays well-kept public gardens on its eastern and southern slopes. A substantial wooden door is set into a high arch at the eastern end of the Praia, which leads to what was then known as 'The Casa', the Company's house, and which is now occupied by the municipal Museum and Art Gallery. The Camoens Gardens (Jardim de Camoens) lie on either side of the house and, behind it is the Camoens Grotto (Gruta de Camoens). Adjoining the arch is a high stucco wall with a balustrade of Chinese banisters in green porcelain. Above a small double door in the balustrade is set a rectangular marble tablet (above photograph).

The year 1814 bears no direct relation to the purchase of either of the parcels of land, nor to the opening of the cemetery, nor to the conversion of the building to a mortuary chapel, nor to the founding of the church. The tablet was not put into position until after the cemetery had been closed in 1858, when the building became a place of regular worship as the 'Protestant Church'. 1814 was the year of the letters-patent that empowered the Company to acquire and maintain church property out of its Indian revenues.

The sole access to the courtyard and its church, and thence to the burial ground, is in the Praia and through the double door that lies below this mar-

ble tablet; beyond it, two steps lead down to the level of a courtyard measuring about 30 metres long by 20 wide. This and the two burial terraces beyond are on three levels, and together form the entire church property.

THE COURTYARD

THE CHURCH IS THE MAIN feature of the courtyard at the north end (or to visitors entering, the left-hand side). It follows a meagre but stern design, lacks a porch, has walls 60 cm thick, and is entered directly by its west door. Above the door is a semi-circular arch, and above it a circular window: the whole front presents an unfinished appearance, to which the reduced extrados around this arch, repeated in the window-arch above, contributes; the impost mouldings extend as a string course above the buttresses and windows round the building. The design of the west window is repeated in the east, which was originally filled with stained glass donated by Gideon Nye, the American merchant of many years' standing in the region, but which because of deterioration has since been replaced. Within the Church are two simple, memorial wall-tablets of identical design (165 and 166), one on each side of its east window.

Well supplied with trees and beds of flowering shrubs, the courtyard is bounded on its west by the Praia wall and the retaining wall of the Camoens Gardens, on its north by the continued retaining wall, on its east by a rough stone wall separating it from one of the Chinese quarters of the city, and on its south by the outer wall of the Canossian Institute.

From the courtyard may be seen two short-limbed Greek crosses above the entrance gate and a

Chinnery: Dr Morrison's Tomb at Macao (1838)

Latin cross above the Church's west gable. These are the only crosses to be found on the property, both of them in the part that was rebuilt in the 20th century. Indeed, not one grave boasts a cross: the memorials were erected for a Protestant community predominantly low-church and non-conformist. The English had a strong missionary and non-episcopal bias, there were many Scots, the Americans were almost without exception from Puritan stock and many of them were Quakers and Unitarians, and the other Europeans were practically all from non-Roman Catholic countries. The cemetery was an extension of Georgian England, of the Protestant fear of Catholic ascendancy and general aversion to the image of the cross, to which pagan symbolism was frequently preferred.[12] Two such symbols decorate the corner-post of the balustrade within the courtyard, two porcelain peaches – Chinese symbols of longevity, in a cemetery more apt to the visitor than to the occupant. By the time the church was being rebuilt, episcopal influence on the Protestant circles of Macao was much stronger and aversion to the cross correspondingly weaker.

In the courtyard to the east of the church a balustrade is set on a retaining wall, and beside it a walk overlooks the burial ground.

THE BURIAL GROUND

NATURAL CONTOURS DIVIDE the burial ground into its two levels, converted into an upper terrace and a lower terrace by a 1.5 metre-high granite retaining wall without either parapet or balustrade. A wide, sloping path interrupted by five single steps set at 3-metre intervals, starts from the porcelain peaches and leads to the two terraces below, with a low wall alongside on its left. Beyond the third step, a gap in the wall and two granite steps to the left lead on to a short, 3-metre-wide ramp and into the upper terrace, which is about 40 metres by 10 and roughly rectangular. The end of the sloping path is the entry to the lower, larger terrace, about 45 metres north-south by 25 east-west and also roughly rectangular.

Near the entry to the lower terrace, set about 2.5 metres high into the south wall separating the courtyard from the Canossian Institute next door, is a small rectangular stone bearing the inscription:

This wall is erected by
permission of the Protestant
Cemetery and this permission
carries with it no rights of light
MDCCCXCIX

The wall cannot have been the first to have been built there. Chinnery's ink and watercolour sketch of 'Dr Morrison's Tomb at Macao' shows quite a different wall there when he painted it in 1838 'to remember the light'. The remains of what was Chinnery's wall seem to have been replaced with the present wall 50 years earlier. The more recent Institute wall closely observes the denial of 'rights of light', being quite devoid of windows. The burial ground is peaceful and pleasing, if not elegant. In August 1844 Rebecca Kinsman wrote of it: 'I had never seen this burial ground, till one evening, when I was out with Capt. Gore & his wife, at the Camoen's Cave Garden, I proposed to them to go in, as it is very near – and we were very much pleased to find it a sweet, shady, secluded spot, containing many handsome monuments.'[13]

In 1839, an American naval chaplain visited what is now the lower terrace, after he had strolled through the gardens at the foot of the Camoens hill and left that 'scene of loveliness and flowers and life, for one of yet deeper stillness, soft beauty and death. It is a spot like most of the burial places I have seen in the East, possessing a rural beauty, and still calm, and green richness and softness, which makes you feel that if you were to die abroad you would choose to be placed in such a spot.'[14]

It has always had visitors, and not all of them have agreed with these verdicts. Some seven years earlier it was visited by 'an idle man ... disposed to scribble' and he drew a very different picture – of 'the most forlorn and cheerless spot imaginable, calculated to inspire the reverse of the reflections which occur in visiting Père La Chaise and other cemeteries, where taste and affection strive to remove from the last resting place of those we love the evidences of the sad uses to which they are dedicated'.[15] This was not dissimilar to the view of an outraged visitor to the upper terrace some four decades later, when neglect was taking its toll, and when 'several tombs were unapproachable on account of the yard being overgrown with trees, grass, and weeds ... The state of the graveyard is a great reproach to those whose duty it is to look after it ... to remove the disgrace which attaches to the place being allowed to get into such a sad state of uncleanliness and filth'.[16]

The memorials themselves take varied forms. There are flat slabs, chest-tombs, pedestal tombs, monuments, headstones and wall-tablets. None of them is elaborate, though one or two have some claim to be noteworthy. None of the epitaphs has title to originality, as do so many of those of the same period in America and England, though two (141 and 146) are just as wordy. Nor is the cutting of the inscriptions of any special merit. More often than not, given the effect of heat and humidity on the corpse, the inscription was composed in haste and was cut by Chinese masons working at speed, unsupervised and in a language strange to them. The community was cosmopolitan, largely transient, and relatively small.

1 MacLeod pp 112ff
2 Downing i p 203
3 Gallagher pp 566–94; and Planchet 1928
4 Planchet 1926
5 Morse iii p 317
6 Staunton (1833) p 103
7 Morse and d'Aquino
8 Morrison
9 Canton R of 15 and 30/7 and 6/8/1833
10 Wilkinson
11 Braga 1940 and Ball 1905. The original name of the hill was Meersberg, which had become corrupted and reflected the name of its oldest occupant, Wilhelm Meeseberg(171), a former supercargo of the Dutch East India Company, who died 1767.
12 Burgess
13 Monroe
14 Taylor
15 Ch Courier of 8/12/1832
16 CelEmp of 12/10/1876 p 420

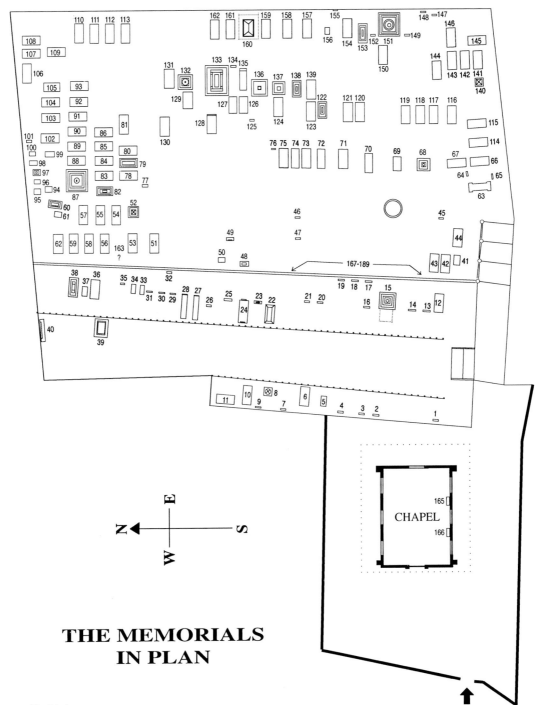

THE MEMORIALS
IN PLAN

After Teixeira

8
The Memorials

OUR WORK ON EACH memorial was in three phases. The inscription was deciphered and inked in with Chinese brush, its stones were measured, and photographs were taken. Information for the biographical entries of the persons buried in the Old Cemetery and about their families and related companies, societies, services, and ships, was sought from newspapers of the period, from libraries, and from family records. All these findings were then collated and recorded.

MEMORIAL DESIGN AND INSCRIPTIONS
RECORDING THE DESIGN of the memorials presented its problems. In the large and varied literature on British churchyard memorials there seems to be no generally accepted nomenclature. For example, some writers regard table-, altar-, high- and chest-tombs as being of the same kind; we have used the classification of Frederick Burgess. Any memorial not being a slab, a headstone, or a chest-tomb, we have classified as a monument, whether its main feature is a pillar, a column, a pedestal, a figure or any of many other designs. More than half of the memorials in this cemetery are chest-tombs, all conforming to a common pattern with small variations, so that in our descriptions only special differences are noted.[1]

The *chest-tomb* is heavy and, like other stone monuments of any size, is built on foundations laid underground and not visible. On these rests the granite slabbing, the podium that supports the visible tomb. The podium invariably consists of four steps forming a rectangle, generally with mitred corners but occasionally butt-jointed. Where there appears not to be a podium, it has been obscured by undergrowth or turf. In some cases it is multi-layered, each layer stepped back. The top layer of this stepped podium supports the main part of the tomb. A stepped podium is more frequently associated with taller monuments than chest-tombs. There are several examples in this cemetery of chest-tombs surmounted by funerary ornaments such as an urn, each invariably carried on a small stepped podium and often carved from one piece of granite. The main part of the tomb is its rectangular box, of which the ends and sides are often cut with the inscription in whole or part. The box may be plain or ornamented, vertical or splayed outwards. Mostly, each corner where a side meets an end is disguised by a vertical moulding or beading, the edge-roll, which may be carried either on the side or the end, so that it rolls in and is flush with the surface of its mate. Only in one or two examples in this cemetery are the edge-rolls patterned. The commonest form of embellishment on sides and ends is the panel, either recessed by a surrounding moat or carved in low relief; the severity of the rectangular shape may be relieved by incised corners, and of course by an inscription. The base of the box, where it rests on its podium, is surrounded with a low, moulded skirting or plinth, which in this cemetery is usually cut in two U-shaped pieces of granite, joined at the middle of the box's ends or less commonly at the middle of its sides. The lid of the box is the table-top, a cap, ledger or slab, and invariably overhangs its sides and ends. The bed-mould, the under-surface of this overhang, is frequently carved with a simple moulding. Of the upper surface of the table-top, the outer edge may be taken up by a raised border, a chamfer or an over-mould; the large surface thus enclosed may be left free, be cut with an inscription or carry an ornament, the most frequent ornament being a funerary urn mounted on a pedestal in the form of a three-tiered stepped podium.

Other memorials in this cemetery are the headstone, the monument, and the ledger or slab.

The *headstones* are nearly always rectangular, though many have arches or gables as the top edges. The arch or gable is often adorned with a device carved in low relief, a device which may be either simply ornamental or symbolic. Unless very old, they generally mark actual burial places, but have been the most liable to displacement. Some of them have been brought in from unrecorded sites and incorporated in the cemetery walls. It is a matter of conjecture whether headstones were carried out to the East as ballast, ready-cut in part, for use in the event of a shore burial; this could explain variations of carving techniques found within one headstone. It is reasonable, as well as tempting, to assume that the American naval headstones of 1, 3, 4 and 7 came from one quarry and were cut by the same mason. An American admiral has described a voyage on the Boston trader *Tsar* to Tahiti in 1848, during which the ship stayed for six weeks in Papeete selling her cargo, which included gravestones: 'one of the gravestones, intended apparently for the Salem market, was already inscribed.'[2] While no other evidence for this has come to light, it seems not unlikely, from the evidence of double standards in the cutting of inscriptions in 17 and others, that on the voyage out some ships would carry headstones, perhaps bearing ready-cut conventional phrases to be completed locally later. Certainly some, for example 86 and 87, were cut wholly by the stonemasons Llewellyn & Co of Calcutta and imported; and 165 and 166 inside the church were both cut by Gaffin of London.

The *monument* is a taller memorial, usually more showy and elaborate in design than the others, and admits of infinite variations, so that the term is hardly exact. Here it subsumes all those few memorials that are not obviously slabs, headstones or chest-tombs. The principal feature of a memorial in this group may be a pillar, a column, a pedestal, a figure or some similar device usually mounted on a stepped podium.

A *slab* is a stone laid horizontally on the ground over a grave, usually rectangular. Of all memorials, the slab is the most easily moved and tends to be unreliable as the marker of a place of burial.

Apart from the 23 memorials sited along the terrace retaining wall, which were set into place in the 1970s, 100 of the other 162 memorials in the burial ground are chest-tombs, 45 are headstones, 11 are monuments and six are slabs. There are also four very small granite markers, of which only one cannot be assigned to its appropriate memorial.

Some lettering in the inscriptions has deteriorated and is hard to read. So badly have a few of the headstones weathered that we had to try several means: feeling grooves, taking rubbings, working outwards from legible key-words, and comparing them with others and finally with the earlier listings. Of the vertical headstones, most face either due east or due west: now and then, we waited for shadows to accentuate the incisions, often clearest in shadows cast by the sun at noon. Midday shadow enlightened our darkness in the cases of 9, 25 and 27, and was useful in the recognition of key-words in texts, poems, and stereotyped phrases. It was by comparing the headstones of the two shipmates 76 and 77 that we managed to confirm the name of their ship and confirm the name and rank of its commander. Where all else failed to yield readable and photogenic results, we picked out the grooves, working not very satisfactorily with charcoal or white chalk, never on the small lettering. Nor did we use the black paint used by some of the earlier investigators, which in some cases not only yielded incorrect results, but obscured the inscription it was intended to illuminate, as in the case of 142.

Some of the granite stones, especially those standing under palms or trees, had become coated with a fine green pigment on which our Chinese ink failed to register, and which we had to remove with soapy water and scrubbing brush: a method from which the pictures were so good that we adopted it for all the inscriptions in the cemetery. Taking rubbings proved the best method for deciphering dates and for decoding and recording the Chinese inscriptions, which are all cut on marble.

MEMORIAL LISTINGS

WITH THE NOTABLE exception of that of J.M. Braga, the four earlier listings made no attempt to quote inscriptions in full: in ours we do, except where we offer a readable photograph. The earliest listing, hung on the north wall inside the church, we refer to as the Protestant Church List. The second is the Official List, made available to us by the late F.J. Gellion of the Macao Electric Company. The third is in Braga's 1940 book, which we use extensively in this study. The fourth is the listing published in 1939 by Captain H.S.P. Hopkinson in *Genealogists' Magazine*.

The memorials numbered from 1 to 162 follow the numbering in the Official List. Each of two graves is occupied by two persons (44 and 140); two others commemorate the same man (16 and 20). To the official list we have added two of what appear to be vacated lots (163–164) and two wall-plaques (165–166). The two vacated lots can with reasonable certainty be identified as the early resting-places of remains later transferred elsewhere, and neither has a memorial. Of one further burial stated in records to have taken place, the memorial and its siting remain untraced: it seems probable that it was occupied by one Captain Joel Woodberry.

Commemorated thus by name are 116 British, 55 American, nine Dutch, three German, three

Mary Clark Sutherland's tomb (15) in the East Row (centre)

Swedish, two Danish, one Armenian, and one Australian deceased.

GROUPING OF MEMORIALS

THE MAJORITY of memorials are sited on two levels of the graveyard, with 40 on the upper terrace immediately below the church and 122 on the lower terrace, approached by a pathway leading down from the church. Two memorial plaques are affixed to a wall inside the church.

Some twenty-two of the memorial stones set into the wall separating the upper terrace from the lower were brought in from elsewhere by Lindsay

and May Ride in 1971, and the circumstance of the shift is set out in Chapter 10 below; the twenty-third, added in 1977, commemorates Sir Lindsay Ride himself, and is numbered 178. Of these the Macao historian, Monsignor Manuel Teixeira, SJ, has published a list supplied to him by the Rides, to which, with the addition of the Ride marble, he assigned numbers from 167 to 189. This numbering has been adopted.

Two concrete kerbs, running its entire east-west length, divide the upper terrace of about 40 by 11 metres into a central avenue and two side rows, one east and one west. The memorials here are dated between 1850 and 1858, except for one of 1888

(30), and the upper level was thus the last part of the churchyard to be used for burials.

1 to 11: The West Row contains 11 memorials, starting near the pathway entrance, extending along the west retaining wall, and ending in the corner formed by the museum garden re-entrant.

12 to 38: The East Row contains 27 memorials, starting near the terrace entrance immediately on the right and extending to the north in two lines, one close to the edge of the terrace and the other close to the kerb of the central avenue, with 17, 18, 19 and 32 lying in the rear line. The total of the deceased in this section, however, is 26, two of the three Danish memorials having been erected to one man.

39 and 40: The central avenue contains the memorials of especially interesting men, one American and one British, who lived in Macao for many years. They are sited conspicuously at the far north end of the terrace, 40 being built against its north wall.

The 122 memorials of the lower terrace have had to be arranged in a far more complex pattern. For ease in tracing them, they are here divided into rows and groups with names derived from recognizable features. Their numbering starts with those to the left, as the visitor steps off the path leading down to the terrace, and ends with the Canning tomb just north of the middle of the east wall.

41 to 62: Bamboo Row derives its name from two large clumps of bamboo, one in the south-west corner of the terrace and the other halfway along the wall separating it from the upper terrace. The clumps effectively divide the row into three sec-tions: South, Middle and North. The South section contains four closely parallel chest-tombs (41–44), with occupants shifted from previous hillside burials and probably all the work of one stonemason at the time of re-interment: one of them has two occupants. The memorials in the Middle section are scattered in the area south of the second clump, and are so grouped for convenience (45–50): North of this clump is the North section with a single monument (52) and 11 unadorned, straight-sided, and somewhat severe chest-tombs (51–62), all similar in general design. Nine of them are ranged in two lines parallel to the inter-terrace wall, one line close to it and the other a few feet east; the 10th and 11th tombs lie at the end of the outer line with axes north-south.

63 to 76: Riddles Row falls into two sections: South and North. The South section is a cluster of five memorials (63–67) at the bottom of the pathway and is dominated by the tomb with which the numbering starts, that of Riddles, which is closely invested with low palms. Separated from it by an uninhabited area, within which the landmark is a well, the North section has nine memorials (68–76) in a line running northwards parallel to the Bamboo Row and sheltered by tall frangipani trees, which during the summer months shed their funereal blossoms profusely on the graves beneath. The numbering continues northwards along the line of the row, with memorials to American naval personnel at each end, from officer Brooke to seaman Tarbox. The 14 are divided equally between British and American deceased.

77 to 113: The central area to the north of the well and west is free of memorials. It is between this vacant area and the northern wall that the Crockett

Group is found, in which appears the most conspicuous memorial in the cemetery, the monument from which it derives its name. Except at the northwest corner of the cemetery, there is a clear boundary between the Riddles Row and this group, which has seven separate lines of memorials running east-west at right angles to that row, except that the last line lies north-south along the cemetery's east wall. The first line holds one memorial, the second and seventh four each, the third five, the fourth and fifth seven each, the sixth nine.

114 to 139: Churchill Group comprises a set of memorials lying east of and parallel to Riddles Row, in two lines running north-south. The west line of 17 tombs (114–130) is numbered from south to north, the east line of nine (131–139) from north to south. With several well-known names in this group, such as Senhouse, Fitzgerald, Rawle, Innes, Churchill, we chose Churchill because it has the most famous connection. The first two memorials are separate from the rest, and stand near the Convent wall in line with the tomb of Riddles (63).

140 to 146: Morrison Group has a strong missionary bias, and is so named because it contains the tomb of Dr Robert Morrison, one of the cemetery's most frequently visited tombs. The numbering starts with a monument cut in 'Canton marble', and four members of the Morrison family are commemorated in the next three tombs.

147 to 162: Cruttenden Row lies along the cemetery's east wall, with the backs of its headstones and the head-ends of its chest-tombs closest to the

wall. Several of those interred in the row were formerly in service with the English East India Company, and we have named it after the most distinguished of them. The row contains three memorials with unusual features: a headstone set into the wall (155); a chest-tomb with an unknown occupant (156); and the sole chest-tomb still boasting its iron railings (160), though there are indications that others once had them. The numbers start at the south near the Morrison Group and continue north. Between this row and the last four of the Crockett Group also lying along the wall, there is so large a gap that the two sections are readily distinguished one from the other.

163 and 164: Two vacated lots, 163 once sited probably between 53 and 56, 164 close to 141.

165 to 166: Two wall plaques, identical in design and form and commemorating persons who died elsewhere, are set on either side of the east window inside the church.

167 to 189: The 23 memorials added later.

---

1 Editor: The Council for British Archaeology and Rescue produces and sells a standard Grave Memorial Recording Form, and also publishes J. Jones: *How to Record Graveyards* (1979). Two other useful publications are: J.L. Rayment, *Notes on the Recording of Monumental Inscriptions*, published by the Federation of Family History Societies, London, 3rd edition 1981, and H.L. White, *Monuments and their Inscriptions*, published by the Society of Genealogists, London 1978.

2 Morison p 265

9
The Entries

EACH MEMORIAL HAS an entry in the next pages, consisting of its official list number and the full name, nationality, date of death, and age at death of the person commemorated (where known). Entries for 1 to 166 and 178 also provide either a photograph or transcript of the inscription, other notes about the person and any events and shipping recorded in the inscription (where information has been found), a description of its size and characteristics, a note on such variants as appear in the other listings, and references to the sources of immediate and further information. The source items are detailed in Sources on page 276.

It was not always possible to identify the person memorialized, because in several cases, especially those of the sea-captains, references in the newspapers and other publications appeared without forenames or initials, and it was known that captains with surnames in common were in command of different ships at much the same time, and sometimes of the same ship at different times. Nor were their nationalities always clear, especially those of the Americans, who were often described as of their country of origin, though they might have been American immigrants. Some (e.g. Duncan-Dunken, 48) appeared in the records with transliterations of a name in two language-versions.

Of the dates of foreign births, the only notices are in the Baptismal Records in London, which cover only the years 1820–38, and in the local newspapers. From time to time in the instance of a seaman, the date of death recorded on a tombstone is not the same as that in his ship's log. Such discrepancies were inevitable before the days of chronometers, particularly if the ship had crossed the international date-line and not called in port where a correction might be made. Also, at that time the ship's day was reckoned from noon to noon; hence the forenoon and afternoon of any one day had different calendar dates in the log. The name of the day changed at midnight, the date of the day changed at noon. There was also, of course, human error due to lapse of memory or lack of precise information.

View of the East Row

The military establishment of the Company was reorganized in 1795, and each of its Native Regiments standardized on a two-battalion basis; but in 1824 the Court of Directors replaced these double battalions with single ones, and this necessitated the renumbering of all the regiments. Old customs die hard, and the old number remained in use for some time, so that the terms New and Old were used to indicate which system of numbering was being employed.

Photographic reproduction of inscriptions in the following pages shows only what has been deciphered and inked in; in some cases, punctuation marks and even letters were not discovered until after the photographs were taken, and therefore do not show in the reproductions. They are our recording of fact as it presented itself to us then, without necessarily being the final truth: our readings of a few of the words and figures still remain guesswork.

Tell us, for Oracles must still ascend,
For those that crave them at your tomb:
Tell us, where are those beauties now become,
And what they now intend:
Tell us, alas, that cannot tell our grief,
Or hope relief.

—Lord Herbert of Cherbury

1. OLIVER MITCHELL *American*

IN MEMORY OF
OLIVER MITCHELL:
SEAMAN:
A NATIVE OF THE STATE OF VERMONT,
U. STATES OF AMERICA, WHO DIED OF
DYSENTERY AT THE U.S. NAVAL
HOSPITAL, MACAO.
ON THE 23 DAY OF JULY 1850
AGED 43 YEARS.
THIS STONE
IS ERECTED BY HIS MESSMATES
OF THE UNITED STATES SHIP MARION
AS A TRIBUTE OF RESPECT

Inscription

THERE IS NO record of a United States Naval Hospital in Macao, but Mitchell's messmates may have assumed the institution was for American seamen (see also 4 and 131). A cholera epidemic was raging at the time, and a large number of Chinese and many Portuguese residents, including the Governor, died. Braga says the cause of Mitchell's death was most likely to have been cholera. Three other members of the crew of the *Marion* lie buried in the cemetery (see 3, 4 and 6). A 16-gun sloop-of-war of 566 tons built at Boston, the ship served on the East Indies station, chiefly in the South China seas, from 1850 to 1852 under Commander William M. Glendy, and sailed back to America from Hong Kong on 25 February 1852. Nothing is known of Oliver Mitchell.

The first memorial in the cemetery, this isolated headstone of rough, coarse granite stands almost hidden by bushes and trees, its back one metre from the retaining wall below the church. It is 102 cm high, 56 cm wide and 10cm thick. Beneath the segmental arched top, with its rise of 15 cm, is a stereotype floral design carved in relief and beneath this a deep inscription whose bottom line is cut in such small italics and is so deteriorated as to be illegible. Correctly cut as VERMONT and MARION, these names have been painted to read incorrectly: reference to 3, 4 and 6 prove the ship's name to have been *Marion*. The whole inscription is difficult to decipher, and the final line illegible.

REFER TO: Braga 1940 p 39; FC&HKG of 25/2/1852; Dixson HKG for 1852.

2.   EDWARDS W. BATES   *American*

EDWARDS WHIPPLE BATES died in the home of Robert Browne, local consul for the Netherlands. His partner Henry Griswold Wolcott had ships trading with Canton as early as 1807; Bates may have worked in the Canton branch of the firm, and may have been one and the same as the American merchant Bates noted by J.M.K. Fairbank as being involved in questionable trading on the coast at the time.

The memorial is a rectangular marble headstone 130 cm high, 107 cm wide and 15 cm thick, supported by a narrow marble block set on a wider, coarse granite base 85 x 38 cm, some six metres north of the first memorial and largely hidden by shrubs and palms. Its surface, disfigured by the aerial roots of climbing ferns, revealed when scrubbed an easily read, well-cut inscription.

After the word 'Born', a crack and moulds have almost obliterated the word 'State', and have contrived to modernize the original 'Shanghae' to read 'Shanghai'; the Christian name is definitely spelt Edwards; the abbreviation 'Sep.' for September is not a mould artefact, but as commonly used a century ago.

TO THE

MEMORY OF

EDWARDS W. BATES,

LATE OF THE FIRM

WOLCOTT, BATES AND CO.

SHANGHAI, CHINA.

Born, State New York, U.S.A.
July 18th. 1818.
Died Macao, China,
Sep. 11th. 1850,

AGED 32 YEARS

OTHER OBSERVERS: PCL, OL, JMB and HSPH: EDWARD W. BATES.
REFER TO: FC&HKG of 14/9/1850; Fairbank pp 332, 334; HKA&D for 1846.

3.   HENRY JONES   *American, possibly Danish*

THE US SHIP *Marion* was visiting Macao from
Hong Kong between 7 and 11 March. Having
fallen ill, Jones was put ashore and died after his
messmate Herman Bollins (Rawlings) had returned
to Hong Kong, and the stone was probably not put
into place before the next visit of the *Marion* in
July-October. The ship's log and muster roll confirm some details of the inscription, but give the
date of Jones' death as 14 March; however, the
ship's days started at noon, so that forenoon and
afternoon of the same day were entered as different
dates.

This grey, medium-grained granite headstone
stands on a step one metre from the retaining wall
in line with and a metre north of No 2. It is 107 cm
high, 61 cm wide and 10 cm thick, and has a
segmental arched top, below which is carved in
relief a device like an open scallop-shell flanked by
wings. The inscription is recessed below and separated from the border by a shallow groove 4 cm
wide.

The italics in the last line of the inscription are
hard to decipher. They read 'Bollins', but Henry
Jones' messmate was named Herman Rawlings,
according to the log and muster roll (in which both
are noted as Danish). The ship's name is painted in
as 'Aiarion', but comparison with No 4 alongside
confirms it to be 'Marion'.

The similarity of stone and design of 3 and
4, and the lack of a 'th' in the dates on both, make
it likely that the headstones of the two shipmates Jones and West were carved by the same
sculptor.

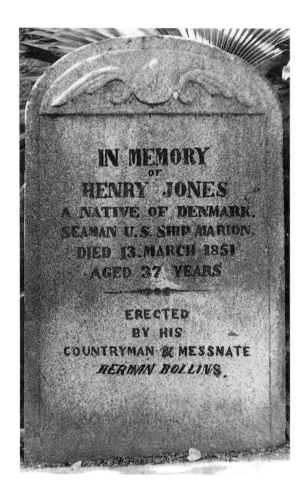

OTHER OBSERVERS: JMB reads HERMAN HOLLINS.
REFER TO: Loomis; FC&HKG during 1851; Dixson HKG for
1851.

81

4.   JOSEPH JAMES WEST   *American*

THIS IS ANOTHER of the four memorials to crew of the *Marion* dying at Macao within a period of 20 months: the others are 1, 3 and 6. The ship left Macao for Whampoa on 5 November and went on to Hong Kong on the 15th. Taken ill, West was put ashore at Macao and died before the ship returned – the ship's log states in the 'Portuguese Hospital, Macao'. This was doubtless the eye hospital founded in 1838 by Dr T.R. Colledge (see 96) of the Medical Missionary Society, the only institution in Macao at the time which could be so referred to, and the same hospital as that in which the other three *Marion* seamen died, despite discrepancies in data on the headstones.

Also standing with its back a metre from the retaining wall below the church and two metres north of 3, and almost hidden by palms, this grey, fine-grained granite headstone is 107 cm high, 56 cm wide and 15 cm thick, surmounted by a segmental arch: the device carved in relief below, in contrast with those of 1 and 3, is not recessed; the whole is enclosed in a grooved border cut 2.5 cm in from its edge. It stands on a coarse granite step 90 x 29 cm.

The device is a small globe placed on a larger one, fluted on its lower half and resting on a pedestal, flanked like the motif of 3 with wings but slightly more curved. The italics in the inscription are hard to decipher.

SACRED
TO THE MEMORY
of
JOSEPH JAMES WEST,
LATE SEAMAN ON BOARD OF
THE UNITED STATES SHIP
MARION, DIED AT MACAO ON
12 OF NOVEMBER 1831

ERECTED
TO HIS MEMORY BY HIS COUNTRYMEN
IN CHINA

REFER TO: Loomis; FC&HKG various issues in 1851; Dixson HKG for 1851.

5. THOMAS A. DENSON *American*

THE CAUSE OF Denson's demise must have seen its onset after 13 July, his ship having already left Macao for the Cumsingmoon passage and not sailing for Hong Kong until 9 September, and he would have been put ashore into the Macao hospital, as were 1, 3 and 4. The US sloop-of-war *Saratoga* of the East India squadron was the biggest of her class, and throughout 1852 was on the move between Amoy, Hong Kong, Macao, Cumsingmoon and Whampoa. In 1853 she joined the historic Japanese mission of Commodore M.C. Perry, the American ambassador to Japan. Nothing is known of Steward Denson beyond his being a native of Portsmouth, Virginia.

Lying two metres north of 4 and about a metre out from the retaining wall with its head end to the west, this memorial is a granite slab 130 cm long by 76 cm wide, with a polished surface. The word 'Sacred' is in Old English capitals; only one punctuation mark is now visible. Note the spelling of 'testamony'.

The grave is listed under the name Pinsets, which should read Purser's, a fact confirmed by the ship's log entry of 30 August recording Denson's death. The ship's days started at noon, and the log entry of the 30th records his death in the morning of the 31st, as in the inscription.

SACRED

to the memory
of
Thomas A Denson Purser's Steward
A native of Portsmouth Virginia
United States. Who departed this
life on board the US Ship Saratoga
Cumsingmoon August 31st 1852
Aged 24 years

This Tomb was erected by his
messmates as a testamony of
their personal regard

OTHER OBSERVERS: OL: THOMAS A. DENAMI PINSETS; PCL: THOS. A. DENAI PINSETS; JMB: THOMAS A DENAMI PINSETS; HSPH: THOMAS A. DEAMI PINSETS.
REFER TO: Loomis; Dixson HKG for 1852; Hawks Wallach.

6.   LIEUTENANT BENJAMIN S. GANTT   *American*

SACRED
TO THE MEMORY
OF
LIEUTENANT BENJAMIN S. GANTT
U. S. NAVY
LATE OF THE U. S. SHIP MARION
WHO DEPARTED THIS LIFE ON THE
14 MARCH 1852

Erected by his brother Officers
on the Station.

THERE IS NO record of where Gantt died: the date 14th was due to misinformation, naval records giving the date as the 12th. The *Marion* left Hong Kong for America on 25 February, some two weeks before his death. It is likely that 'his brother officers' in other ships of the squadron which were still serving in the area were given the task of erecting his memorial. Nothing is known of Gantt other than his service record.

Lying 1.5 metres north of 5, this granite memorial takes the form of a grey, medium-grained granite chest-tomb without ornament or inscription on sides and ends and stands on a shallow coarse granite base, its long axis running east and west, its head close to the west wall.

The inscription on the top has weathered well. A narrow groove parallel to the sides and bottom runs round it in a border 8 cm wide. The groove crosses the top in four curves, the two in the middle embellished with a simple winged design. As in 5, the word 'Sacred' is in Old English style. Two of the lines are in italics, sloping in opposite directions. The 'e' in the word 'Memory' lacks its upper limb, either omitted by the mason or deleted by the weather. The memorial is more elaborate than 5, but both are probably from the same mason's yard.

In the word 'Gantt' the letter 'n' has been painted over the first 't', making the 'Gaunt' shown in other listings. Gantt is correct, as confirmed from official records.

OTHER OBSERVERS: OL, PCL, JMB and HSPH: BENJAMIN S. GAUNT.
REFER TO: Loomis; FC&HKG of 28/2/1852; Dixson HKG 1852; Alexander 1845 p 34 and 1848 p 42.

7. **DANIEL CUSHMAN** *American*

DANIEL WAS A direct descendant of the Robert Cushman who, with John Carver, was responsible for organizing the *Mayflower* emigration of 1620 to America, and followed himself the next year. Daniel Cushman was born on 5 October 1828, and was therefore 23 when he died, not 33 as in the inscription. The US frigate *Susquehanna* was a side-wheel vessel built of white oak and wrought iron and launched in 1850.

In January 1852, visiting Singapore during her first cruise, she was described as 'wonderful', the largest vessel ever to visit the city. On 24 April she set out on the tour on which she would lose her quartermaster, sailing from Hong Kong to Macao and Whampoa, and arriving back at Hong Kong on 22 May. He may have been put ashore into hospital in Macao when his ship called, or his remains may have been brought from Whampoa if he died there. The ship later joined Commodore Perry's mission to Japan.

Cushman's granite memorial stands one metre to the north of 6 behind a 89 x 43 x 13 cm step with its back close to the wall. It is 91 cm high, 56 cm wide and 13 cm thick, and of similar design to 1, 3 and 5. Its top forms an ogee arch, with small lower curves giving it a shouldered appearance. A design combined from those of 3 and 4 but in higher relief is cut on the segment below the arch.

The surface, with all but the last line of the inscription, is set lower than the border, separated from it by a groove cut 2.5 cm from the edge. Weather and attempts to distinguish the letters by painting them, have made deciphering difficult, especially the name of the ship, divided as it is between two lines.

REFER TO: Loomis; DAB; Pierce; SFP&MA of 23 and 30/1/1852; FC&HKG of 7/2 and 1–26/5/1852 and 10/8/1853; CM of 16/4/1854.

8.   MRS DISHKOONE SETH   *Armenian-British*

A NEWSPAPER REPORT records Mrs Seth as being 44 and 4 months when she died. Her husband Seth Anst Seth, with her aged mother and his two sons, moved to Hong Kong and continued trading there until he died; he was buried in the Colonial Cemetery in 1875. Until the late 1980s, his name continued to feature in the title of the firm of accountants Percy Smith, Seth & Fleming. Mrs Seth was Armenian by birth, but may have been a British subject. Nothing has been discovered of her father, Arathoon J. Marooth.

The most conspicuous in the row, and standing close to the kerb and away from the wall, this 183 cm-high, medium-grained granite memorial comprises two parts: a square, bonded, coarse-grained granite box set on a podium without a plinth but up two steps; and a truncated, pink, medium-grained granite pyramid with chamfered under-surface, its lower measurement conforming to those of the box beneath. Attached to its east face is a slab of marble, in length and width the same size as the box face, but 4 cm thick.

Two inscriptions are cut on the marble slab: the upper in Armenian, the lower in English. Neither is of good workmanship, especially the Armenian script. A member of the family has confirmed that the name Marooth (without a final 'e') is correct. The larger size of this letter suggests that the mason was to have cut 'Esq.' but ran out of space. The inscription in Armenian renders precisely the

meaning of that in English, except that the biblical quotation translates as 'In the passing wind, we are left to wither like grass'.

OTHER OBSERVERS: HSPH: MRS. DISKOONE SETH. **REFER TO:** Seth; FC&HKG of 18/7/1857.

9.   WILLIAM ELLIS   *British*

INFORMATION ABOUT Ellis from Perth is meagre. Briefly in Hong Kong at the time were two ship's captains with his surname, but it is unlikely that he was either, since he was appointed a Justice of the Peace either in January 1846 or early in 1849. There were three Ellises in the Company's marine service: there is no evidence that he was related to any of them. The early links of Perth with the Indian jute trade led the search to Calcutta, where his death in 1853 in Macao was reported in the *Indian Mail*, establishing some connection with India.

Half a metre north of 8 and behind it, its back against the wall, this memorial headstone is of very coarse-grained granite, as is the 91 x 38 x 14 cm step in front of it. Partially hidden by bushes, it stands 152 cm high, 81 cm wide and 13 cm thick. Its segmental arched top is 76 cm in diameter, set on horizontal shoulders 2.5 cm wide.

Except for the biblical text, which is difficult to read – as is its reference (Rev. III.II) – the inscription, now illegible, is here supplied as observed by Braga over 50 years ago. This sort of stone weathers fast.

REFER TO: FC&HKG of 30/6/1843 and 23/7/1853; CM of 21/7/1853; HKR of 4/7/1843; Kyshe i pp 25, 91 and 230; Ind M of 20/9/1853.

10.   WILLIAM THOMAS BOWEN EVANS   *British*

THE NAME OF the ship *Futty Mombarruck* means 'victory celebration', and was a favourite name in India for ships, especially those of the Arab trade (or *futeh*, *futtey*, *futtay*, *futtel*, *futtek*, *fattle*, and the Dutch version *foedal*; and what seems an infinite set of variations on *mombarruck*). The ship was British, and from 1843 to 1850 her captains were called Moore (or More), Morrison, and Lurgin, and she was absent from the China waters during the whole of 1851. Captains of the name Evans, but without initials and on other ships, were in formidable number at the time. This Captain Evans arrived at Hong Kong as a passenger in the P&O ship *Pekin* on 10 September 1851; he was the same Evans who was master of the *Charles Grant* when it was in port at Whampoa from 29 June 1852. The *Futty Mombarruck* was there at the same time, but lacked a master, and Evans transferred to her early in July. The year (and possibly the day) of his death on the headstone does not accord with newspaper reports that it occurred on the 5th, and is in error. When the *Charles Grant* sailed from Whampoa on 14 October, it sailed under the command of a different Captain Evans.

A chest-tomb made of very coarse-grained granite and lying east-west with its head near the west wall, the sides and ends of this memorial box are vertical and unadorned on a plinth 259 x 145 x 30 cm; its table-top is bordered by a wide, gently-sloping chamfer, and on the narrow central surface so framed is cut the inscription, the top line of which is curved. The variations in the names of the deceased and of his ship given in other lists occur because the stone is not well preserved.

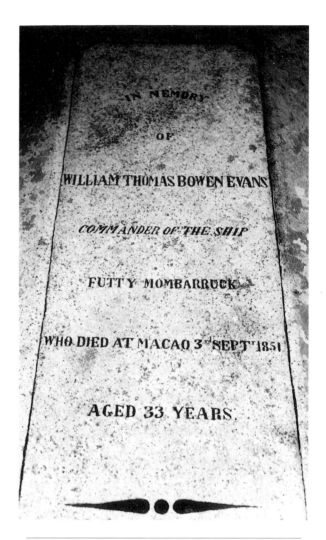

OTHER OBSERVERS: OL, PCL and HSPH: WILLIAM THOMAS; JMB: WILLIAM THOMAS ...
REFER TO: FC&HKG of 28/8 and 14/9/1844, 10/9/1851, 16 and 30/6, 3/7, 7/7, 29/9 and 20/10/1852; CM of 20/6/1850 and 11/9/1851.

11. CHAS. JOHN WOOD BARTON, B.A. *British*

BARTON WAS BROUGHT out from England as a recent graduate of Worcester College to be the chaplain to the Anglican community in Macao and Canton. He was the first neither employed by the Company, which had ceased operations in China in 1834, nor a missionary having other duties. He arrived with his wife by the steamship *Malta* on 11 May 1851, and died at the home of W.W. Dale less than four months after taking up his duties in Canton, following a fainting fit in the pulpit while paying a visit to Macao for the sake of his health. His widow left for England on the 29th.

The last memorial in the row, this pink, coarse-grained granite chest-tomb lies north-south at the corner of the wall, head to the north. It is of similar design to 10, with the top having no bed-mould, but differs in having a slightly splayed plinth 254 x 147 x 30 cm, and a table-top surface with broad chamfer within which is cut a border groove 2.5 cm wide. The inscription surface is recessed 6 mm below this border, at each inner corner of which a small and simple design is cut, an unusual feature in the chest-tombs in this cemetery.

The mason has miscalculated the space for the end of the fourth line of the inscription, which is otherwise well-cut, and has encroached upon the border. The letters being too narrow to withstand the effects of weather, some names – such as Saxby – have now become very hard to decipher.

IN MEMORY
OF
THE REVEREND
CHAS. JOHN WOOD BARTON, B.A.
Of Worcester College, Oxford.
CHAPLAIN TO CANTON COMMUNITY,
ELDEST SON OF
Reverend CHARLES BARTON,
Of Saxby, Lincolnshire

BORN APRIL 21, 1823.
DIED SEPTEMBER 2, 1851

OTHER OBSERVERS: HSPH: CHARLES WOOD BARTON.
REFER TO: FC&HKG of 14 and 21/5, 10/9, 1 and 13/10/1851; CM of 11/9 and 2/10/1851.

12.   EUPHEMIA ISABEL BARTON   *British*

IT IS EXTRAORDI-
NARY that 11 and 12
commemorate two un-
related contemporaries of the same surname, and
that they are very similar in design. Euphemia
arrived in Macao with her parents, Charles and
Sarah Barton, from Singapore. He was either the
Charles Barton who was in the shipbuilding or
chandlering trade in Singapore, or the Charles
Barton who kept a tavern in Penang, or both. He
died aged 52 in 1852, his wife in 1861, and both
are buried in the Hong Kong Colonial Cemetery.
Two press reports give a date for Euphemia's death
different from that shown on her memorial – 1
September.

Sited immediately to the right of the upper
terrace entrance and ly-
ing east-west, its head
towards the lower ter-
race, this granite chest-tomb has no podium; a
moulded plinth supports the box, the ends of which
are jointed in the middle and its sides are slightly
splayed. There is a marked chamfer on its top in the
manner of 11, though its inscription is of better
craftsmanship: the curve of the word 'SACRED' is
balanced by the inverted curve of the deceased's
name.

REFER TO: FC&HKG of 20/9/1851, 9/6/1852 and 14/9/1853;
CM of 10/6/1852 and 15/9/1853; SFP&MA of 15/7/1841; EIR&D
for 1827–1831.

13. CAPTAIN SHAMGAR HUNTINGTON SLATE *American*

SLATE WAS CAPTAIN of the *Wizard*, a newly built advanced clipper which, according to an advertising poster, was of a speed 'unsurpassed by any Clipper afloat'. With Slate in command, her maiden voyage from San Francisco to Hong Kong took only 44 days, and on her third voyage back she came in 'ahead of some six vessels which sailed before her'. Following his fourth voyage to Hong Kong, struck low at the age of 47 with dysentery, Slate died in Macao on 20 November 1854. His wife Maria remained at home at Sag Harbor. Newspapers both in Hong Kong and Sag Harbor wrongly assign his death to 29 November.

Standing on a step 81 x 34 cm about half a metre to the north and level with the foot of 12, this coarse-grained granite headstone is 99 cm high, 76 cm wide and 10 cm thick, with a low gabled top starting from its incised upper corners and rising 10 cm above its sides. The inscription is well cut but has poor spacing, the mason having run out of space at the ends of two lines.

Pits in the stone have made reading some letters difficult, including the deceased's surname. Painters have not helped, to the extent that his birth-place has been recorded as Saghablor and problems have arisen in his age and the date of his death. The versions given above are from family records and the family monument at Sag Harbor.

The short approach from the central avenue is between two small hedgerows of box plants, taken as cuttings from a hedge planted by Captain Slate in his garden at home, before his last journey out to China. The cuttings were given by his grand-daugh-

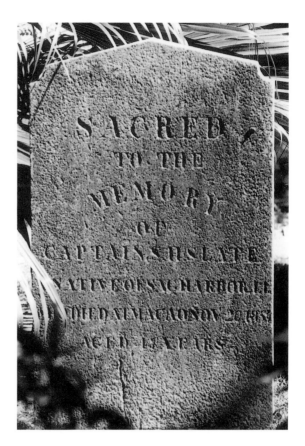

ters to Lindsay and May Ride during their visit to Sag Harbor.

OTHER OBSERVERS: PCL: S.H. STATE; JMB: CAPTAIN S.H. STATE; HSPH: H. STATE.
REFER TO: Sleight pp 109-10; Peabody; Dixson HKG for 1854; Cutler p 341; FC&HKG of 23/9 and 2/12/1857; *The Corrector* (Sag Harbor) of 20/2 and 13/3/1858.

14.   GEORGE H. DUNCAN   *British*

Sacred
TO THE MEMORY
of
GEORGE H. DUNCAN
Who Departed This Life
May 9th 1857
AGE 32 YEARS
The Port is reached
The sails are furled
Life's voyage now is over
By faith's bright chart
He has reached that world
Where storms are felt no more
This stone was erected by his
Old and esteemed friends

Inscription

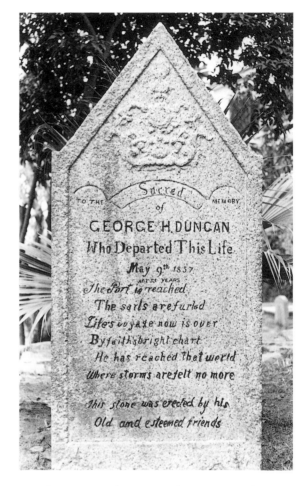

DUNCAN'S IDENTITY cannot be determined; it may be inferred from the verses that he was closely concerned with the sea in some capacity.

Some half a metre to the north and in line with 13, the pink, coarse-grained granite headstone is 175 cm high, 76 cm wide and 9 cm thick, with an inscription surface recessed 13 mm below a border of 8 cm at its top and sides and 20 cm at the bottom. Its steep gabled top forms an equilateral triangle 51 cm high and carries an elaborate device in high relief resembling a coat-of-arms or a military badge, beneath which is a scroll on which is cut the word 'Sacred' in the middle and 'TO THE' and 'MEMORY' at the sides.

The workmanship of the scroll is poor and unfinished, the lettering and spacing of the whole inscription ill-crafted. The age is almost illegible – the above may be wrong – but the border and device are expertly cut, giving the impression that a master mason was helped by an apprentice.

OTHER OBSERVERS: OL and PCL: GEORGE A. DUNCAN; JMB: GEORGE A DUNGAN: HSPH: GEORGE A. DUNGAM.

15.   MARY CLARK SUTHERLAND   *British*

SACRED TO THE MEMORY
OF
MARY CLARK
The beloved and lamented Wife
OF
W. SUTHERLAND
WHO DIED AT MACAO
January 10th, 1858.
BELIEVING ON HER SAVIOUR
AGED 51 YEARS.

Inscription on the west face

Beloved and respected by all who knew her

Inscription on the north face

MARY CLARK'S husband, William Sutherland, was the master of the British ship *Hero* on the Calcutta-Macao run, the cargo from India probably consisting largely of opium, from which the profit would account for so expensive a monument. Mary sailed with him from Calcutta on 1 October 1857, arrived at Hong Kong on 2 January, and moved to Macao two days later, probably very ill, for she lasted only another six days. Nothing has been unearthed to connect Sutherland with any of the many captains of the same name. Some five weeks after her death, he sailed away in the *Hero*.

In all 3.7 metres tall, this conspicuous memorial, constructed of pink, coarse-grained granite throughout, takes the form of an interrupted column supporting a small obelisk, set on a podium of three steps, the lowest being 198 cm square. The vertical line of the column is interrupted by an inverted, truncated pyramid 30 cm high supporting an ob-elisk 91 cm high, above which is a small table and an urn. Leading to it from the avenue is a short approach flanked by two rows each of three octagonal granite posts 71 cm in height with 9 cm sides tapering abruptly to the top, where on each there still remains an iron ring that once supported the iron chains that formed the approach.

There are inscriptions on three of the column faces: the main inscription is clearly cut and its letters have weathered well; not so the other two, whose letters are very small and have weathered.

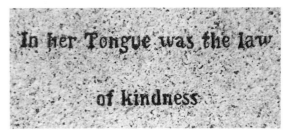

Inscription on the south face

REFER TO: CM of 14/1/1858 and 18/2/1858; Dixson HKSL for 1858; SFP&MA of 12 and 19/11/1857.

16.   CHRISTIAN JOHANN FRIEDRICH JPLAND   *Danish*

'HERE SLEEPS Christian Johann Friedrich Jpland born at Apenrade, the 30th June 1818, died in Macao on the 5th October 1857. May thy ashes rest in peace, thou weary wanderer.' There are two headstones for the one man (see 20). A tall palm 1.2 metres north of 15 shelters two headstones. This is one of them, in line with 13 and 14, sited nearest the central avenue.

Of grey granite, rectangular in shape and 130 cm high, 61 cm wide and 11 cm thick, it is surmounted by a segmental arch rising without shoulders to 14 cm above its sides. The inscription surface is slightly polished and this and the border are marked by a groove running 4 cm from the edge round the whole stone.

The craftsmanship is clearly that of a master mason and unlikely to have been that of a local man. The top line is in Gothic script. Beneath it is carved an ancient Christian all-seeing eye encased in an equilateral triangle – the Trinity – from the sides of which radiates a glory, a symbol commonly used in Austrian Renaissance churches. The other lines are in Roman capitals and either in lower case or in a running hand. Beneath the inscription is cut a simple but ornamental sheaf representing the gathered harvest.

OTHER OBSERVERS: OL, PCL and JMB: IPLAND; HSPH: UPLAND.

17.   JOHN DINNEN   *American*

NOTHING HAS BEEN traced of Dinnen or his family, beyond that he was a native of New York and was serving on the *Powhatan* when he died. Sited beneath the palm that shades 16, this slightly polished, grey, medium-grained granite head-stone 122 cm high, 61 cm wide and 11 cm thick, is set behind a granite step 89 x 36 x 13 cm close to the edge of the wall dividing the two terraces. Its upper edge is a low gable of 6 cm rising from two shoulders 4 cm wide.

The word 'Memory' is not only carved on a curve but shaded, and all the upper part of the inscription is artistically spaced and cut; both parts have worn well and are almost all easy to read. But the letters in the lower part are much smaller and poorly spaced, and New York has a small 'y', suggesting (as in 14) a division of labour between mason and apprentice.

One wonders, too, if ships carried as ballast an assortment of headstones bearing ready-cut conventional opening phrases, for completing later and locally; there is no evidence to confirm this conjecture, except that Admiral Samuel Morison has described the voyage of a Boston trading ship, the *Tsar*, when it sailed for Tahiti in the spring of 1848 with gravestones included in its cargo.

OTHER OBSERVERS: JMB and HSPH: DUNNEN.
REFER TO: Morison p 265.

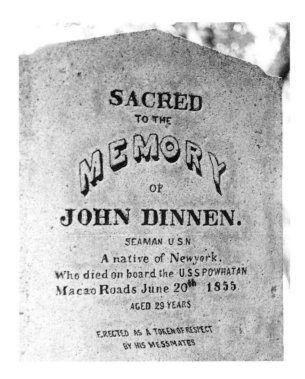

18. WASHINGTON F. HICKMAN *American*

IN LINE WITH, alongside, and a metre further north than 17, this headstone is precisely similar in size, shape and polished granite texture. The similarities are to be expected, as they were both erected by the men of one ship. The frigate *Powhatan* is of particular interest. It was one of the six American naval craft assigned to the East India Squadron to serve with six vessels sent out from America, all under the command of Commodore Perry for his commercial and diplomatic mission

to Japan, where he transferred his flag to the *Powhatan*.

It was during her visit to Macao when returning from Japan that Seaman Hickman died. While under repair in Hong Kong, its equipment and men were lent to the Royal Naval sloop *Rattler* for an anti-pirate action of 4 August 1855 in local waters, which is commemorated at Happy Valley by one of Hong Kong's few public monuments. In 1864–5, the *Powhatan* took part in Civil War operations on the Potomac River and in Chesapeake Bay, in the attack on Fort Fisher and in the blockade of the Mississippi, and was in service during operations against Charleston.

Some of the smaller letters in the inscription offer difficulty, while the line 'Who died' was at first recorded as 'Wrecked', and the date of death as 1853. Rank and date of death (in 1855) are as found in the *Powhatan*'s log.

OTHER OBSERVERS: OL, PCL, JMB, HSPH: WASHINTON F. HICKMAN.
REFER TO: FC&HKG of 27/7/1853 and various issues from May to July 1855.

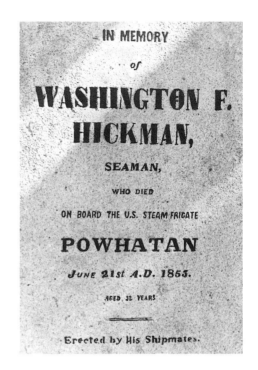

19.   CHARLES WOODBERRY   *American*

WOODBERRY WAS BORN on 20 February 1817 in Beverly, Mass.; newspapers reported his death in 1855 (not 1854), and he was aged 38, not 36 (Braga and Hopkinson both give it as 37). The references to American captains named Woodberry in Chinese waters are many at this time, and some of them may have been to Charles. He signed a notice dissolving a firm of chandlers and general agents, which re-opened in the name of H. Fogg & Co of Shanghai, and he started a Canton river-boat career in association with J.B. Endicott (166) and W. Endicott, for whom his last voyages were in command of the American steamer *Spark*. The ship boasted a particularly shrill whistle, which was celebrated in the following verses appearing in the *China Mail* – verses that effectively silenced the whistles on both the *Spark* and the *Canton*, another river steamer:

What a screaming, screeching, shrieking,
In the dark,
From the rattling, roaring, reeking
Ranting Spark!
Gongs and guns and ghosts are listening
To the revel –
While she's whirring, whirling, whistling
Like the devil!
Truly, when they cross the Atlantic,
Yankee boys
Make the very ocean frantic
With their noise!
That pert, probing, pricking, piercing,
Thrilling tune,
Might put down the winds rehearsing
A Typhoon!
I would give the Spark a mission,
Which should claim
For her eagle-voiced ambition
Noise and name!
Like an eagle let her light on
Proud Pekin,
And the 'Son of Heaven' shall frighten
With her din.

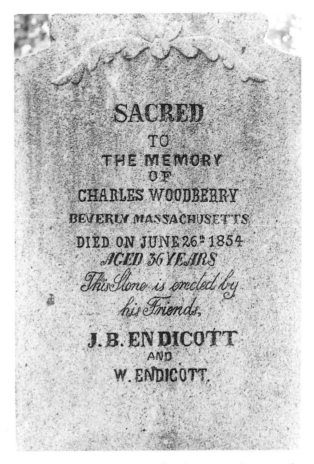

This Woodberry memorial is last in a line of three headstones on the edge of the wall overlooking the lower terrace and stands 1.2 metres north of 18, is of the same granite, but a little larger than the two others, being 127 cm high, 66 cm wide and 12 cm thick, and stands behind a granite step 91 x 27 cm with an 8 cm slot. Its top is flat, 51 cm wide and rises 11 cm above corner shoulders; the rise carries a simple symmetrical leaf motif in relief.

The inscription, which includes two lines of running hand and one of italics, is well cut and pleasingly spaced, probably under the supervision of the two Endicott friends who were residing in Macao.

OTHER OBSERVERS: JMB and HSPH: CHARLES WOODBERRY BEVERLY.
REFER TO: FC&HKG of 26/5/1849 and 18/7/1855; CM of 28/3/1850, 6/6 and 4/7/1850, 9, 16, 23 and 30/1/1851 and 19/7/1855; Dixson HKG for 1852.

20. CAPTAIN CHRISTIAN JPLAND *Danish*

'HERE RESTS Captain Christian Jpland from Apenrade died 5 October 1857.' The family now spells its name Ipland; Apenrade is now Abenraa, at the head of a fiord on Denmark's east coast. There were two Danish Captains Jpland in Macao in the period late September-early October 1857, but communication with Michael and Jacob Jebsen and with the Ipland family has satisfactorily established that this headstone and 16 both commemorate one man.

It was the captain of the barque *Camilla* who died in Macao (the other was captain of the *Dido*). The captain who succeeded him seems not to have known much about him when he had this memorial erected – the inscription is so coarse and sparse.

Meanwhile, once the news of his death reached Apenrade, the family sent a headstone from Denmark (16, a very well-made and well-informed memorial).

His father Hieronymus had been the younger of two brothers, through whom the family accounted for no less than nine ship's captains. He had two sons who became captains, as did his son-in-law, all of them in the service of Jebsen & Co. An early, blue version of the present Jebsen house-flag (red, with three mackerel) was designed by a member of the family for her Jpland husband, and later adopted by the Jpland captains.

The stone is in line with 13, 14 and 16 and stands 4.6 metres to the north of 16. Of grey, very coarse-grained granite, 104 cm high, 53 cm wide and 14 cm thick, it is behind a granite step 71 x 30 cm with a 2.5 cm slot. Its top is a high segmental arch of 24 cm rise on horizontal shoulders 2.5 cm wide. The stone has flaked and pitted badly, making for difficult reading, some letters scarcely recognizable; moreover, the letters used are too small for the type of stone. Nor is the inscription artistic, as its top line hardly follows the arched top of the stone.

OTHER OBSERVERS: OL and PCL: IPLAND; JMB and HSPH: not listed.
REFER TO: FC&HKG of 6/9/1856 and 13 and 20/5/1857; Dixson HKG for 1856–7; SFP&MA of 18 and 25/6 and 3 and 10/9/1857; Dixson HKSL for 1857; Ipland.

21. HARRIET DUDDELL *British*

THERE ARE TWO Duddell headstones, this and 27 (Frederick Duddell) further along the row, both similar in stone, design and layout. Harriet was the widow of Frederick. In 1854 Harriet was running her own business from showrooms on Queen's Road in Hong Kong let to her by her husband, with 'a large and choice selection of fancy goods, both millinery and haberdashery'. They moved to Macao, where Frederick became proprietor of the Oriental Hotel on the Praya Grande. He died in 1856. She announced that she would re-open her business and also have riding horses and phaetons for hire. She died only six months later.

Standing in line with and larger than 13, 14 and 16, and about half a metre north of 20, this rough, pink, coarse-grained, granite headstone, badly pitted with age, measures 168 cm high, 97 cm wide and 15 cm thick; its height is accentuated by a steep gable top 53 cm high with sides 69 cm long rising from horizontal shoulders 4 cm wide. The biblical text is extremely difficult to read. The following is the reading made by Braga:

**FOR IF WE BE DEAD WITH HIM
WE SHALL ALSO LIVE WITH HIM**

OTHER OBSERVERS: HSPH: No. 20.
REFER TO: JMB p 42; Dixson HKG for 1854; FC&HKG of 28/2/1857 and 1/8/1857.
NOTE: Between 21 and 22 is a gap of 4.5 metres, in which stand two small rectangular stones each 30 cm high, 23 cm wide and 8 cm thick, temporary markers discarded at the time complete tombs were built, and replaced at random during a churchyard restoration. On the side of the first facing the avenue, are engraved the letters E L, clearly a marker for 90: EDWARD LARKIN; the other is without any identification.

22. MAJOR MARK BEALE COOPER *British*

SACRED TO THE MEMORY
OF
MAJOR MARK BEALE COOPER.
12th REGIMENT
MADRAS NATIVE INFANTRY.
Who died at Macao, 26th July, 1857.

ERECTED AS A TOKEN OF RESPECT BY HIS
BROTHER OFFICERS

Inscription

WHEN HE DIED, Brevet-Major Cooper had been for a short time in command of an advance detachment of his light infantry regiment at Hong Kong, in what is now Stanley Village, where he probably contracted malaria. Given sick leave to recover in Macao, he was staying at Shaw's (later Wade's) hotel on the Rua do Campo when he died.

Just north of 21, this large chest-tomb of pink coarse-grained granite is similar in size to 10, 11 and 12, but lacks an inscription on the table-top, has no visible podium, and its box has splayed sides and ends and corner edge-rolls carved on the ends. The table-top is not supported by a bed-mould, and on its upper surface there is a 30 cm-wide chamfer, its inner edge forming a horizontal border 29 cm wide around a sunken panel, at each corner of which an ogee trefoil is cut in low relief, possibly a family or regimental symbol. Each of the sides and ends has a relief panel trapezoidal in shape, with incised corners but no inscription. To the west end is fixed a marble tablet conforming to the shape of the panel 30 cm high, 36 cm wide at its top and 30 cm at its bottom. Carved in Calcutta, the inscription is finely executed on the marble tablet, but in such small letters that they were deciphered only with the aid of a rubbing.

OTHER OBSERVERS: HSPH: No. 21.
REFER TO: FC&HKG of 21 and 25/3/1857 and 1/8/1857; CM of 26/3/1857; Dixson HKSL of 21/3/1857; SFP&MA of 23 and 30/10/1856; EIR&AL Madras 1836 p 41, 1831 p 92, 1837 p 41, 1847 p 63 and 1857 p 35.

23.   JOHN P. WILLIAMS   *American*

IN MEMORIAM
JOHN P. WILLIAMS
OF UTICA
STATE OF NEW YORK
U.S.A.
DIED AT MACAO
JULY 25, 1857,
AGED 31 YEARS.
HE ASSISTED IN SETTING
UP
THE FIRST
MAGNETIC TELEGRAPH
IN JAPAN IN 1854.

Inscription

WILLIAMS, A MERCHANT captain from Utica who joined Commodore Perry's expedition to Japan, was among those who were permitted to keep gifts from the Japanese Commissioners: in his case, a length of dyed and figured crepe and 10 sets of lacquer-ware cups and covers. Perry returned the compliments by offering gifts to senior officials, among them two modern machines that attracted much interest, a miniature railway driven by steam and an electro-magnetic telegraph, both on show in Yokohama Park.

As the inscription states, Williams helped to instal the first magnetic telegraph in Japan and was one of two men who demonstrated its use. The two terminals which comprised the telegraph were set up about 1.5 km apart at each end of wires, along which messages were sent in English, Dutch and Japanese, greatly to the amazement and amuse-ment of the spectators who thronged the exhibition daily, 'eagerly beseeching the operators to work the telegraph', and watching 'with unabated interest, the sending and receiving of messages'. Communication by telegraph as a commercial operation came to Japan somewhat later than 1854. Hawks was also a member of the expedition and has told how the passenger car of the railway train was 'so small that it could hardly carry a child of six years of age'. The Japanese, however, 'unable to reduce themselves to the capacity of the inside of the carriage, betook themselves to the roof', where dignitaries were on view 'whirling around the circular road at the rate of twenty miles an hour ... loose robes flying in the wind'.

Captain Williams remained in the Orient to take command of the river steamer *Spark* owned by J.B. Endicott (165), probably on the death of Charles Woodberry (19). In 1856 he took command of one of Endicott's new steamers launched that March, the *Lily*: she was registered as a Portuguese vessel, her agent at Canton was W.C. Hunter (after whom one of Endicott's daughter's was named: 34) and in Hong Kong Sandwith Drinker (39), and her name was given to another of Endicott's daughters (33). At the end of 1856 the *Lily*, his last command, was fitted out to sail to Hainan Island to tow the disabled barque *Africa* to Hong Kong.

A pleasing, grey, fine-grained granite memorial – showing raised lettering, rare in this cemetery – this headstone of local granite stands between two steps just north of 22 and in line with 20 and 21; it is 114 cm high, 61 cm wide and 10 cm thick. A device is carved in low relief beneath its blunted gable top 15 cm high, comprising flowers surrounding a central urn, above a small rectangular panel. Set back in a deep recess cut into the granite below this, a white rectangular marble tablet carries a perfectly preserved inscription. The inscription is so much better than other examples of local craftsmanship that the marble inset must have been imported ready-cut, probably from the US.

OTHER OBSERVERS: PCL: JOHN P. WILLIAM; HSPH: No. 22.
REFER TO: Hawks Wallach pp 189 and 295; Hawks p 416; Dixson HKSL for 1855, 1856; FC&HKG of 23/4 and 9/8/1856 and 29/7/1857; CM of 11/8/1856; Dixson HKG of 22/10/1856.

24.   WALTHER SCHAEFFER   *German*

THE INSCRIPTION translates: 'To the memory of Walther Schaeffer of Altena in Westphalia who died 1st July 1857. God preserve thy blessed soul.' In Macao either on a health visit, or as a minor merchant in a business in which his brother Herman was a partner, Walther died of pulmonary tuberculosis shortly after arriving. A son was born to his wife in Hong Kong, in 1852.

Set behind a coarse granite step facing the central avenue and in line with and 1.2 metres to the north of 23, this rough, medium-grain granite headstone is 137 cm high, 61 cm wide and 17 cm thick, with a segmental arched top 28 cm high above horizontal shoulders 2.5 cm wide; of the inscription the first line follows the curve of the

arch. Much of the inscription itself is illegible, the penultimate line above being reconstructed from Braga's earlier observation, confirmed by an obituary notice in the press.

OTHER OBSERVERS: OL: WALTER SCHAEFFER VON ALTENA; HSPH: WALTHE. SCHAEFFER.
REFER TO: FC&HKG of 1/7/1857.
NOTE: There are two small, grey granite foot-stones between 24 and 25, both the same size as those between 21 and 22, but both bearing large, indistinct letters on their western aspects, as follows:
The first: E W E, DE, VOGEL
The second: F.D. 185-
The first was used as a marker for 25 alongside; the second for 27, that of FREDERICK DUDDELL, the date on whose memorial is 1856.

25. E.W.E. DE VOGEL *Dutch*

PROBABLY DYING during a round trip from Java, Emile Willem Eugéne de Vogel, aged 19, was born there on 28 February 1838, son of Willem de Vogel (then serving in Java as Director of Finance) and Frederique Jeanne Louise Bousquet (née de Froideville). There appears to be no connection between this young man and either the Rev Carl Vogel who was in Hong Kong in 1850–2 or the Vogel buried in the Hong Kong Colonial Cemetery at about the same time.

This rectangular headstone stands behind a step 84 x 38 cm, both of pink coarse granite, and lies 2.4 metres beyond and in line with 23 and 24, measuring 107 cm high, 64 cm wide and 13 cm thick, with rounded shoulders and a flat top. It is so badly worn that deciphering the last line is impossible: it may be a biblical quotation. The first of the two foot-stones noted in 24 refers to this grave.

OTHER OBSERVERS: OL and PCL: OVERLEDEN; JMB and HSPH: not listed – for the rest of the memorials in this terrace, HSPH's numbering is two less than that of the corresponding official list.

26. MARIA BALL FRENCH *American*

THE QUOTATION: 'I was dumb, I opened not my mouth; because thou didst it' is taken from Psalm 39:9. This infant was the second child and only daughter of the Rev John Booth French, who had married Mary Lucy Ball at Canton in 1851, with Dr Peter Parker officiating. Posted to Canton, he sailed out from New York in 1846 in the company of the Speers (140). His wife Mary was one of the two daughters of the American missionary and sinologue, the Rev Dr Dyer Ball and Lucy (née Mills). Lucy's mother and her two young brothers lie buried in the Hong Kong Colonial Cemetery. Mary's half-brother, James Dyer Ball, famed as the author of the popular reference work *Things Chinese* and several guides to Chinese dialects, was thus the uncle of this infant.

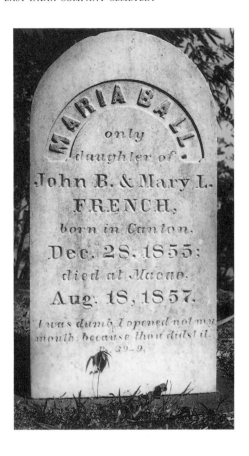

Mary was seven months pregnant with their third child when little Maria died. Their house at Canton had been burnt down in the Taiping disturbances of 29 October 1856, and French and his family were evacuated to Macao on 4 November (see also 32) on board the river steamer *Spark*, when under the command of Captain J.P. Williams (23). It was during this visit that Maria died. On the way home in November 1858 with his family, her father died and was buried at sea off Java.

Standing on a sunken plinth of red igneous rock with a chipped edge, a metre north of and in line with 25, this small and pleasing marble headstone is 69 cm high, 38 cm wide and 6 cm thick, its sides passing without shoulders into a semi-circular arched top. Letters in the first line of the inscription are cut by a skilled chisel, in high relief within a moat round the arch, so that their surface is flush with that of the stone.

OTHER OBSERVERS: JMB: MARIA BALL; HSPH: Numbered 24.
REFER TO: Dean; FC&HKG of 8/11/1851 and 18/2, 19/8 and 21/10/1857; CM of 6/11/1851, 22/9/1853, 18/11/1847 and 19/8/1857; Wylie; Monroe lxxxvi p 276.

---

27.   FREDERICK DUDDELL   *British*

FREDERICK WAS ONE of two brothers resident in Hong Kong. The other, George, appears to have preceded him in the Colony, and being better known was probably the Duddell whose name was given to Duddell Street in the city centre. Both

were members of the first volunteer corps, which was formed for Hong Kong's defence in 1854 with 99 members. That year, Frederick had opened a store in Queen's Road from which to set up in business on his own as an auctioneer. He abandoned this business after one year to open a hotel in Macao, the Oriental on the Praya Grande near the corner of the Rua do Campo, moving it in June 1856 to more commodious premises formerly known as the Macao Hotel, on a site later occupied by the Riviera Hotel. Lodging at the former, with board, was advertised at $2 a day, at the latter $3. A typhoon in July 1855 blew his cutter ashore on the Praya, where thieves stripped it bare. He was married to Harriet Duddell (21) and died on 1 November 1856 aged 38.

This badly weathered headstone of grey coarse-grained granite with a steep gable top stands 157 cm high, 74 cm wide and 13 cm thick, behind a granite step 41 x 89 cm, in line with its neighbours, and appears to have been hewn from the same quarry as his wife's in 21, proving equally unsuitable for inscribing and at least as hard to read. The first words were recognized mostly by guesswork and the verses were very troublesome before Mary Visick of the University of Hong Kong identified them as the last stanza of a poem by Thomas Moore (1779–1852) from the *Sacred Songs No. 1* dedicated in 1824:

> *Poor wand'rers of a stormy day*
> *From wave to wave we're driven*
> *And Fancy's Haste and Reason*
> *Serve but to light the troubled way.*
> *There's nothing calm but Heaven.*

The second of the two foot-stones noted in 24 belongs to this memorial.

OTHER OBSERVERS: HSPH: FRED. DUDDEL, Numbered 25. **REFER TO:** Dixson HKR for 1854-6; FC&HKG of 25/7/1855 and 25/6/1856.

28.   ELIZABETH LEWIS HADDON   *British*

THERE APPEARS the following quotation below the main inscription: 'Lord Jesus receive my spirit.' At the time of Elizabeth's death, her husband Thomas Haddon was an engineer on the new steamer *Remi*, which sailed to Shanghai the day she died – it is not known if he left with it. They had arrived at Hong Kong on the British barque *Mary Graham* in May 1852. Soon after her death, at the end of March 1857, he left for Ceylon in the steamer *Erin*.

Standing half a metre to the north of and in line with 27 behind a granite step 33 x 79 cm, this finely textured, grey granite headstone is 99 cm high, 61 cm wide and 14 cm thick, its top a low segmental arch 6 cm high rising direct from the sides. The lettering is well-preserved. The word 'Memory' follows the curve of the arch and the deceased's Christian names are cut in an ogee curve below, in artistic balance with the upper curve.

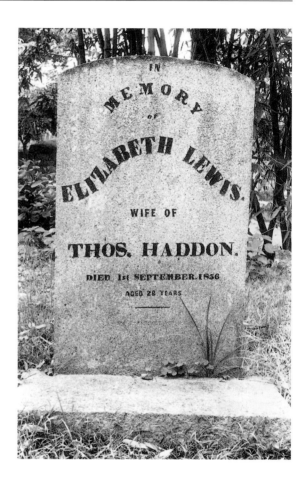

OTHER OBSERVERS: HSPH: Numbered 26.
REFER TO: FC&HKG of 3/9/1856; CM of 27/5/1852; Dixson HKSL for 1855-7; Dixson HKG for 1856.

29.   ABBY L. KERR   *American*

THE QUOTATION, 'As for God, his way is perfect', is taken from Psalm 18: 30. The date of death appears, but some weeks after it, in two Hong Kong newspapers as 25 August. John Glasgow Kerr and his first wife Abby (née Kingsbury) left New York in December 1853 in the American ship *Horatio* with Captain Crocker in command, and arrived in Hong Kong five months later on the way to Canton, where, with Dr Peter Parker going on leave, he was to take over on behalf of the American Presbyterian Mission the hospital of the Medical Missionary Society. It is unusual in this cemetery that the date of landing in China is recorded. Kerr's contributions to Western medicine during almost half a century in China were immense: he consolidated the pioneering introduction of smallpox vaccination by Dr Pearson of the Company; he was associated with the Canton hospital for over 40 years, and recommissioned its operations after it had been burnt down during the Anglo-Chinese hostilities of 1856–60; he taught in the medical school which he founded and wrote and updated Chinese medical texts; and among his pupils was Sun

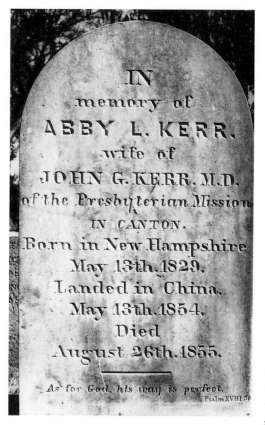

Yat-sen, during the year before he moved to the new medical college founded at Hong Kong by Drs Patrick Manson and James Cantlie to complete his training. In 1886 Kerr was elected the first president of a new Medical Missionary Association of China; and in 1898 he started the first hospital for the insane. He died in 1901.

The second in a group of three headstones of marble, 26, 29 and 30, which stand in line at intervals of about a metre, all mounted on granite plinths facing the central avenue, and from the similarities of design and execution probably the work of one stonemason, this is of white marble, rectangular, surmounted by a segmental top rising directly from the sides, and stands on a granite base of two steps, the upper step 69 cm long, 28 cm wide and 22 cm high and the lower 81 x 36 x 11cm.

OTHER OBSERVERS: HSPH: No. 27.
REFER TO: FC&HKG of 15/9/1855; CM of 20/9/1855; Dixson HKR for 1855; Wylie.

30.   AGNES GILMAN   *American*

IT WAS NOT legal to bury in this cemetery after 1857, 30 years before Agnes' memorial was erected in it in 1889. Her father, the Rev Frank P. Gilman, was a missionary in Hainan, and it seems likely that his infant daughter died there and the parents erected a memorial to her during a visit to Macao, where there was a more reasonable hope of permanence than Hainan offered. Her mother, Marion (née McNair), married the Rev Gilman in December 1885, and died at the American Presbyterian Mission in Hainan three months after Agnes.

The third of a trio of marble headstones of similar design, this stands shakily on a granite plinth and podium and measures 71 x 43 x 10 cm, with a semi-circular top rising direct from the sides. The plinth is moulded, 20 cm high, with a splay reducing to a top of 10 cm less on each side from a bottom of 71 x 38 cm. Its lettering differs from the other two, and the precise age and the contractions of month and day are more in the conventions of New England monuments cut a few decades earlier.

OTHER OBSERVERS: HSPH: AGNES GIMAN, No. 28.

31.   CHARLES HODGE PRESTON   *American*

THE FATHER OF THIS infant was the Rev Charles Finney Preston, who joined the American Presbyterian Mission at Canton in 1854 and married Mrs M.C. Brecoster late that year, in a ceremony at which Dr Peter Parker, who was then American Commissioner to China, officiated. Preston died on 17 July 1877 and was buried in the Colonial Cemetery of Hong Kong beneath a monument erected by his three brothers in America. His religious books, pamphlets and articles in Cantonese included a life of Christ and colloquial translations of two gospels.

Much smaller and simpler even than No 30, this charming pink marble headstone, 58 x 30 x 4.5 cm, is on a rectangular granite plinth 51 cm long, 20 cm wide and 18 cm high, which is surrounded by a concave moulding and mounted on a granite step 58 cm long by 28 cm wide. It is sited in the rear line of the row, on the edge of the wall and facing the central avenue. Devoid of embellishment, its charm lies in the clearly cut lettering and well-spaced lines, combining some of the features of 26 and 29. It is scarcely usual for a biblical text to be ascribed to Christ; and the abbreviation for months is more in keeping with the 1850s than with the 1880s of 30. The stone has suffered a fracture at some time, the two pieces of which have been rejoined without damage to either inscription or appearance.

OTHER OBSERVERS: OL: CHARLES RODGE PRESTON: HSPH: Numbered 29.
REFER TO: FC&HKG of 23/12/1854, 9/12/1857 and 7/9/1861; CM pp 191ff; Wylie.

32.   HELEN BAPTISTA GAILLARD   *American*

THE FATHER OF this infant, the Southern Baptist missionary Charles Washington Gaillard, married Eva (née Mills) shortly before they left for Hong Kong and Canton, arriving in the autumn of 1854. In 1856, the family took temporary refuge in Macao from the troubles then starting at Canton. After returning to Canton, Gaillard opened the first chapel within the city walls, and introduced there a daily service in Cantonese. He was killed at home in July 1862 when his house collapsed during a typhoon.

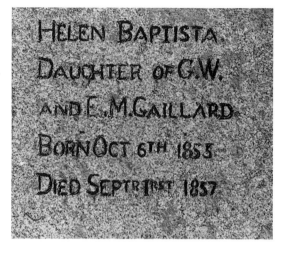

Standing apart in the back line of the row and behind 29 and 30, this crude rectangular headstone of rough grey granite is 97 cm high, 48 cm wide and 11 cm thick, and lacks a step.

The inscription is badly cut and poorly finished with letters of irregular size, showing the mason's inability to distinguish between C and G. Its quality indicates that it was a temporary memorial to be replaced at a date which never came. Only with the help of an obituary notice could the full date be reconstructed.

OTHER OBSERVERS: OL and PCL: HELEN BAPTISTA CAILLARD; JMB and HSPH: Numbered 30, HELEN BATISTA CAILLARD.
REFER TO: FC&HKG of 12/8/1854, 9/9/1857, 21/11/1857 and 10/4/1858; Dixson HKG for 1854; Wylie.

33–34. FIDELIA BRIDGES ENDICOTT *Americans*
and ROSALIE HUNTER ENDICOTT

The twin tombs of the Endicott sisters

**SUFFER LITTLE CHILDREN TO COME
UNTO ME
AND FORBID THEM NOT**

33. Inscription on west end

**HE SHALL CARRY THE LAMBS WITH HIS
ARM AND CARRY THEM IN HIS BOSOM**

34. Inscription on west end

OBITUARY NOTICES give Rosalie Endicott the second name of Hunter, so called after the American merchant and diarist W.C. Hunter, who was a close friend of the parents. Fidelia Endicott's second name was that of her paternal grandmother, née Fidelia Bridges (see 108), and in family circles she was called Lily after one of the Canton steamers built and operated by her father (166). The mother of these two girls was Sarah Ann, née Russell, married to J.B. Endicott at Macao in October 1852, the Rev E.A. Washburn officiating.

111

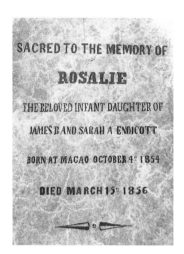

SACRED TO THE MEMORY OF

ROSALIE

THE BELOVED INFANT DAUGHTER OF

JAMES B AND SARAH A ENDICOTT

BORN AT MACAO OCTOBER 4ᵗʰ 1854

DIED MARCH 15ᵗʰ 1856

Side by side and in line with 17, 28, 29 and 30, heads towards the lower terrace, the memorials to

the two sisters are small, simple, medium-grained granite chest-tombs similar both in size and design and both on podia 110 x 151 cm. Sides and ends are vertical and unadorned, each supporting a bed-mould and table-top carved from a single block of stone. The top inscriptions are easy to read, the west ends less so. The granite of 34 has discoloured more than that of 33, and weathering has made its inscription less easy to read.

OTHER OBSERVERS: HSPH: Numbered 31 and 32 respectively.
REFER TO: FC&HKG of 23/10/1852, 31/8/1853, 7/10/1854 and 22/3/1856; CM of 25/8/1853.

---

35.   MEDHURST   *British*

HERE LIES
THE INFANT DAUGHTER
OF
WALTER HENRY
AND
ANN ISABEL
MEDHURST,
BORN
9TH NOVEMBER 1854

Inscription

THE FATHER, a sinologue, writer, and distinguished consular officer of Amoy, Foochow and Shanghai, was the son of a well-known member of

the London Missionary Society of the same name and the first of the Protestant missionaries to work in north China; both father and son published books about their experiences in China. The mother, who in 1854 became his second wife, was a granddaughter of the American S.B. Rawle (134) and died in Singapore the following year. There being neither name nor date of death in the inscription, the infant was probably still-born, or she died before a name could be given. Early in February 1841, the father had been one of a group of eight missionaries who hired a Portuguese lorcha and made a two-day excursion from Macao to the newly acquired colony of Hong Kong, where they walked the island through Wongneichong Gap as far as Stanley and Tai Tam. In 1852 he was appointed Chinese Secretary to the Superintendent of Trade, and it was only three days after he married for the second time that he was sent north to Shanghai, joining his brother-in-law, the Hon C.B. Hillier, and Horatio Nelson Lay in the mission of the Governor of Hong Kong, HE Sir George Bonham, in connection with the disturbances. The young Lay was moving to Shanghai to take up appointments as acting interpreter and then concurrently as acting vice-consul; both postings were far more senior than his 22 years would suggest, for which he was bitterly dubbed the 'Boy Consul' by those in the consular service over whom he had been promoted. Five years later he was selected by the Chinese mandarins to be the first Inspector-General of the new Chinese Imperial Customs Service. Medhurst remained in the consular service from 1854, when he became British Consul at Foochow, until his retirement. He had married for the third time before 1858, and retired from Shanghai in 1876.

In line with 33 and 34, this rectangular, fine-grained, grey granite headstone is 91 cm high, 43 cm wide and 9.5 cm thick with a low gable top rising only 4 cm direct from the sides, and is set on a granite plinth 58 x 28 cm. Much of the inscription is boldly incised and can be easily read: it boasts two curved lines that add a touch of gracefulness.

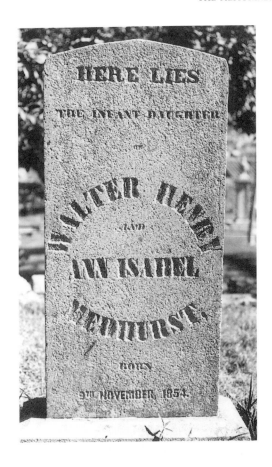

OTHER OBSERVERS: OL: MEDHUBST; HSPH: Numbered 33.
REFER TO: CM of 4/1/1849, 19/2/1852, 23/2/1854 and 8/3/1855; SFP&MA of 22/2/1855; CM of 15/7 and 28/11/1876 and 14/12/1876 pp 72, 727, 664 respectively; Canton R of 16/2/1841; Canton P of 27/2/1841.

36.   ELIZABETH C. VROOMAN   *American*

North side

**SACRED TO THE MEMORY OF
MRS. ELIZABETH C. VROOMAN
WIFE OF REV. DANIEL VROOMAN
MISSIONARY OF THE A.B.C.F.M.**

Inscription on south side

DANIEL VROOMAN and his wife arrived at Canton in March 1852, responding to a call to mission work in China issued by the American Board of Commissioners for Foreign Missions – the A.B.C.F.M. of the south side inscription above – a call the mission was urged to make by Dr Morrison (141). Daniel re-married in 1857 and retired from this mission in 1867.

Meanwhile, in 1860, Daniel had published a map in English of the city and suburbs of Canton, and in 1863 his own phonetic alphabet of Cantonese. In 1878 he was appointed to superintend a new mission to the Chinese in Victoria, Australia, a post which he held until his final retirement in 1881.

Some six metres beyond 35 lies this large chest-tomb set on a 241 x 127 x 25 cm podium with mitred corners, both in pink, coarse-grained granite, as is the plinth around the box base, which is carved with a large ogee moulding in its upper part. Sides and ends are slightly splayed, on each side a rectangular panel in relief with incised corners. The inscriptions on the panels are deeply cut, but not all easy to read. The ends are without panels, but to the east end is attached a tablet of Belgian black marble shaped to match its trapezoid, carrying the neatly cut Chinese inscription, of which the English translation is as follows:

'Mrs Vrooman was born in the USA in 1826, came to Canton in 1852 and died in Macao in 1854. It is said that the principle of womanhood lies in the four virtues, while the excellence of a woman is her chastity and gentleness. Is not this saying true also even in foreign lands? Mrs Vrooman came to Canton from America. She fully understood the Way and worshipped the true God. Seeing that the Chinese ladies, though pure and refined, could do nothing but embroidery, she wanted to open their minds to the teaching of Jesus of Judea. But though her good intention was great, Heaven did not allow her to achieve her aim. She was in China

114

"MY DEAR, HEAVEN IS A HAPPY LAND."

"Tell them all to love the Savior more."

East side

for less than three years when she was called by God to enter into the Kingdom of Heaven. Through Jesus, her sins were forgiven. That she could share the joys of Heaven and dispense with all the labour on earth make us envy her now. Since there is at present no possibility for the people on earth to catch sight of her who is in Heaven we write this biography to commemorate her that the world may know such a virtuous woman once existed in this world.'

OTHER OBSERVERS: OL, PCL, JMB, HSPH: ELIZABETH G; HSPH: Numbered 34.
REFER TO: FC&HKG of 21/6/1854; CM of 11/3/1852 and 22/6/1854; Wylie; CelEmp of 22/6/1878 p 595; Drake.

37.   ARTHUR WILLIAM URMSON   *British*

THE FINAL LINE of this inscription on the south face reads 'Born 18 November 1853 Died 1st March 1854'. The father of this infant, George Urmson, for more than 15 years in business in Shanghai, Canton and Hong Kong, was born in 1827 and married Martha (née Tarrant) at Hong Kong in May 1850. The infant was thus the grandson of the William Tarrant who shortly afterwards bought the newspaper *Friend of China and Hong Kong Gazette* (FC&HKG) from John Carr and became its publisher.

Urmson was associated with Endicott (166) in the Hong Kong Steam Packet Company. The couple's first son, George Harold, was born at

South side

Canton in 1853; the infant Arthur William was the second. Later a daughter Mary was born, also in Macao. Urmson, then a partner in the Hong Kong firm of Birley & Co, died on board the packet ship *Cadiz* and was buried at sea near Penang while on his way home to join wife and family, who had left before him in February 1857. He is remembered in a tablet in St John's Cathedral, Hong Kong. He should not be confused with Urmston (115).

Too close to 36, this small chest-tomb of coarse-grained, local pink granite, sides and ends slightly splayed, displays badly weathered lettering. Supporting its moulded plinth is a podium 76 x 145 x 18 cm with mitred corners. The main inscription is cut on a panel, some of it difficult to read. On the table-top, which has no bed-mould, the secondary inscription is in such small letters that it may readily be overlooked.

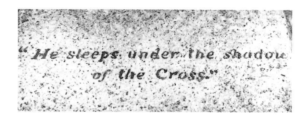

OTHER OBSERVERS: JMB: URMSTON; HSPH: Numbered 35. REFER TO: FC&HKG of 8/5/1850, 3/7/1850, 18/11/1850, 15/2/1851, 19/11/1853, 8/3/1854 and 11/5/1861; CM of 2/5/1850, 20/2/1851, 24/11/1853 and 9/3/1854.

38.   LIEUTENANT JOSEPH HAROD ADAMS   *American*

West end and south side of the tomb

DIED ON BOARD U S STEAM FRIGATE
POWHATAN OCTOBER 4th 1853 AGED 36 YEARS

Inscription on north side

LIEUTENANT ADAMS belonged to a New England family of outstanding public service in America and abroad. From it came two Presidents of the United States: John Adams (1797–1801), second president and grandfather of the deceased, and John Quincy Adams (1825–29), sixth president and his uncle. John Adams also served as Vice-President (1789–97) under George Washington, the godfather of 58 (George Washington Biddle).

His father, Thomas Boylston Adams, was the youngest brother of John Quincy and was a distinguished lawyer and politician; his mother was Ann (née Harod), after whom he received his second name Harod. He died on the *Powhatan*, a frigate in the East India and Japan Squadron, at anchor in the Cumsingmoon Passage, and his remains were taken to Macao for burial.

Conspicuous at the north end of the row is

his medium-grained, grey granite chest-tomb; mounted on its table-top, in common with nine of the others that are in the Lower Terrace, is a closed, fluted urn mounted on a small three-tiered podium. Its long axis is east-west. The box itself rests on a grey granite podium of 152 x 249 x 28 cm, the bases of its vertical sides and ends surrounded by a moulded plinth, and its podium supports a table-top on a bed-mould. Carved in relief on the sides and ends are rectangular panels, three of them

Anchor device cut in relief on the east end.

boldly inscribed and the east end boasting in relief a foul anchor: one of the few devices in the cemetery that denotes a profession. It is the fluted urn and its podium, carved from one piece of granite 72 cm high, that give so pleasing an aspect to the memorial.

OTHER OBSERVERS: HSPH: Numbered 36.
REFER TO: Loomis; FC&HKG of 8/10/1853; CM of 13/10/1853; Alexander 1848.

---

39.   SANDWITH B[udd]. DRINKER   *American*

DRINKER WAS ONE of twin brothers born on 19 November 1808 to Henry and Elizabeth Drinker (née Sandwith), and the last in the family. By the marriage of a sister, he became related to the Biddle family (see 58). As a ship's captain he had brought his wife Susanna (née Budd) with him to Macao, where he had been under medical care in 1838. They had started living in the area at least from 1837. By 1845 he had abandoned the seafaring life and became well established at Canton and Hong Kong, as the Hong Kong and adjacent-ports agent

for underwriters not only at Philadelphia, but at New York and Boston.

The products he distributed through his agencies ranged from ice cut from Wenham Lake in Massachusetts to chandlery for American warships. A freemason, he was Worshipful Master of Zetland Lodge in Hong Kong (1850–1), and moved to Macao during 1857. A newspaper report had it that he and Williams (23) died "from the effects of poison administered in the bread ... by the Esang Bakery". They were among over 400 foreigners, including the wife of the Governor of Hong Kong, who were either suffering or dying from the effects of arsenical poisoning, victims of a notorious plot directed at British residents of Hong Kong; the owner of the bakery had fled to Macao whence he was extradited to be charged in Hong Kong with nine others, on evidence so circumstantial that they were discharged. (See Chapter 6 page 57.)

After his death, his wife left for Baltimore and died the same year, probably of the same cause. It is unlikely that she had time to plan and supervise the cutting and erection of this memorial. There are two likely errors: the date of death, which was reported in the papers as on 17 January; and the initial B in his name, which members of his family in America are adamant that he did not have, and which may have become transposed from Susanna's own surname, since she usually signed herself 'Sue B.D'.

The sole memorial within the central avenue, this medium-grained granite chest-tomb lies with its long axis east-west at the north end, solidly based on two tiers of a grey, coarse-grained granite podium with mitred corners, one 130 x 206 x 28 cm and the other 183 x 256 x 25 cm. It reveals many unusual features: as they rise to support the bed-mould, the sides of the box curve outwards; the edges of the table-top are also curved, within their camber the inscription surface. There are no edge-rolls on the box's corners, and while its sides and ends are carved with panels in 12 mm relief and with incised corners, they do not carry the inscription, which is cut in the table-top, head towards the Lower Terrace east. The lettering is well-preserved and artistically spaced, two lines being in Old English script.

OTHER OBSERVERS: JMB: SANWITH B. DRINKER; HSPH: SANWITH DRINKER, Numbered 37.
REFER TO: Nye Morning; Drinker; Canton P of 8/9/1838, 23/3/1839 and 3, 10 and 24/2/1844; Monroe lxxxvii pp 148, 149, 269, 270 and 281–3; Wood p 75.

40.   **GEORGE CHINNERY**   *British*

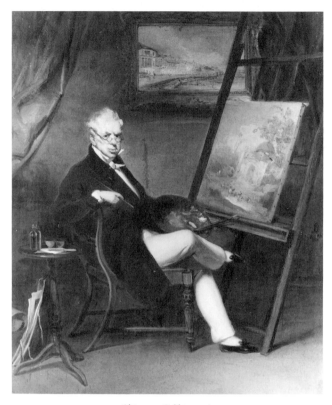

Chinnery: Self-portrait

CHINNERY THE ARTIST was born in London soon after the start of 1774. He married his Dublin landlord's unlovely daughter Marianne Vigne, from whom he fled in frustration first to London and then, in 1802, to Madras, where he was immediately listed among the residents as a painter of portraits, soon collecting a clientele among the members of high society. In 1808 he shifted his operations to Bengal, where he embarked upon one of his most productive periods, and whither his wife sailed in 1818 in an attempt to mend fences.

Indifferent to the value of money, he was always in debt and, by the time he left his wife again in 1822, was said to owe over $40,000.

When he saw that Serampur, where he had moved, was still far too near his wife and his creditors for safety, he sailed in September 1825 to Macao, where he remained painting from then until his death in 1852, apart from six months in 1846 painting in Hong Kong, and apart from a brief, panic-stricken flight to Canton when he heard it said his wife was following in another attempt to engineer a reconciliation. She died in England in 1847, after a life of disappointment and disillusion.

Chinnery was an ugly man: in local British theatrical productions, he was invariably chosen to act as a female oddity – 'what an ugly fellow', he once said of his own face. He led a wholly disorganized and improvident personal life. He was so grossly overweight by the time he died, in his 80th year, that he had long been forced to depend on others for many of life's necessities. Among them were Patrick Stewart (44) and William C. Hunter, who recorded in close detail the daily events of some six weeks of the life they were leading.

His paintings demonstrate the elegance and grace his person so sadly lacked, and many were hung at Royal Academy exhibitions in London. Several local artists, as well as his pupils, adopted his style and technique to such effect that the term 'belonging to the school of Chinnery' was applied to their works. Among his pupils and portrait subjects in Macao were his friend the French opium trader, J.A. Durran and the diarist Harriet Low. The accuracy of his paintings and of his pencil sketches of people and animals and places has made his work an invaluable check of historical and biographical detail. Extant are his pencil sketches and aquarelles and oils of landscapes, riverscapes and seascapes; of Chinese fortune-tellers, fishermen and farmers dressed for all weathers, traders, black-smiths, barbers, a surgeon with his patients, builders, beggars and boat-women, with their pipes and hookahs, their watering cans, nets and catches, of card-players and shuttle-cock players, of streets, pagodas, bridges, forts and factories, markets and merchants' houses, an eye hospital, churches, temples and tombs, of junks, ships and sampans, of cows, pigs, dogs and cats, and many single and group portraits of people with children, with Chinese assistants, with books and a scroll, a sewing basket, a bird-cage, a fan, a piano or a harp; and several of himself, including one from behind. Among this prodigious output are portraits of prominent local residents who are buried in the cemetery, including Dr Morrison's (141) second wife Eliza, her son John and his son by his first wife, John Robert (143), and Sir Andrew Ljungstedt (60). Of a portrait of Morrison with his acolytes, he wrote that 'the gentlemen of the Factory have sent it home to be engraved at their expense'.

Among his close friends were the Americans,

the merchant W.W. Wood, a life-long correspondent, and Hunter, who told of Wood's reading out to Chinnery a notice in a Bengal newspaper, in which he was described as 'George Chinnery, an absconding debtor', and of his towering rage, not because of the description, but because he was simply 'George Chinnery, neither Mr. nor Esquire ... without head or tail; that is too much to bear!' The inscription on his memorial is no less simple.

The memorial, of medium-grain granite, stands against the Camoens Garden wall at the north end of the avenue. In standard of design and craftsmanship, none other in the cemetery can compare with it: of the other stonemasons whose work is represented, none shows the technique needed to plan and produce it.

It stands 168 cm high and 118 cm wide. An oval panel of grey, finer grain is carved in low relief on a flat niche set between the pillars of a semi-circular arch rising from imposts above two main pilasters; the pilasters are flanked by engaged, unfluted Tuscan columns of grey medium-grained granite; the columns support an entablature in form not strictly classical, for the place of an architrave is taken by a secondary plinth. An exaggerated frieze is cut on this plinth, the recessed centre of which exhibits in low relief an inner panel between two low pilasters, on which are embossed roundels. Simple designs are cut in low relief on the keystone of the arch and its spandrils; both Tuscan columns and main pilasters rest directly on a medium-grained granite step without a base. Despite the high finish of the surface of its oval panel, however, there is no other inscription, and indeed no visible sign of an intention to attach to it a tablet or plaque. It is on the inner panel that Chinnery's name, in large block capitals, is commemorated.

Gideon Nye said in a lecture at Canton on 31 January 1873, that after Chinnery's death a 'fund was raised for a Memorial Tablet to his memory; but it has not yet been received from England'. The 20-year lapse may in some way account for the lack of any other inscription. No further reference to the memorial from England has been traced.

The balustrade above it belongs to the cemetery wall. At the time of writing, parts of the wall had been brought down by typhoon rains, including that behind the Chinnery memorial, which itself stood undamaged.

OTHER OBSERVERS: HSPH: Numbered 38.
REFER TO: DNB; Hunter pp 271–3; Redgrave; Bapt R 6541/1; Nye Morning pp 30 and 32; EIR&D for 1803–7; China J viii of 6/1928 p 297; Bovill; Bengal P&P xxv p 127; Cotton pp 53-4; Loines pp 118, 181–2 and 184; Canton R of 30/5/1852; Downing iii pp 220–1; Dixson HKG of 9/7/1852; FC&HKG of 29/8/1837 and 2/6/1852; FInd of 8/7/1852; CM of 9/9/1852; Morrison ii p 424; Guildhall Library MS 6541/1; Hutcheon passim; Coates 1966, 1978; Conner passim.

41. CHARLOTTE M. LIVINGSTONE *British*

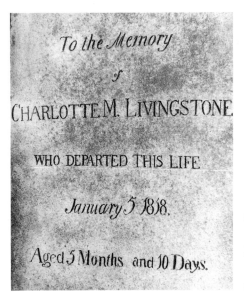

To the Memory
of
CHARLOTTE M. LIVINGSTONE
WHO DEPARTED THIS LIFE
January 5 1818.
Aged 5 Months and 10 Days.

CHARLOTTE WAS THE infant daughter of John and Janet Livingstone. John, a surgeon employed from 1807 in the Company's service, stationed at Canton and Macao after a career afloat on the Company's ships, also had a son, Charles Patrick , who followed his father into the service as a surgeon. While still in Macao in 1821, John received the degree of MD in absentia from Marischal College, Aberdeen. In June of that year he was in constant attendance on Mary Morrison (142) during her sudden and fatal illness, while Janet saw to the needs of the family. He was, with Sir William Fraser (62) and George Urmston (115), a pall-bearer at her funeral, and he and his wife took the Morrison daughter Rebecca to live with them, until she sailed to England with her brother John Robert (143) for schooling.

John, like so many other medical men of the time, was also a botanist and, as an expert in the knowledge and use of Chinese herbs and drugs, he asked Morrison to arrange translations of important Chinese botanical works into English. He died on board the Company ship *Waterloo* on their way home on leave in 1829.

Alike in design and lying close and parallel to 42 and 43, the three memorials mark the re-interment of bodies buried on the hillside before the cemetery was brought into use. No records of the earlier burials have emerged.

The sides and ends of the box of this chest-tomb, encased in a moulded plinth, stand on a mitred podium and rise vertically to support a substantial bed-mould and an unchamfered table-top. They are each carved to form recessed panels with incised corners, but none carries an inscription. On the table-top, the inscription is of tasteful design, its figures particularly well cut. It has withstood weathering and can be read with ease.

OTHER OBSERVERS: HSPH: Numbered 1.
REFER TO: Hardy pp 144, 155, 173, 186, 200 and 228; Crawford pp 440 and 624; Morse iii pp 117 and 229 and iv pp 110 and 187; Morrison ii p 101; EIR&D.

42.   THOMAS CHARLES PATTLE   *British*

SACRED
To the Memory of
THOMAS CHA.ˢ PATTLE Esqᵗᵉ.
Who Died
On the 26ᵗʰ of November 1815
Aged 44 Years

PATTLE'S FAMILY was connected with the Company from the middle of the 18th century. After serving in Bengal, he joined the China branch at Canton in 1789 as a writer at the age of about 18, and despite Chinese restrictions he was taught to speak Cantonese. He became in 1807 second supercargo and member of the Select Committee, several of whose decisions he objected to – 'his sagacity was of the *ex post facto* type', but his opposition was often reinforced by strong anti-opium principles.

For the part they played in 1810 in heightening tension between the British and the Portuguese, he and the other members of the committee – the president and the third supercargo – were all relieved of their posts in 1810. The committee had concluded that the French were planning to take advantage of the weak Portuguese defences and attack Macao, and persuaded the Company in India to send troops to forestall them. An attack did not take place, however, and the arrival of troops from India was strongly resented by the Portuguese. Pattle was back on the committee again the next year and remained on it until his death. His last years were spent in Macao, where he was responsible for the exporting of the uncoined silver used by the Chinese as a medium of exchange: a responsibility that brought him great profit from commissions, its export being prohibited from Canton, but not from Macao. James Molony knew him as 'a man of remarkably convivial Habits and of great Conversational Powers which rendered him very popular with some of the young men'.

Its head near the wall and lying alongside 41, closely resembling it in design but with slightly larger dimensions, his chest-tomb has at its sides and ends, uninscribed, rectangular, square-cornered panels surrounded by moats. The table-top carries an inscription, is well cut and easily read.

OTHER OBSERVERS: HSPH: Numbered 21.
REFER TO: Bengal P&P xxv p 137; COPR viii p 423; Bengal Obit for 1848 p 31; Morse ii p 209 and iii pp 36ff, 79, 132, 176 and 226; EIK/AR for 1792 p 171; Molony.

43. JOANNI HENRYCO RABINEL *Dutch*

South side

RABINEL WAS OF Huguenot descent, as was Pierot (45), which accounts for their being interred in a Protestant cemetery. He was a member of the trade council of the Dutch East India Company's factory at Canton as early as 1787, becoming its head in 1798.

Along with John Henri Bletterman and Bernardus Zeeman (114), he was chiefly responsible for the arrangements for the visit of the Dutch Embassy to the Chinese Emperor in 1794–5.

This granite chest-tomb stands close alongside, similar in orientation and ground measurements, and parallel to 42 but a few centimetres to its north. It stands noticeably higher, however, being 91 cm from base to table-top. Like it, the panels on sides and ends have incised corners and are surrounded by moats. The lettering of the inscriptions on the sides is competently cut, deeply incised, well preserved and easy to read. One is in Latin, the other in Dutch, and both are freely translated below, with some necessary comment.

Dutch: In memory of the Honourable Mr Jean Henry Rabinel, Chief of the Netherlands trading station at Canton, China. Born, Deventer 24 December 1759. Died Macao 24 March 1816.

Latin: Sacred to John Henry Rabinel leader of the Dutch traders in China, born at Daventre, nine days before December Calends 1759, died at Macao nine days before March Calends, 1816.

The variants in the spelling of his place of birth are accounted for in that Deventer, the town's present name, was the name used at the time of death, while Daventre was its name when founded in the 9th century.

The Dutch version gives old forms of the spell-

North side

ing of *opperhoofd, gebooren, overleeden* and *Maart,* still commonly used in epitaphs.

The two versions supply different dates of death. The actual month of his death is not the Calends month of the Latin version, but the same as that of the Dutch version; the deceased died nine days before the April Calends.

OTHER OBSERVERS: PCL and JMB: ROBINEL; HSPH: ROBINEL, Numbered 3.
REFER TO: Canton R of 20/3/1833; Dutch Archives No. 42; Osselen; Green.

44.   PATRICK AND LOUISA STEWART   *British*

SACRED TO THE MEMORY OF PATRICK STEWART
WHO DIED ON THE 20 APRIL 1857.
AND OF HIS WIFE LOUISA STEWART
WHO DIED ON THE 10 APRIL 1857.

PATRICK STEWART, a friend of Chinnery (40), was purser on Company ships on the India-China run, including the *Vansittart* and the *London*, for 12 years from 1815, with a six-year hiatus when he was trading from Bombay, first concurrently then as a merchant there, until he left for China in 1835, still retaining his business connection with Bombay.

He probably left Canton for Macao in the British exodus of 1841. At a time when the Royal Mail had not yet started overseas deliveries of personal mail, he was authorized by the administrator of the newly founded colony of Hong Kong to open and distribute ships' packets in Macao – this was a measure of his status, which one writer equated with that of Resident, and a death notice called him the British Consular Agent. In 1843, while still residing in Macao, he was appointed Justice of the Peace in Hong Kong, and in 1844 foreman of the Grand Jury, being especially transported to and from Hong Kong for his duties. At the funeral of John Robert Morrison (143), he was one of the pall-bearers and was there to comfort George Chinnery (40) on his death-bed.

Louisa was the daughter of Isaac Cotgrave, born

the year of his promotion to Captain in 1802, the year after he had served as commander of a division in a 'cutting out expedition' sent by Nelson to head off a French invasion flotilla assembling under the guns at Boulogne. Her three brothers also served as naval officers.

The couple's granite chest-tomb stands on a wide, mitred podium, immediately to the left of the end of the path leading from the church. The sides and ends of its box, encased in a moulded plinth and rising vertically to the bed-mould of the table-top, are ornamented with rectangular panels carved in relief and surrounded by borders. The inscription on the top, its lines running lengthways west-east, is neatly cut and in excellent condition.

OTHER OBSERVERS: HSPH: Numbered 4; JMB and HSPH: husband's death recorded as in 1837.
REFER TO: Hardy pp 325, 340, 350 and S41; EIR&D for 1824 p 347, 1826 pp 345 and 339, 1827 p 344 and 1829 p 344; ACK for 1835, 1836 and 1838; SFP&MA ii of 20/7/1837; Canton R of 30/11/1841 and 4/7/1843; Morse iii pp 356–61; FC&HKG of 30/6/1843 and 15 and 25/4/1857; Canton P of 2/9/1843 and 9/3/1844; HKA&D for 1846; Hunter p 273.

45. JACQUES PIEROT *Dutch*

HIER RUST

JACQUES PIEROT

Med. D.

Geboren te Leiden

den 29 February 1812

Overleden te Macao

den 16 Augustus 1841.

LIKE RABINEL (43), Pierot was of Huguenot origin, the son of a minor official at Leiden, born on Leap Year Day in 1812. He joined the Dutch East India Company's medical service, where he might indulge an interest in medicinal and rare plants. A new Institute of Horticulture had been founded at Leiden, where he had graduated in medicine, and he was granted a one-year monopoly in 1841 to export plants, vegetables and seeds from the Dutch factory in Japan to the Institute and to the Company's gardens at Batavia (Jakarta).

The ship *Middelburg* took part in that year's expedition to Japan, and sailed on 10 July 1841 with Pierot on board. Nearing the Formosa Channel a fortnight later, the ship ran into a typhoon, was dismasted and sprang a leak. The captain made for Macao, and with all aboard safe, anchored in the Macao Roads on the 31st. On 16 August, with the crew repairing the damage, Pierot died, either from illness or from an injury sustained during the incident.

His is the sole headstone in the south section of the row, standing near the well and further east than the line of the Stewart tomb (44), behind a rough step of the same stone – a coarse biotite granite. It measures 152 cm high, 76 cm wide and 18 cm thick, and its top is formed into a low segmental arch below which is cut an elaborate design in high relief. Round the inscription surface runs a deep, cornered groove 19 mm wide, leaving a 5 cm border. The inscription is artistically executed and has lasted well, except that the surface is covered with lichen which renders the small letters difficult to read.

OTHER OBSERVERS: HSPH: Numbered 5.
REFER TO: Dutch Archives of 27/7 and 13/11/1841 (Nos. 24 and 16) and of 22/1/1841 (Nos. 20/32); Canton P of 7/8/1841.

46.   CHRISTIAN BOECK   *Danish*

A NOTICE OF HIS death states that 'the Hon. E. [sic] Boeck, member of his Danish Majesty's government at Serampore' died on 10 September 1836 at the house of the Rev Charles Gutzlaff, at that time in the employ of Jardine, Matheson & Co as translator and interpreter. Stegepaamoen, the place of his birth, is an island some 100 km south of Copenhagen. Boeck died two days after disembarking from the *Victory*, while on a health visit to Macao, seeking to repair the strain of office as judge, magistrate and administrator of government estates at Calcutta, after the anxiety experienced while breaking up 'an extensive combination of robbers' combined with the fatigue of subsequent criminal procedures.

The ship went on to Manila, where she was condemned as unseaworthy. Boeck's burial ceremony was performed by the Rev G.H. Vachell, chaplain to the superintendent of trade. As the inscription says, James Matheson was acting in his official capacity when he arranged to erect the memorial.

The headstone stands in the open apart from others in the row, and is in line with 45, which it closely resembles in form and size, the similarity even extending to the design in high relief under the arched top, though the back is more rough-hewn. The inscription is on its east face, and the letters, which are well cut and well set out, have resisted the weather better.

OTHER OBSERVERS: HSPH: Numbered 6.
REFER TO: Canton R of 20/9/1836; FInd of 11/2/1836 p 43, 14/7/1836 p 224, 15/12/1836 p 394 and 1/6/1837; Bengal Obit for 1848 p 250; Burial R 11,218.

47. WILLIAM HAVELOCK *British*

THE BURIAL RECORDS in London state that Havelock was a native of Guisborough in Yorkshire, died in Macao while his ship was in the Cumsingmoon Passage, and was buried by the Rev G.H. Vachell, chaplain to the Superintendent of Trade. There were three ships named *Eleanor* in the region at that time, but no link has been established between Macao and any of them.

Standing just northwest of 46 and in line with the Stewart tomb (44), slightly south of the middle bamboo clump, his granite headstone measures 147 cm high, 75 cm wide and 15 cm thick, this rectangle being heightened by the further 29 cm of a semi-elliptical arch. Beneath the arch is cut in high relief a design very similar to those on 45 and 46. Like them, it remains rough-hewn at its back. A deep groove surrounds the inscription surface on the east face. Though its lettering is well cut, spacing is faulty through avoiding encroachment on the groove.

OTHER OBSERVERS: HSPH: Numbered 7.
REFER TO: Burial R,11,218; Bateson pp 229 and 300; SFP&MA of 27/4/1837; Heard.

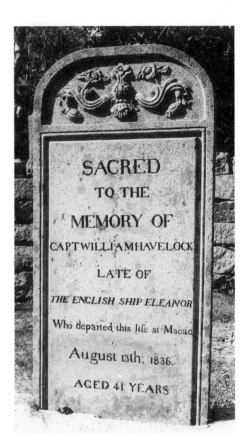

SACRED
TO THE
MEMORY OF
CAPT WILLIAM HAVELOCK
LATE OF
THE ENGLISH SHIP ELEANOR
Who departed this life at Macao
August 13th, 1836.
AGED 41 YEARS

48.   J. GEORGE DUNCAN   *British*

RECORD OF THE burial sent to London gives his name in two versions, John George Duncan as above and a German alias, Johann Yungen Dunken, and states that he was buried on 11 August in the 'Company's Cemetery' by Charles Wimberley, then officiating as the Company's chaplain. As the commander of a ship registered at Hamburg, he must have found it convenient to take a German alias. By the 1839s, the number of ships belonging to owners living in the Low Countries and the Baltic States was diminishing. In order to evade the Company's monopoly, some British-owned ships were registered elsewhere than in England and India, and Duncan's Hamburg barque the *Reform* might have been one of them. In 1833, shortly before he died, Duncan brought his wife out to Macao with him in the *Reform*.

The verses are cut with slight variations on the memorials of seafaring men in Stepney, Ipswich, Ilfracombe and other English burial grounds. 'Boreas' was the ancient Greek god of the north wind.

> *Though Boreas blows and Neptune's waves*
> *Have toss'd me too and fro*

> *By God's decree you plainly see*
> *I'm anchor'd here below*
> *Where we at anchor safely ride*
> *With many of our Fleet*
> *But once again we must set sail*
> *Our Savior Christ to meet*

The headstone, similar in size, design and the faults in its inscription to 47, stands south of the bamboo clump, its rough-hewn back close to the wall. As on the other stones in this group the extensive lichen growths make the letters difficult to read, particularly the eight lines of verse on the lower half, cut in an indifferent running hand. The semi-ellipse of the upper part was cut from a different stone from the rest, as revealed by its displacement in the typhoon rains of 1957, later repaired. The spelling of 'too' in the quotation is a mistake, of course, but not 'Savior', which like harbor, honor and humor, was commonly so spelt in the Orient: Burgess describes it as 'the usual sailor's epitaph', but offers a different version.

OTHER OBSERVERS: HSPH: No.8.
REFER TO: Burgess p 253; Burial R 11,218; Canton R of 15/7, 6/8 and 16/9/1833.

49.   WILLIAM BARNETT   *British*

BURIAL RECORDS in London show that Barnett, a native of London, died while his ship the barque, *Royal Sovereign*, was lying in the Macao Roads, and was buried the next day by the Rev G.H. Vachell, chaplain to the Superintendents of Trade.

Standing behind a rough granite step about three metres from the wall and in line with 47, this headstone is similar in design to its preceding neighbours but is elaborately carved.

Once a heavy infestation of lichens was scrubbed away, the inscription was revealed as well cut and legible enough.

OTHER OBSERVERS: HSPH: Numbered 9.
REFER TO: Burial R 11,218; ACK for 1835; Canton R of 14/6/1836.

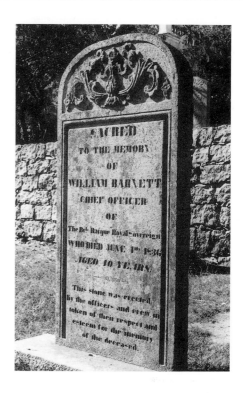

50.   FRANK SCOTT   *British*

THIS SEEMS TOO humble and unpretentious a memorial for someone who was a first cousin once removed of the novelist Sir Walter Scott (then at the height of his fame) and the son of James Scott, the partner and great friend of Sir Stamford Raffles, founder of Penang.

Its small size, meagre wording, unfinished edge and unusual shape, the use of the soubriquet Frank for Francis (the name given in the burial records in London), and the unusual spelling of Malacca, taken together suggest that he was visiting as a tourist, not known and without close friends locally. The Rev Charles Wimberley, then officiating as the Company's chaplain, presided over his burial.

His granite slab, something over 60 cm square, lies on the south edge of the bamboo clump close to the wall, its inscription well cut, spaced and preserved. The absence of any sign of plinth or foundation indicates that its location may not be the actual site of burial.

OTHER OBSERVERS: HSPH: Numbered 10.
REFER TO: Burial R 11,218; Winstedt p 102; Scott p 153; Rogers; Fielding; Hardy a p 13; Lennox p 53; Clodd pp 35–6; Gannier p 5; Makepeace i p 491; Buckley p 310; RCoArchers.

---

51.   CHARLES HAWKINS   *British*

UNIQUELY IN THIS cemetery, this memorial perpetuates the memory of the entire crew of a cutter: Hawkins's seven amiable and deserving shipmates, John Brazier, John Crowley, James Samuels, John Hilton, Thomas Jerry, John Belotti and Edward Johnston, and also of his friend, Surgeon Middlemass, on a visit from the *Mangles*, who all perished together. Hawkins entered the Company's maritime service in 1825, and it was on his third voyage to China on board the *Atlas* that the catastrophe struck. The ship's cutter, returning to its anchorage after sunset from a visit to Lintin, was upset in a squall off Tung Koo Island and its whole crew drowned.

'The cries of the sufferers,' said a contemporary newspaper report some two weeks later, 'were heard from the longboat of the *Duke of York* which was passing at some distance ... It was perfectly dark at the time.' When the longboat arrived at the scene, all that could be found were a few hats of the crew, and the stretchers of the boat. Both Hawkins and Surgeon Middlemass were reported as buried in the cemetery; but there is no Middlemass tomb, and the statement that the Rev G.H. Vachell buried Hawkins on 21 January makes no mention of Middlemass. There were two Surgeons Middlemass in the Company's maritime service; both are recorded as serving at various times on board the *Mangles*, and both as being still active after the date of the tragedy, one not dying before 1886, and the other retiring in 1850.

Hawkins's granite chest-tomb is the first memorial in that section of the row which lies immediately north of a bamboo clump, head-end close to the wall. It stands on a mitred podium, with a moulded plinth that surrounds the base of the box. The sides rise vertically to a heavy bed-mould and a table-top, on which a raised rectangular panel with concave, excised corners holds the inscription. The lettering is deeply cut and well preserved.

OTHER OBSERVERS: HSPH: Numbered 11.
REFER TO: Burial R 11,218; Hardy a – pp 80, 99, 109, 120, 311, 326, 340, 351 and 338, b – p 35, c – pp 9, 22, 25, 33–4, 45, 57, 59 and 69, and d – p 16; Canton R of 3/2/1830; Crawford p 320; EIR&D for 1816 and 1822; Bateson pp 214–8; Morse iii pp 373–9 and iv p 380; Canton P of 6/9/1838 and 13/9/38.

52.   BENJAMIN ROPES LEACH   *American*

BENJ^N R. LEACH ESQ.
Born in Salem Mass. U.S.A.
Dec. 16. 1802.
Died at Macao
Aug. 26. 1838.
He was long
the active and intelligent
Agent in India of
MESSRS. NEAL & CO.
of Salem Mass. U.S.A.
who have caused this
Monument to be erected
over his Grave.

BENJAMIN LEACH sailed from Salem in July 1836 for the Far East in the schooner *Theodore*, to join the Indian office of the merchant house of Neal & Co. When he died, he was trading from Manila to Java and Canton, whence he had sailed to Macao on 17 January 1837 on the same ship. His death followed a brief bout of 'diarrhoea contracted by his exertions and exposure', and he was buried the next day by the Rev G.H. Vachell, then chaplain to the Superintendent of Trade.

This distinctive monument stands about four metres from the wall in line with 45 and 46 on the other side of the bamboos, lying diagonally northeast of 51, its low, square column surmounted by a pyramid and rising from a double-tier podium, the lower tier of which has mitred corners, the upper tier bonded. Faced with marble, now badly discoloured, its east side bears the above well-cut, well-spaced inscription.

OTHER OBSERVERS: HSPH: Numbered 12.
REFER TO: Burial R 11,218; Leach i and ii; Salem G of 12/2/ 1839; Canton P of 8 and 29/9/1838; FInd of 3/1/1839; Neal; Dermigny iii p 1194; Morse iii p 158; Canton R of 17/1/1837; Forbes p 152.

53.   SAMUEL GOVER   British

CONFIRMATION OF THIS reading of the surname, and the date of Gover's death on 26 October 1829, is in the local press and in the burial record sent to London, which also gives his birth date as 19 January 1790, his residence as Macao, and his burial ceremony as performed the day he died, at the age of 40, by the Rev G.H. Vachell, the Company's chaplain. He appears to have been one of three brothers who left home separately for India, and then went further east to enrich themselves.

Samuel's chest-tomb lies alongside and immediately to the north of 51, to which it is similar in size and design, with no ornamentation on the top, ends and north side, with its head end close to the wall on an east-west long axis.

The inscription is on the south side, and its letters are not all easy to read, though they are deeply cut and generally well preserved.

OTHER OBSERVERS: PCL, HSPH and JMB: SAMUEL COVER; HSPH: Numbered 13.
REFER TO: Burial R 11,218; Canton R of 13/12/1828, 11/11/1829 and 22/3/1830; Morse iv pp 187 and 254; Hunter p 269; Parkinson pp 362–4.

54.   RODERICK FRAZER ROBERTSON   *British*

SACRED
to the memory of
RODERICK FRAZER ROBERTSON
Son of
F. ROBERTSON ESQ.
of Dundee
who died at Macao on the
16. day of January 1839.
AGED 20 YEARS.

Top inscription (above) East end (right)

ROBERTSON'S FATHER was Patrick Francis Robertson, who was living at Canton through the third decade of the 19th century as partner in Turner & Co, from at least 1835 until the death of Richard Turner (see 93) in 1839. Roderick died after a long and painful illness.

His well-proportioned, granite chest-tomb lies immediately to the north of and in line with 52, its long axis running east-west, head at the west. The box stands on a mitred podium, its bottom encased in a heavy, moulded plinth, rising vertically to a table-top that lacks a bed-mould; its severity is relieved only by the rounded edges, which merge into a raised moulded border 4 cm high, framing the top inscription surface. The sides and ends of the box have recessed panels with incised corners, and an auxiliary inscription on the east-end panel. The words are artistically cut and well spaced.

OTHER OBSERVERS: HSPH: Numbered 14.
REFER TO: Canton R of 5/2/1839; Dundee P&CA of 17/5/1839; Dundee D for 1840–1; ACK for 1835–9; Canton P of 30/11/1839.

55.   FREDERICK PERCEVAL ALLEYN   *British*

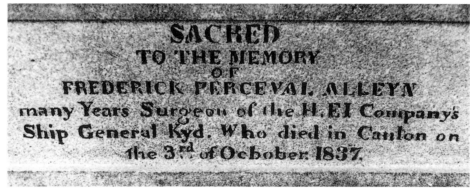

Inscription on south side

Erected by his Widow
ANNE PERCEVAL ALLEYN

Inscription on west end

THE COMPANY'S SHIP *General Kyd* carried 26 guns and a complement of 130 men, and made in all nine voyages to China up to 1832. Dr Alleyn served as full-time surgeon on the first eight, between 1815 and 1830. He appears then to have retired from the Company (the H.E.I. of the inscription) on his return to London. His service was not without incident. Apart from trouble over customs dues on two watches which he was carrying illicitly on his fifth visit to Canton, his eighth in 1829 brought him considerable fame during the suspension of British trade and the evacuation of personnel to Macao. The one Western-trained doctor then living at Canton was too ill to stay behind, and Dr Alleyn offered to take his place lest the members of the foreign community remaining in Canton should be wholly cut off from medical advice. His services were given gratuitously and irrespective of nationality. The Americans, by far the largest group of Westerners not to leave, presented him with a handsome piece of plate and an address at the end of the emergency, in recognition of his kindness and professional services.

He was acquainted with Dr William Jardine, who let him know that Magniac & Co would in 1832 become Jardine, Matheson & Co, and in 1834 he responded to the firm's search for a tea-taster: a venture which seems not to have been as unqualified a success as his medical career, for in July 1837 Matheson wrote from Macao to Jardine, then in England, saying that Dr Alleyn was suffering from hypochondria. He was unwell all that summer, and when at the start of October he complained of constipation 'and medicine would not act on him', more serious symptoms developed. He died at Canton, from where his remains were brought to Macao and buried two days after death by the Rev G.H. Vachell, chaplain to the Superintendent of Trade. On 1 February 1838, his widow sailed for England in the *Sophia*, commanded by Captain Macnair.

Alleyn's chest-tomb stands in the east line of the row along with 52 and 54, its long axis east-west, standing on a substantial podium with mitred corners. The ends and sides of the box, resting upon and not enveloping the base of a moulded plinth, show sign in their butt-jointed corners of the strain of carrying so thick a table-top. The top has neither bed-mould nor inscription, but like 54 boasts rounded edges and elaborate over-moulding.

The letters of the main inscription on the south side are deeply cut and of good craftsmanship. Since his widow did not leave Macao for four months after her husband had died, it may be assumed that she was responsible for the composition and cutting of the inscription and the erection of the memorial.

East end

OTHER OBSERVERS: HSPH: Numbered 15.
REFER TO: EIR&D for 1815; Hardy a – pp 271, 326, 337 and 341, b – pp 9, 20, 31, 37 and 56, and c – p 66; Morse iv p 81; Canton R of 10/10/1837 and 30/1/1838; Burial R 11,218; Chatterton p 303; Williamson.

56.   SAMUEL H. MONSON   *American*

MONSON OF NEWHAVEN was chief clerk to Thomas Forbes (163), the head of Perkins & Co. He and Forbes drowned off Macao on board Forbes's yacht the *Haidee* during a typhoon. They had returned from near Lintin Island, some 30 kilometres away, after an unsuccessful attempt to anticipate the mail delivery. The yacht anchored in the outer harbour close to the Praya Grande beach. Monson having become too seasick to be moved, Forbes remained with him for the night on board. Just before daylight the wind increased to hurricane force. They failed to gain the inner harbour and were forced to try anchoring once more, but the anchors failed to hold and the yacht was blown across the Macao Roads to Taipa and wrecked. After the gale had subsided, boats sent from Macao found the yacht on the bottom, its mast above water. The bodies of Monson and Forbes were taken to Macao. Both appeared in the list of casualties given by the diarist Harriet Low, which also included the name of J.P. Cushing, who had left China 16 months previously and was at the time living safely in England. Monson was buried the day after Forbes by the Rev G.H. Vachell, the Company's chaplain.

His chest-tomb is next to the space once occupied by the body of Forbes (see 163), in the west line of the section, its long axis lying east-west. A

SACRED
TO THE MEMORY
OF
SAMUEL H. MONSON ESQ.ʳ
OF
NEW HAVEN (U. S. OF AMERICA)
WHO WAS DROWNED NEAR MACAO
AUGUST 9ᵀᴴ 1829
AGED 28 YEARS.

granite podium with mitred corners, moulded plinth and vertical sides, follows the pattern usual in this cemetery. The square-edged table-top is supported by a bed-mould. The unusual orthography of Esquire may be due less to spelling than to flaking of the stone. Otherwise the inscription, on the south side of the tomb, is easy to read.

OTHER OBSERVERS: HSPH: Numbered 16.
REFER TO: Loines p 30; Burial R 11,218.

57. LOUISA ILBERY *British*

LOUISA ILBERY was buried by the Rev G.H. Vachell, chaplain to the Superintendent of Trade, who had also baptized her daughter, Louisa Crockett Ilbery, born in Macao on 27 May 1836. Her aunt was the wife of Captain John Crockett (87) of Lintin. Her husband was James William Henry Ilbery, a country trader of Macao and close business associate for 30 years of Charles Magniac, who once wrote to his partner William Jardine at Canton that Louisa was a strong-willed lady, unwilling to be blistered or take any of her doctor's prescriptions for the obstinate constipation from which she suffered. Early in the century, there seem to be three separate members of the Ilbery family recorded: a James Ilbery who was the partner of Louisa's husband in Ilbery & Co, and Frederick Ilbery (110): James W.H. Ilbery of the inscription may have been the Ilbery who was Hanoverian consul resident at Canton in 1825–8, having Christopher Fearon, the husband of Elizabeth Fearon

SACRED
TO THE MEMORY OF
LOUISA
THE BELOVED WIFE OF
JAMES W.H. ILBERY
WHO DEPARTED THIS LIFE AT MACAO
ON THE TWENTY FIRST DAY OF AUGUST
IN THE YEAR ONE THOUSAND EIGHT
HUNDRED AND THIRTY SEVEN DEEPLY
AND DESERVEDLY LAMENTED BY
HER FOND AND AFFECTIONATE
HUSBAND.

Inscription

(84), as his vice-consul and partner in the firm, then called Ilbery, Fearon & Co. The timing makes it impossible, before the days of steam, for him to have been the J.W. Ilbery of Canton who married at Calcutta but one month after Louisa had died.

Louisa's chest-tomb lies immediately north of and parallel to 55, which it closely resembles except for its plinth, which surrounds the base of the box so that the sides and ends are better supported, and show no signs of strain. The one inscription is cut on its table-top.

The last line contains the one word, displaced to the left as if the stonemason had added more, though there is no longer sign of it if he did.

OTHER OBSERVERS: In his transcript, JMB adds 'Aged 20 years and 4 months' to the last line, which does not accord with the age of 25 years and 4 months given in the burial records at London; HSPH: LOUISA ILBERT, Numbered 17.

REFER TO: Braga 1940 p 29; Burial R 11,218 p 353; Bapt R 11,218 p 347; Canton R of 31/5/1836 and 16/9/1833; ACK for 1835–9; Morse iv pp 128, 163, 187, 190 and 295; FInd of 27/9/1837, 19/9/1839, 22/10, 19/11 and 17/12/1840, 11/2, 1/4 and 9/9/1841, and 28/7/1842; EIR&D for 1842 p 151, for 1845 p 203, and for 1847 p 203; Williamson.

139

58. GEORGE WASHINGTON BIDDLE *American*

GEORGE BIDDLE'S middle initial stands for Washington. His Quaker father, Clement Biddle (1740–1814), was the Commissary General and close friend of American president George Washington, and served under him with distinction at Valley Forge and the Battle of Trenton, with particular effectiveness during the terrible winter of 1778–9.

One of his 13 offspring by his second wife, Rebekah Biddle (née Cornell), was born near the end of this win-

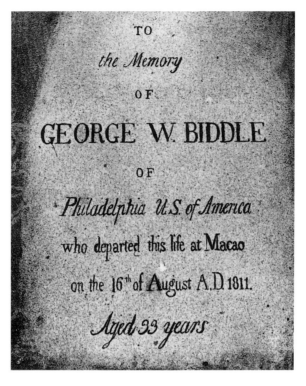

TO
the Memory
OF
GEORGE W. BIDDLE
OF
Philadelphia U.S. of America
who departed this life at Macao
on the 16th of August A.D. 1811.
Aged 33 years

self was in Macao on a merchant venture, and was the Biddle who was reported to have been attacked by pirates in the Pearl River on his way back from Canton in August 1805.

His chest-tomb of local granite lies immediately to the north of 56, between 57 and the wall, standing on a very narrow, mitred podium, its moulded plinth and box much higher than is usual, giving it prominence. A substantial bedmould supports the table-top, whose edges only very slightly overhang the

ter and took the surname of the president, who stood as the infant's godfather at the christening. There is an American adage that Philadelphia was 'a city founded at the confluence of the Biddle and Drexel families'. When Biddle died in 1811, which was 10 years before the cemetery was opened, his remains were given the customary hillside burial, and were re-interred in the Old Cemetery when a member of the family was visiting Macao many years later. As his grandfather in Philadelphia was a well-established importer, and other members of the family had trading connections with China, it is likely that Biddle him-

vertical sides and ends of the box, adding to the general severity of the design. The panels on sides and ends are surrounded by rectangular moats 2.5 cm wide and half that deep, their surfaces devoid of ornament and lettering.

The inscription is on the table-top, badly discoloured by weathering, but once cleaned, it was easy to read. It not only commemorates the death of a godson of America's First President, but the earliest death of all those at rest in the cemetery.

OTHER OBSERVERS: HSPH: Numbered 18.
REFER TO: Burt passim; Morse iii p 8; Frost; AmJNB.

59. FRANCIS WILLIAM BACON *American*

TO THE MEMORY
OF
FRANCIS W BACON
DIED
IN MACAO NOVEMBER 1ˢᵗ 1845
AGED 25 YEARS
BORN IN BARNSTABLE MASS
UNITED STATES N A.

Top

FRANCIS W. BACON
East end inscription

A FAMILY MEMORIAL at Barnstaple, Massachusetts gives his second name as William; his family knew him as Frank. He appears to have been in business at Canton and had gone to Macao for health reasons, clearly with no great success. He was taken care of in Macao by James Perkins Sturgis and, in gratitude the next year, Bacon's uncle sent Sturgis 'two half-barrels of beef and one of pork' via his cousin Ebenezer Bacon, on board the *Vancouver*.

Lying alongside and parallel to 58, this granite chest-tomb is the more pleasing in appearance, having a larger mitred podium and shorter box-height. Its sides and ends, carrying rectangular panels carved in high relief, show incised corners, are vertical, and support a substantial bed-mould and a square-edged table-top. The upper part of the inscription is cut without a moulding frame.

The name at the top is in Old English script and all the lettering is well-carved, well-preserved and easy to read.

OTHER OBSERVERS: HSPH: Numbered 19.
REFER TO: Lothrop; Barnstable Epi i p 157; Barnstable Marr; Swift.

60.   SIR ANDERS LJUNGSTEDT   *Swedish*

South end (above), west side (below)

Here lie the remains
of
ANDREW LJUNGSTEDT
Knight of Wasa, Scholar and Philanthropist
born in
Linköping March 12 1759
Died at Macao November 10 1835
Inscription on east side

AFTER SOME YEARS working as a tutor and interpreter in Russia, Ljungstedt had sailed for China on the Swedish East India Company's ship *Drottningen*, arriving at Canton in 1798 to take up an appointment as resident in charge of the Swedish factory there. He acquired such wealth that when he returned to Sweden he was able to endow an industrial school in his home town, and there it flourishes to this day. Lindsay and May Ride recorded seeing a small Chinnery portrait of him taken from a drawer in the Mayor's office in Linköping, and a poor copy hanging in the school assembly hall: others are the Chinnery portrait reproduced on the next page, which is in the Peabody Essex Museum, Salem, Massachusetts, a

His granite chest-tomb lies with its long axis north-south between the north wall and the north-west corner of 87 (which dominates the whole area) and is readily identifiable by the closed, fluted, funeral urn on its table-top. From position and orientation it should, with 61, be included with the Crockett group: the official numbering, however, puts them both in the bamboo row. The box is of the usual pattern here – a mitred podium, moulded plinth, vertical sides and ends supporting a bed-mould under a table-top with square edges but no over-moulding; but it also carries a small three-tiered podium and the urn, all cut out of one piece of granite, adding distinction to what is a pleasing memorial.

In all the inscriptions on sides and ends, the mason has used an unusual mix of block capitals and running script.

copy of which is in the National Museum at Stockholm. Knighted for his benefactions, Ljungstedt returned in 1815 as Swedish consul at Canton, where he was commonly referred to among the Europeans as 'Sir Andrew'. He had withdrawn from active business by 1821, making Macao his place of permanent residence, and remained there as a leading member of its foreign community until his death. He was affectionately known among his China friends as the 'philosopher from the north', and was the author of a *Historical Sketch of Portuguese Settlements in China* and of *The Roman Catholic Church and Missions in China* (1836). Like many others at rest in the cemetery, he was buried by the Trade Superintendent's chaplain, the Rev G.H. Vachell.

North end

OTHER OBSERVERS: HSPH: Numbered 20.
REFER TO: Morse iii p 228; Morrison ii p 102 (where the name is misspelled Ljoungstedt); Montalto pp 23ff; Canton R of 24/11/1835; Burial R 11,218.

61.   JOHN HAMILTON RITCHIE   *American*

SACRED
to the memory
JOHN HAMILTON
the third Son
of
ARCHIBALD A. and MARTHA H. RITCHIE
who died at Macao
March 14th 1844.
AGED 11 MONTHS, 19 DAYS.

TOLD OF THIS infant's death, Rebecca Chase Kinsman recorded on 17 March that she and her husband Nathaniel (112), called 'to sympathize with our friend Mrs Ritchie, in the loss of a dear little boy of 15 [sic] mos. old, one of twin brothers, her youngest children – I have been a good deal with her during his sickness & since his death, for in this small community as you may imagine, the few individuals composing it, felt themselves bound together by stronger ties than would exist between the same people under other circumstances, and our sympathy in each other's joys & sorrows is proportionally strong'. By 1843 Mrs Kinsman had gained the reputation of being, for her general kindliness, the doyenne of American ladies in Macao.

A.A. Ritchie was head of the American firm bearing his name, which traded in Canton from the late 1830s until it was dissolved in June 1850. He had commanded the ship *Champlain* when it voyaged to China in 1837, and then entered business at Canton. Martha, daughter of the Philadelphian lawyer John Hamilton (after whom the infant had been named), sailed out with her younger sister Sarah in the *Zenobia*, under the command of Captain Kinsman (112), to join him, and took up residence in Macao. Ritchie himself fell out of a carriage and died towards the end of 1856 – 'whether a fit or not is not known'. Sarah was married to the Englishman John Holliday in October 1841, in a ceremony at the Ritchie house at Canton by the Rev E.C. Bridgman.

The infant's small, granite chest-tomb is simple in design and pleasing in proportions, and lies immediately to the west of 60, between it and the wall, its axis north-south, with head to the north. A small, moulded plinth stands on its mitred podium, which envelops the bases of the vertical sides and ends of the box supporting the bed-mould and table-top; the top has vertical edges but neither upper moulding nor carving to frame the inscription surface.

The inscription is carved in well-cut but very small lettering and, though there is flaking, has weathered well.

OTHER OBSERVERS: HSPH: JOHN HAMILTON, Numbered 21.
REFER TO: CM of 25/5/1848, 4/4 and 11/7/1850, 1/1, 26/2, 4–25/3, 1/4, 9/9, 23/9 and 28/10//1852, and 27/1/1853; SFP&MA of 1/6/1837 and 30/7/1852; FInd of 16/12/1841; Monroe lxxxvii pp 119 and 127 and lxxxviii pp 50 and 52; Nye Friends.

62.   SIR WILLIAM FRASER, BART.   *British*

SACRED
TO THE MEMORY OF
SIR WILLIAM FRASER BART.
CHIEF OF THE BRITISH FACTORY IN CHINA :
who died at Macao sincerely and deservedly lamented, on the 22 December 1827
IN THE 40" YEAR OF HIS AGE.

WILLIAM WAS THE eldest son of a large Inverness family. His father was in the Company's service, visiting India and China on several voyages between 1764 and 1785; one of the first to fix the longitude at sea through lunar observation, he was made a Fellow of the Royal Society in 1791 and created baronet in 1806. William's mother was Elizabeth (née Farquharson). On his father's death in 1818 of apoplexy, the day after he attended the Prince Regent's levee, Fraser succeeded as second baronet and sixth Fraser of Ledeclune. There is a memorial tablet to William Fraser senior on the north wall of the Parish Church of St Mary-le-Bone in London. In 1801, William junior followed his father into Company service but ashore, and was posted to Canton, where he was promoted to follow J.B. Urmston (see 115) as 'chief' in China (chairman of the Select Committee). Dr Morrison (141) wrote to a friend on 22 December 1827, that his mind was 'much agitated by the present condition of our chief, Sir William F. About a fortnight ago he was seized with mental derangement, and wearied nature now sinks under the perpetual excitement, night and day, to which he has been subject. His life is despaired of ...' A close friend of Morrison, Fraser had been a pall-bearer, with John Livingstone

(father of 41) and Urmston at the funeral of Morrison's wife Mary (142), and Morrison conducted the service at Fraser's funeral on Christmas Day 1827, attended by all the Westerners in Macao.

A chest-tomb of local granite and the last in the row, this memorial occupies the extreme northwest corner of the terrace and lies alongside to and parallel with 59 and at right angles to 61 and 60, its position and orientation taking the numbering sequence back to the line of tombs along the wall. A mitred podium, moulded plinth, box with vertical sides and ends supporting a substantial bed-mould, all conform to the general design of tombs, except that the table-top has curved edges and a plain, unadorned, upper surface. The main inscription is cut on the south side of the tomb; its letters are becoming indistinct. Fraser's initials and date of death are clearly cut on the recessed rectangular panel on its east end, pictured above.

OTHER OBSERVERS: PCL: SIR WILLIAM FRASER BART; HSPH: SIR WILLIAM FRAZER, BART, Numbered 22.
REFER TO: Burke 1980 p 457; Mackenzie pp 564 and 567; Hardy a – pp 9, 23, 30, 42, 57, 75, 85, 103 and 121; Gent Mag lxxxviii pp 379–80; Morse iii pp 68, 117, 177, 346 and 368 and iv pp 1, 7, 52, 70, 87, 122 and 144; Canton R of 15/1/1828; Morrison ii pp 393–4; Burial R 11,218.

63.   T.W. RIDDLES   *British*

**SACRED TO THE MEMORY
OF
T.W. RIDDLES,
MASTER MARINER,
WHO DEPARTED THIS LIFE.
AUGUST 21st, 1856,
AGED 41 YEARS.**

Inscription

WHEN HE DIED, Riddles was chief officer of the ship *Cama Family*, then lying in the Cumsingmoon Passage. He was sailing the China coast to and from Shanghai and Whampoa between 1846 and 1848, as captain variously of the *Royalist*, the *William IV* and the 300-ton barque *Sir Edward Ryan*, all operated by Murrow & Co of Hong Kong.

He had scarcely transferred to the British schooner *Torrington* when she was dismasted off Amoy in the heavy gales of October 1848. After repairs in Hong Kong, she continued her coastal distribution of opium until June 1849, when she ran aground and, with no more than enough time for the crew to save themselves, sank in the Woosung River with 400 chests of opium still in the hold. Riddles sailed in command of the 160-ton British brig *Corsair* from Hong Kong to the Sandwich Islands via Shanghai in 1850, after which information dries up until the time of his death in 1856.

This conspicuous chest-tomb and podium of coarse-grained granite stands directly opposite the bottom of the pathway leading from the upper terrace and courtyard. The sides and ends are vertical, and on each corner are terminal pilasters, each carved with an engaged baluster. On a substantial

146

bed-mould, the table-top is slightly plano-convex in section round its longitudinal axis, its cambered, upper surface carrying neither lettering nor ornament.

Identical inscriptions are cut on the west and east sides of the tomb, each on a three-tiered panel with incised corners set between its lateral pilasters.

OTHER OBSERVERS: JMB and HSPH: RIDLES; HSPH Numbered 23

REFER TO: FC&HKG of 4/2, 9/9 and 3/10/1846, various issues from 5/1847 to 1/1848 and from 24/5 to 16/9/1848, 19/4, 3/5, 23 and 27/9, 18/10 and 13/12/1848, 10/1, 23/5, 23/6, 8/7 and 28/11/1849, 12/1, 1 and 15/6 and 20/7/1850, and 23/8/1856; Dixson HKG for May 1857

64.   JOHN P. GRIFFIN   *American*

IN MEMORY
OF
JOHN P. GRIFFIN
SEAMAN BORN IN NEW YORK
AND DIED ON BOARD THE U.S.
SHIP PLYMOUTH, MACAO ROADS.
BY A FALL FROM ALOFT
JUNE 19 1849
AGED ABOUT 35 YEARS.

————

THIS IS ERECTED BY HIS
MESSMATES
Inscription

THE DATE IS the day Griffin fell. His ship's log assigns his actual death to the following day. The *Plymouth* was a sloop-of-war carrying 22 guns commanded by Captain T.R. Gedney, and flagship of the American East Indies Squadron. She put into Macao in December 1848, and returned on 30 May 1849 for a stay of two months after visiting Manila, Whampoa and Shanghai. It was in the course of this longer visit that Seaman Griffin fell from her rigging. August was spent in Whampoa, and it was after she returned to Macao in September that Surgeon John F. Brooke (68) died. Later the ship was detailed to participate in Commodore Perry's expedition to Japan. She was scuttled at the Norfolk naval yard in April 1861, to forestall her capture by the Confederate forces. Griffin's messmates were Valentine Swearlin (65) and Samuel Smith (147).

The granite headstone, with a rough-hewn back, stands behind a step immediately east of and in line with the northern end of 63. It is 119 cm high, including the 20 cm rise of its segmental arched top, 56 cm wide and 15 cm thick; the rectangular inscription surface is slightly recessed below the level of a 5 cm border. The surface beneath the arched top is flat, and carries a botanical design in low relief. The inscription is not easy to decipher.

OTHER OBSERVERS: HSPH: Numbered 24.

REFER TO: Loomis; CM of 17/8/1848 and 4/1/1849; FC&HKG from October to December 1848, throughout 1849 and of 2/3/1850; Dixson HKG of 2 and 9/8/1850 and 1854; SFP&MA of 6/2 and 19 and 23/3/1852; Hawk Wallach pp 4 and 42.

65.   VALENTINE SWEARLIN   *American-German*

**SACRED TO THE MEMORY
OF
VALENTINE SWEARLIN MARINE
NATIVE OF NEWSTADT GERMANY
WHO DIED ON BOARD THE U.S.
SHIP PLYMOUTH MACAO ROADS
JUNE 20 1849.
AGED 27 YEARS.**

———

**THIS MONUMENT IS ERECTED BY HIS
MESSMATES THE MARINE GUARD**
Inscription

THE SHIP'S LOG records the date of his death as 30 August 1849. The date on the headstone coincides with the correct date of his messmate Griffin's death (64). Their memorials are similar in design, size, type of granite and wear. The messmates of the Marine Guard must have been common to them both, and one stonemason probably cut both stones: either mate or mason may have been responsible for the error in the date. The *Plymouth* was in Whampoa the whole of that August, and was not reported as back in Macao until early in September, when it would have carried Marine Swearlin's body to be buried alongside that of Seaman Griffin. There is no evidence of his nationality at the time of death, but, serving on an American naval ship, he is more likely to have been American than German.

The headstone stands, its rough-hewn back near the south wall, in line with the south end of 63 and some two metres in front of 64. Its top is a semi-elliptical arch – not a segmental arch like that of 64: this gives it an extra 20 cm in height above the sides. Carved under the arched top in low-relief is a design similar to that of 4 in the upper terrace.

OTHER OBSERVERS: HSPH: Numbered 25.
REFER TO: Loomis; FC&HKG of 1 to 29/8 and 5/9/1859.

66.   CHARLES GRAHAM   *British*

CHARLES GRAHAM made the first of his 14 trips to the Orient as an officer in 1792. It is likely that most of his service, if not all, was on the Company's ships (the H.C. of the inscription). His last voyage was the *Bombay*'s sixth. The Company was increasing the size of its ships carrying tea, for which demand was rising rapidly in Europe: by 1800 it had 22 ships of over 1,200 tons, including the *Bombay*. A vessel of this displacement could carry a load of tea twice that of a ship two-thirds the size. The senior officers who contributed to the erection of the memorial were the *Bombay*'s first, second, third and fourth mates – respectively Joseph Stanton, Walter H. Whitehead, John Burt and Ludovick Grant, its surgeon James Don and its purser David Coulthard. There was a good number of Company commanders in Macao that season, when at least 20 of its ships visited Canton waters.

A coarse-grained granite chest-tomb in the pattern usual in this cemetery, the Graham memorial lies to the east of 64 and 65, its long axis parallel with that of 63, the

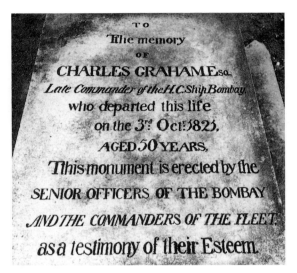

TO The memory OF CHARLES GRAHAM Esq. Late Commander of the H.C.Ship Bombay who departed this life on the 3rd Oct. 1825, AGED 50 YEARS. This monument is erected by the SENIOR OFFICERS OF THE BOMBAY AND THE COMMANDERS OF THE FLEET as a testimony of their Esteem.

four of them enclosing a small grassed quadrangle of 2.5 x 1.5 metres. Moats 5 cm wide, some 10 cm in from the edges of sides and ends, frame rectangular panels without ornament. The table-top, on which the inscription is cut, has vertical edges and square corners.

OTHER OBSERVERS: HSPH: Numbered 26.
REFER TO: Hardy pp 148, 161, 175, 195, 213, 230, 248, 270, 285, 315, 329, 342, S11, A11, A31 and A156; Morse iv pp 373–5, 377, 380 and 382.

---

67.   JOHN WILSON   *British*

NO INFORMATION has come to light about John Wilson's brief career before he died of fever, nor how and why he had come to Macao.

His memorial is a chest-tomb of coarse-grained granite, on a podium almost hidden in the turf. It lies with long axis north-south, the head close to the foot of 66. A moulded plinth surrounds the vertical sides and

SACRED
TO THE MEMORY OF
JOHN WILSON
OF WHITWELL YORKSHIRE ENGLAND
WHO DIED OF FEVER
ON THE
21ST Nov. 1844
AGED 21 YEARS
DEEPLY LAMENTED BY ALL WHO KNEW HIM

ends of the box, and its table-top, set on a heavy bed-mould, has vertical edges and square corners. Its proportions are taller and narrower than others, as is the lettering.

OTHER OBSERVERS: PCL and JMB: JOHN WILSON H. WHITWELL; HSPH: Numbered 27.
REFER TO: FC&HKG of 4/12/1844.

68. JOHN F. BROOKE *American*

HE DIED IN MACAO THE 17.
DAY OF OCTOBER 1849 AGED
59 YEARS
Inscription on north side

**TO THE MEMORY OF
JOHN F. BROOKE M.D. FLEET
SURGEON TO THE UNITED STATES
EAST INDIA SQUADRON.**
Inscription on east end

Erected
by the
Officers of the Squadron.
Inscription on west end

BEYOND THAT OF the inscriptions themselves, confirmed by US naval records, information about Surgeon Brooke is lacking. Being a Fleet Surgeon, he is here assigned to no particular ship. There were, however, only two American naval craft in Canton waters, the *Plymouth* and the brig *Dolphin*, and both were in Macao when he died.

Of granite throughout, the memorial is conspicuous because of the multiplicity of inscriptions, its size, position and proportions, and the fluted funeral urn on its table-top. It stands on a substantial, bonded podium about six metres east of the well, its long axis running east-west. The overall height is 198 cm. The vertical sides and ends of the box are butt-jointed, and edge rolls are carved on the ends. A rectangular panel is carved in relief on each box-face, with a fluted shell or scallop in each corner, and each carries an inscription.

Under-moulded, the table-top has vertical edges and supports two rectangular steps cut out of a single block, this in turn supporting the closed urn with its own rectangular base. There is no doubt that the name is Brooke, as two listings offer, and not Brooks.

OTHER OBSERVERS: JMB and HSPH: BROOKS; HSPH: Numbered 28.
REFER TO: Loomis.

150

69.   THOMAS J. OSBORNE   *British*

IN THE WEEKLY shipping reports between 1843 and early 1846, the frequency of the references to the *Calcutta* (and her captain, Osborne) suggests that the barque was an opium storeship. A news item relates that the Chinese crew of a boat returning to the *Calcutta* overpowered, murdered, and threw both the second mate and their Lascar overseer into the sea, and made off with a booty of 14 chests of opium. Two of the Lascars not in the plot had managed to escape with the story; but since opium was contraband, no action was taken.

The first of the notices announced that anyone seeking London bottled beer might do worse than approach Osborne on board, which was probably an oblique invitation to negotiate an opium sale. At various times, the Company had owned three ships of this name; Osborne's might have been built in India for the 'country trade', and in 1845 was flying a Spanish flag of convenience. In February 1846 her sails, anchors and other equipment were auctioned

SACRED
TO THE MEMORY
OF
THOMAS J. OSBORNE
LATE COMMANDER OF THE
BARK "CALCUTTA"
3: Son of George Osborne Esq.
of Singleland County Limerick
who died at Macao June 2.ⁿᵈ 1847.
Aged 30 Years.

off before she was broken up.

Singleland County Limerick may refer to the chapelry of Singland sited in the parish of St Patrick in the city of Limerick. Captain Osborne's younger brother is also buried in the cemetery (71).

Some three metres north of 68, head towards the east, Osborne's chest-tomb, its podium and plinth almost hidden by the turf, has a thick bed-mould supported on vertical sides and ends of a box 41 cm high, each carrying a rectangular panel carved in high relief with incised quadrant corners. The inscription has two small incised motifs, one above and one below the lettering.

OTHER OBSERVERS: HSPH: Numbered 29.
REFER TO: Canton P of 4/2 and 24/6/1843; Hardy a – p 221; CM of 3/4 and 5/6/1845 and 1, 22, 8/1 and 5/3/1846; FC&HKG of 24/12/1845 and 7, 10, 14 and 17/1, and 4/2/1846.

70.   **WILLIAM HENRY LEGGETT**   *British*

WHEN HE DIED, Leggett was clerk both to the Chief Justice and the Supreme Court of Hong Kong – to which his appointment was confirmed only three weeks before he died – and drew two annual salaries totalling $450, to which he was able to add inquest fees when acting as Coroner. He was not a Justice of the Peace, as has been stated. His health began to fail soon after arriving, and he died when seeking to restore it in Macao.

The Leggett memorial is an attractive chest-tomb on a double-tiered granite podium – the upper step with mitred corners and the lower with bonded corners – supporting a moulded plinth and the vertical sides and ends of the box, which rise 51 cm to the bed-mould and table-top and account for the unusual overall height of the tomb. The sides, ends and table-top are of white marble shot with an irregular dark pattern. The inscription is carved on a marble table-top.

SACRED
To the Memory of
WILLIAM HENRY LEGGETT
Who Departed this Life
23 September 1845
AGED 43 YEARS

OTHER OBSERVERS: JMB and HSPH: LEGGET; HSPH: Numbered 30.

REFER TO: CO 129/9 v of 1844, 129/12 of 1845; Kyshe; FC&HKG of 1/10/1845.

---

71.   **HENRY JAMES OSBORNE**   *British*

HENRY JAMES was the brother of Thomas J. Osborne (69), younger by two years. The date of his death was 23 July 1845. Contacts between western Ireland and the Orient were few and infrequent, and in the cemetery they alone are of Irish descent. There is no further information to hand.

The design of this chest-tomb and its inscription are almost identical with those of his brother's memorial (69). The use of the word Remains as a collective noun is now obsolete.

HERE LIE THE REMAINS
OF
HENRY JAMES OSBORNE
4TH Son of Geo Osborne Esqur.
of Singleland County Limerick
Aged 26 Years

OTHER OBSERVERS: JMB: HARRY JAMES OSBORNE; HSPH: Numbered 30.
REFER TO: Gent Mag for December 1846 p 665.

72.   LEWIS HAMILTON   *American*

LEWIS HAMILTON first arrived in China on an American ship as a ship's carpenter. He settled in Macao to set up his own shipbuilding yard, in the late 1830s building the schooner *Harriet*, 'a small fore and aft craft of nominally 100 tons', for Jardine, Matheson & Co's opium trade on the China coast.

His small, granite headstone stands facing west three metres to the north of 71. Facing it is its footstone carved with the letters L. H. in bold capitals. The headstone, 114 cm high, 76 cm wide and 11 cm thick, is on a rectangular granite podium protruding 25 cm above the ground, 81 cm wide and 25 cm thick. Its top is a semicircular arch rising direct from the sides, and the inscription surface is bounded by a beading 1.2 cm wide and 2.5 cm high.

The composer, or the sculptor, has mixed together the openings of two common epitaphs. Careless provision has resulted in some omissions: *the* from the second line, *of* from the fifth, and the suffix -*ed* from the word 'Depart' on the seventh.

OTHER OBSERVERS: HSPH: Numbered 32.
REFER TO: Hunter 1911 b pp 71–2.

73.   ISAAC E. ENGLE   *American*

SACRED
To The Memory of
CAPTAIN
ISAAC E ENGLE
LATE COMMANDER OF THE
American Barque Valparaiso
AND A NATIVE OF
CHESTER
PENNSYLVANIA
Who Died At Macao
On The 3ᴰ Day of November 1844
Aged About 46 Years
Inscription

THE FIRST REPORT of visits to China made by Engle appeared in March 1844, when he arrived at Lintin Island from Ecuador, in command of the American barque *Pearl*; on another trip he was master of the American ship *Richard Alsop*, in which he sailed back to America from Whampoa in the summer of 1838. He moved his command to the American ship *Hopewell* in 1842 and arrived for a two-month stay in Macao, from January 1843, then sailed again for America. His next, eventful, and final voyage was as captain of the *Valparaiso*: while visiting Hawaii in her, he took on board two Japanese who had been landed from a whaler after being found adrift on a junk, and 480 kilometres out rescued seven Sandwich Islanders blown off-course. Sick with a nervous fever, he died on 23 October 1844, soon after arriving back in Macao, leaving 'a wife and two children to mourn his loss'.

Captain Engle's memorial is a granite chest-tomb just to the north of 72, head to the east. A granite podium with mitred corners supports a moulded plinth below the vertical, 51 cm sides and ends of a box, on which are 2.5 cm-high rectangular panels with incised corners carved in relief; the table-top, supported on the box by a substantial bed-mould, carries the inscription.

OTHER OBSERVERS: PCL: ISSAC ENGLE; HSPH: Numbered 33.
REFER TO: Canton R of 18/3/1834, 28/8/1838, 9/10/1838; Canton P of 3/9/1842 and 7 and 14/1 and 4/3/1843; Stackpole p 33; FC&HKG of 2, 13 and 20/11/1844 and 26/10 and 9/11/1844; Monroe lxxxvi pp 257 and 315; Cutler pp 404, 478 and 480; ACK for 1839; Fairbank i p 211; Heard.

74.   R.V. WARREN   *British*

SACRED
TO
THE MEMORY OF
R.V. WARREN.
Aged 22 Years.
Who was Murdered on Board
The Schooner "KAPPA"
By Chinese
Whilst on her way
To Whampoa from Macao.
On the Night of
The 29th October, 1844:
This Tribute to his Memory
Is erected by
His affectionate Brother
H.V. WARREN.
Inscription

WARREN WAS the captain of the British brigantine *Fair Barbadian* which, on the day he came to his end, he had left lying in the Macao Roads, and taken passage in the teak-built, 31-ton schooner *Kappa* for a visit to Hong Kong. The *Kappa*, carrying a valuable cargo of 40 chests of opium, was the subject of a planned attack by pirates who had followed her from Taipa; there was a struggle, the captain was so badly wounded that he died shortly afterwards, and Warren and a Lascar were killed. While transferring the cargo, the pirates were disturbed by a French steamer but escaped with 26 or 27 of the chests. Warren's body was recovered and taken to Macao for burial. His brother was probably the Henry Warren, former master of the *Privateer*, who died in Hong Kong four years after R.V. – from the DTs, as concluded at the inquest.

A chest-tomb of rough granite, the memorial lies parallel to its neighbours, which it closely resembles, though smaller. The podium is underground, so that the vertical sides and ends of the box seem to rise direct from the moulded plinth; they are cut with rectangular panels. The table-top has a substantial bed-mould and vertical edges and is unadorned except for the inscription, which is thinly incised and pleasing.

OTHER OBSERVERS: HSPH: Numbered 34.
REFER TO: FC&HKG of 6/11/1844, 9/6 to 15/12/1842, 2 to 20/4/1844 and 19/3/1845; Canton P of 21/8/1841, 15/7, 19/8, 4/11 and 30/12/1843; Canton R of 27/4/1841; CM of 7/10/1847, 8/6 and 27/7/1848, and 2/1853; SFP&MA of 15/4, 16/7, 3 and 17/12/1846, 18 and 25/3, 20/5 and 30/12/1853; Dixson HKG for 1850; Dixson HKSL for 1856.

75.   THOMAS WESTBROOK WALDRON   *American*

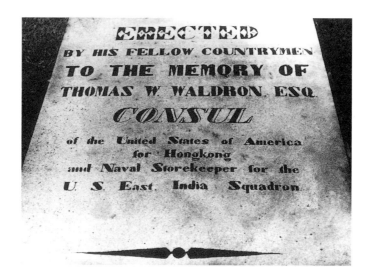

Born in Portsmouth, New Hampshire U.S.A.

Inscription on north side

He died in Macao in September 1844 Aged 52 Years

Inscription on south side

BORN ON 21 May 1814, Thomas Waldron was given the second name of Westbrook after his paternal grandfather, Colonel Westbrook Waldron, and in his maturity seems to have been called 'Samuel' by his friends. His appointment as Naval Storekeeper was made in June 1843, and he arrived in Hong Kong early in February 1844 as the US Government Agent, the Royal Exequatur approving his consular appointment delayed until August by procedures in London and the mail. Neither naval nor an ex-naval officer, he assumed the responsibilities of storekeeper only until a suitable

naval officer was due to arrive in Hong Kong later that year. The revoking letter from the Navy Department is unlikely to have reached him before he left on an official visit to Macao, where he died suddenly of 'the first instance of Asiatic cholera which our physicians have ever known in China', as Mrs Kinsman noted.

Last in the row, like 73 and 74 with its long axis east-west, its head to the east, and of the same design and size, this is a granite chest-tomb with the main epitaph on its table-top, the word 'Erected' being decorated and 'Consul' incised in shaded, forward-sloping italics.

OTHER OBSERVERS: HSPH: Numbered 35.
REFER TO: Wentworth ii p 310; FC&HKG of 6/2 and 11/9/ 1844; Eller; Monroe lxxxvi pp 110, 258 and 280; CO 129/4 and 5; Stackpole p 25.

76.   HIRAM TARBOX   *American*

IN MEMORY
OF
HIRAM TARBOX
ORDINARY SEAMAN
died 31 May 1844
on board of the
U.S. Frigate Brandywine
Commodore F.A. Parker

Requiescat in pace
Inscription

THE DECEASED WAS the fourth of the nine children of Jotham and Olive (née Haley) of Biddeford, Maine, born probably in 1814 and thus about 30 years of age when he died. Both parents were from families with seafaring members.

This unpretentious headstone stands at the end of the row and in line with the head end of 75. It is rectangular, 94 cm high, 51 cm wide and 10 cm thick, rough-hewn at the back, and its top is in the form of a flattened segmental arch, rising from the inner sides of semi-circular shoulders of 8 cm diameter.

OTHER OBSERVERS: PCL and JMB: TABBOX; HSPH: Numbered 36.
REFER TO: Loomis; Tarbox.

77.   CHARLES F. GANGER   *American*

IN MEMORY
of
CHARLES F. GANGER
a Musician
of the
U S Frigate Brandywine
Commodore F A Parker
died 15 October 1844
Aged 50 Years

May he rest in piece
Inscription

NO INFORMATION ABOUT Charles Ganger has come to light beyond what is on the headstone, but the ship's log gives the date of his death as 16 October. Hiram Tarbox (76) died during the same period when the *Brandywine* was patrolling the waters around Hong Kong, Macao and Whampoa, while it was with the American East India Squadron as the flagship of Commodore Parker, from 1843 to 1845. Some four months before Ganger died, the frigate had put into harbour with the Commodore and Caleb Cushing, the American Commissioner to China, on board. A guest has left a lively description of a 'long anticipated' dinner-dance on the ship.

The headstone is nearly identical in size, design, material and inscription to 76. There is also extensive and progressive weathering damage on their surfaces; the lettering on the one has helped in deciphering that on the other. Its delightful variation of the old prayer 'May he rest in piece [sic]' is rescued for posterity.

OTHER OBSERVERS: HSPH: Numbered 37.
REFER TO: Loomis; Monroe lxxxvi pp 110n, 128, 131 and 142; FC&HKG of 31/8/1843 and 27/2, 5 and 9/3, 20/4, and 22/5/1844; Canton P of 2/3/1844; CO 129/4 No. 102.

78. JOHN LEATHLEY *British*

SACRED TO THE MEMORY
OF
JOHN LEATHLEY ESQ.
who died at Macao 15 January 1844
Aged 28 Years.

Inscription

THERE IS ONE reference to the deceased in a press advertisement dated 29 June 1843, announcing that he had received for sale, from Giesler & Co of Rheims and Cologne, sparkling champagne and Johannisberg. A John Leathley was a passenger on the Spanish ship *Rafaela*, sailing from Macao for Manila on 26 January 1841 – the day the British flag was raised at Possession Point in Hong Kong. It is no more than an assumption that he was British – solely from the designation 'esq.' in the inscription.

This is the most westerly of the four chest-tombs that form this line in the Crockett Group, its long axis running north-south; they are nearly identical in size and design, each standing on a mitred podium surmounted by a moulded plinth, each with vertical sides and ends carrying panels with incised corners, cut in high relief, and each with a table-top that rests on a substantial bed-mould and has vertical edges.

OTHER OBSERVERS: PCL: LEATHIEY; HSPH: LEATHLY, Numbered 38.
REFER TO: FC&HKG of 10/8/1843; Canton R of 26/1/1841.

79.   SARAH ANNE BALLS   *British*

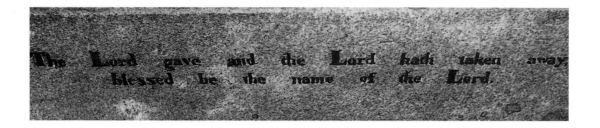

SACRED TO THE MEMORY
OF
SARAH ANNE BALLS
wife of Captain George Balls who was born at W.Cowes, Isle
of Wight, and died at Macao 23 June 1844
Aged 23 Years.

Inscription

NO REFERENCE either to Captain Balls or his wife has come to light.

For a note relevant to this chest-tomb, see 78. Both Braga and Hopkinson give her age as 28.

Intensive weathering leaves it now as 23. Deciphering is no longer easy, and either may be correct.

OTHER OBSERVERS: HSPH: Numbered 39.

80.   THOMAS SCOTLAND   *British*

BECAUSE THOMAS SCOTLAND was a member of the grand jury at the first session of the Criminal and Admiralty Court held in Hong Kong on 4 March 1844, it is clear that he was an established resident of Hong Kong or Macao or Canton for some time before that. The foreman of the grand jury at the time was Patrick Stewart (44). The local

SACRED TO THE MEMORY
THOMAS SCOTLAND ESQ
who died at Macao 10th July 1844
Aged 21 Years.

press confirms the date and place of his death. Nothing else is known of him.

For a note on the four chest-tombs in this line see 78. The lettering, which is carved on the east side of this tomb, is well cut and readily legible.

OTHER OBSERVERS: HSPH: Numbered 40.
REFER TO: Canton P of 9/3/1844; FC&HKG of 20/7/1844.

81.   JANE SPENCER   *British*

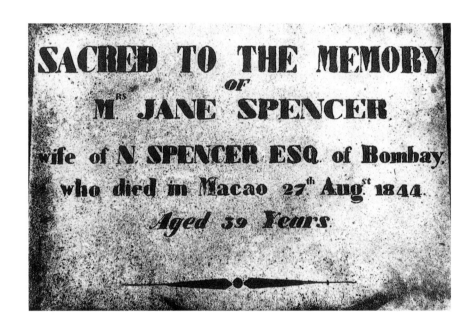

NO INFORMATION HAS been found about either Jane Spencer or her husband, N. Spencer. Her age at death is here taken to be 29; other observers have suggested it as 39. Either may be correct, as the inscription is unclear.

The last chest-tomb in the line, this is very similar in measurement and design to the other three, different only in that its long axis lies east-west, and that no inscriptions are cut on either sides or ends. Except for the italics of the last line, the lettering is well cut.

OTHER OBSERVERS: HSPH: Numbered 41.

82.   ANDREW PATERSON   *British*

West side

**SACRED TO THE MEMORY OF
ANDREW PATERSON**
late Commander of the Barque Lady Hayes
who departed this life July 22nd 1842
Aged 43 Years
Inscription on east side

APART FROM THE inscriptions, newspaper confirmation of his place and date of death, and a notice of claims to his estate, nothing has come to light about Paterson. On the other hand, the operations in south China waters of his ship the *Lady Hayes* were well known over many years. A barque of 313 tons, she was a Company country ship, and had arrived in China for her agents Jardine, Matheson & Co not later than 4 September 1833, thereafter plying between Calcutta, New South Wales and Canton in the face of typhoons and piracy. She was not broken up until 1868.

The first of the five granite chest-tombs lying parallel in the second line of the Crockett Group and very similar in design, the memorial's long axis runs north-south, its box resting on a mitred podium, which in turn supports a moulded plinth surrounding the bases of its incised, perpendicular sides and ends, all of which are carved with rectangular panels with incised corners; the whole is capped by a substantial bed-mould and a table-top with vertical edges. It lies directly south of the Crockett memorial (87), and differs from the others in the closed, fluted urn which is supported by the table-top on a three-tiered podium, granite slabs positioned side by side forming the lower steps.

West side inscription

OTHER OBSERVERS: HSPH: Numbered 42.
REFER TO: ACK for 1835; Canton R of 18/8/1835 and 26/7/1842; Canton P of 4, 11 and 18/6 and 30/7 and 29/10/1842; FInd of 22/9/1842; Braga 1940 p 32.

83. **GEORGE KENNEDY** *British*

SACRED
to the memory
of
CAPTAIN GEORGE KENNEDY
who died at Macao
28th September 1844
AGED 40 YEARS

OTHER THAN THE date and place of his death, very little further is known about Captain Kennedy. He became part-owner of the brig *Governor Findlay*, which had formerly been engaged in the Atlantic slave-trade until it was intercepted and sold. Having sailed in her to south China, he fell on bad times and Jardine, Matheson & Co took her over, but left him in command.

In company with a Chinese boat, she rescued 19 of the 68 passengers from the wreckage of a junk in 1835, the others having perished. In a bad typhoon later that year, the brig and several other ships were dismasted and some were driven ashore or wrecked in the Pearl River delta area. From 1835 to 1838 or 1839, Kennedy was in command of the English brig *Psyche*, sailing with her to India, Singapore and China; he shifted his command to the *Emily Jane* for a trip from China to England and back in September 1840, and sailed for Manila as a passenger aboard the *Thomas Lowry*. He seems to have alternated commands with Captain Thomas Rees (husband of 109) during 1838–40. He died after a long illness.

His tomb stands so close to 82 that their podia almost touch. Its table-top has been fractured across at some time, and the fracture-line makes the last figure of Kennedy's death look as much like a four as anything; other evidence reveals that it must originally have been a one. The lettering, cut on the table-top, has wide shallow grooves, and has weathered well.

OTHER OBSERVERS: HSPH: Numbered 43.
REFER TO: China R of 5/10/1841; Canton P of 8/9/1838, 2/11/1839, 5 and 12/9/1840, and 2/10/1841; Canton R of 18/4, 9/6, and 18/8/1835; FInd of 15/2 and 16/3/1837; SFP&MA of 6 and 13/4/1837 and 26/3/1840; Williamson.

84.   ELIZABETH FEARON   *British*

IN MEMORY
OF ELIZABETH FEARON, WHOSE TRULY AMIABLE
DISPOSITION HAD ENDEARED HER TO ALL WHO KNEW HER,
AND WHOSE CONDUCT AS A WIFE AND A MOTHER DURING AN
UNION OF
20 YEARS WAS MOST EXEMPLARY. THIS MONUMENT
IS ERECTED BY HER SORROWING HUSBAND
Llewelyn & Co

Inscription on west side

"THE LORD GAVE, AND THE LORD HATH TAKEN AWAY:
BLESSED BE HIS HOLY NAME."

Inscription on east side

North end

ELIZABETH FEARON (née Noad) married Christopher Augustus Fearon in England on 14 May 1818, shortly after his third visit to China and some 10 weeks before his fourth. When they were living in Macao, they were reported to have occupied the Company's official house for some time, next door to the plot which was to become the Company cemetery, now occupied by the Camoens Museum. Lintin, where she died, was the anchorage for storeships awaiting opium from India. It is said that George Chinnery (40), who became her youngest son's godfather, lived with the Fearons for some years, and was so taken with Elizabeth's features that he made several portraits of her. She was renowned, not only for her beauty, but for her high spirits. In April 1830, she and two other British women flouted the Chinese regulations that excluded foreign women from Canton. They attended a service at the English Chapel at Canton, almost provoking a suspension of trade. Their exploit was later repeated by Harriet Low and three other American women.

Her husband's family boasted a record of continuous service in the Far East, lasting over a century and a half. Before finally settling in the East, Fearon made five more trips as a Company purser, chiefly in the opium run between Calcutta and China. It is not known when his wife joined him. Operating from Canton and Macao, he traded in the firm of Fearon & Co, which may have been founded by his father. He joined with J.W.H. Ilbery, the husband of 57, under the name of Ilbery, Fearon & Co. One of his sons, Charles Fearon, came to the East at the end of 1844 to begin trading in Shanghai in partnership with Augustine Heard. Another son, Samuel Fearon, became the first Professor of Chinese in Britain, and was based in King's College, London (1847–52).

Christopher Fearon emigrated to New South Wales at the end of 1844, taking a male servant with him. He married as his second wife Grace Adriana (née du Moulin or Mulin), daughter of the Duke of Wellington's staff surgeon, and became a Justice of the Peace at Parramatta, where, after a long illness, he died in 1866 aged 79.

Elizabeth Fearon's chest-tomb of local granite, similar in design and orientation to the others in the third line, differs in that it has no inscription on its table-top. The inscriptions on the sides and ends of the box are cut on Belgian black marble tablets set in rectangular recesses. The end of the text on the east side is a misquotation of 'Blessed be the name of the Lord'. The letters are cut V-shaped: those on the west side are smaller and more deeply incised. The tablets were cut in Calcutta by Llewelyn & Co, formerly Simpson & Llewelyn. Some observers differ in the dates of death, including even 1858, by which time Lintin, where she died, had long faded from the China trading scene, and Christopher Fearon had already remarried and was raising his second family in Australia.

OTHER OBSERVERS: HSPH: Numbered 44, FEARSON.
REFER TO: Liddell; Hunter p 120; Morse iv p 254; FC&HKG of 5/6 and 14/8/1841, 26/3/1842, 8/1/1845, and 7/2/1846; CM of 5 and 12/2/1846 and 17/6/1847; Sydney MH of 18/12/1845 and 1/9/1866; NSWG of 26/7/1864 p 35.

South end

85.   MARIA J. ORTON   *American*

S A C R E D
TO THE MEMORY
OF
Miss Maria J Orton
WHO DIED AT MACAO ON THE XXIII OF SEPT^{ER} 1839
In the XXII Year of her age
This is erected by a friend
Inscription

MARIA ORTON was staying in Macao with the American missionary Rev Jehu Lewis Shuck when she died on 23 September 1839, 'of relapsed dysentery', at the age of 21 (or 'in the XXII Year of her age'). The Rev Shuck and his wife were the first Baptist missionaries to work in China, settling at Canton in 1836. The troubled times forced them to move first to Macao, then in 1842 to Hong Kong, and in 1847 to Shanghai, where they remained until they retired in 1851. It is reasonably likely that Maria was an American, and either a missionary herself or connected with an American mission. Nothing more is known of her.

Her chest-tomb is of granite and identical in composition and layout to its lineal neighbours, except that here the inscriptions are on recessed panels at both ends. Varied lettering, used indiscriminately, yields a result quite inartistic.

OTHER OBSERVERS: HSPH: Numbered 45.
REFER TO: Canton P of 28/9/1839; Dean p 119; CMH of 1896; FInd of 29/3/1838; CM of 23/12/1858.

86.   DONALD MACKENZIE   *British*

THERE IS LITTLE information about Captain Mackenzie, other than references to his voyages in command of vessels in the country trade during the Company's final operations in China and the first of its successor, the Superintendents of Trade. He arrived in south China from Bombay as master of the *Hormusjee Bomanjee* in September 1833. He left London with the English ship *Tamerlane* for Calcutta in 1839. He transferred command to the *Poppy*, bound for China via Singapore, probably on opium runs, arriving in Hong Kong in October 1839, then on to Macao, where he fell ill and left his ship. The *Poppy* was back in Hong Kong waters from 26 October for the next two weeks.

SACRED TO THE MEMORY
OF
DONALD MACKENZIE.
LATE COMMANDER OF THE BRIG POPPY:
WHO DEPARTED THIS LIFE AT MACAO
ON THE 30TH OF OCTOBER 1839. AGED 49 YEARS.
THIS MONUMENT IS ERECTED BY A FRIEND.

LLEWELYN & CO
CALCUTTA
Inscription

His resting-place is the easternmost chest-tomb of the five in Line 3 of the Crockett Group, cut in local granite. The inscription is carved on a rectangular Belgian black marble tablet affixed to its south end, with large, incised quadrants at each corner. Llewelyn & Co of Calcutta were responsible for cutting the tablet, and like all their other work in the cemetery it is of superior craftsmanship. The first line is in Old English script.

OTHER OBSERVERS: JMB: MACKENSIE; HSPH: Numbered 46.
REFER TO: Canton R of 14/9/1833 and 22/10 and 26/11/1839; FInd of 27/6/1839 and 23/1/1840; Canton P of 31/8, 19 and 26/10, 9, 16, 23, and 20/11 and 21/12/1839.

---

87.   JOHN CROCKETT   *British*

CAPTAIN CROCKETT, who was resident at Bombay from at least 1817, arrived with his wife in China, in command of the *Charlotte*, in June 1830. Within a few years he gave up his command afloat and was appointed to the more lucrative command of one of the 'Lintin Fleet' anchored at Lintin Island, the opium storeship *Jane*, from which he was able to supplement his salary by selling salvage opium. 'Capsing Moon', shown as the place of his death, is an erroneous composite of names. There were two permanent anchorages for the opium fleet at Lintin Island on the eastern side of the Pearl River Estuary equidistant from both Macao and Hong Kong, and their names were often confused: the Capsuimoon Strait, where according to burial records in London Crockett died, probably on board, and the Cumsingmoon Passage.

Of the widow and their five children, information has been found only on two daughters (98 and 100), and her niece is buried in the cemetery (57).

John Crockett's monument is of granite and the most westerly in the fourth line of the group bearing his name. The tallest in the cemetery, it comprises a large cube supporting a square column, on the sides of which are carved grooves forming vertical, rectangular panels with incised corners but unadorned, and this in its turn supports an overhanging table carrying a closed, fluted urn. Moulded plinths encase the bases of both column and cube, of which the east, west and north sides are grooved to form rectangular panels, also unadorned. The south side of the cube is faced with a large square tablet of Belgian black marble, on which the inscription was cut by Llewelyn's of Calcutta. The column is not

one of the established architectural orders.

This is one of the few monuments once to have been protected by iron railings, the holes to which they were anchored still visible; the rails disappeared during the metal shortage of the Second World War. It is perhaps significant that Crockett, Paterson (82), and Turner (93) were all in the opium trade, and therefore could afford such distinctive additions.

OTHER OBSERVERS: HSPH: Numbered 47.

REFER TO: EIR&D for 1817; Canton R of 15/6/1830, 28/4/1835, and 1/8/1837; ACK for 1836; Burial R 11,218 p 353.

SACRED
TO THE MEMORY OF
CAPTn. JOHN CROCKETT.
WHO WAS BORN THE 1ST OF DECR. 1786
AND DIED AT CAPSING MOON ON THE 25TH. OF JUNE 1837,
IN THE 51ST. YEAR OF HIS AGE,
LEAVING A WIFE AND FIVE CHILDREN, TO DEPLORE
THE LOSS OF A KIND HUSBAND & AFFECTIONATE FATHER.
THIS MONUMENT WAS ERECTED
WITH THE CONSENT OF HIS FOND AND BEREAVED WIDOW
BY THOSE BELONGING TO THE LINTIN FLEET
WHO DEEPLY LAMENT THE DEATH OF SO SINCERE AND GENEROUS
A FRIEND.
LLEWELYN
Inscription

88. EDMUND ROBERTS *American*

THE REMAINS
OF
EDMUND ROBERTS ESQ
SPECIAL DIPLOMATIC AGENT
OF THE UNITED STATES
TO SEVERAL ASIATIC COURTS
WHO DIED AT MACAO
JUNE 12ᵀᴴ 1836
AET. 50
Top upper half

He devised and executed
for their law
under instruction
from his Government
treaties of amity
commerce between
the United States
and the Courts of
Muscat and of Siam
Top lower half

BORN LATE IN June 1784, Edmund Roberts of Portsmouth, New Hampshire, was almost 52 when he died, not 50. Scion of an old Portsmouth shipping family, to whose business he succeeded at the age of 16, he is historically the most important American buried in the cemetery,

In 1808 he married Catherine, a daughter of Woodberry Langdon and of the shipbuilding family famed for its privateers during the Revolutionary War and later for its large trade with the Orient. He acquired strong political connections

through her: Henry Sherwin and Sarah Warner were her maternal grandparents. A diplomatic future opened for Roberts when his fortunes were reduced by heavy losses at the hands of French and Spanish privateers, and for some time his career veered between diplomacy and merchant shipping. During his efforts to expand his interests to Zanzibar, the friendship he formed with the Sultan of Muscat resulted in his being appointed special U.S. agent in January 1832, to negotiate a treaty of amity and commerce with Muscat. At this time the American Consul at Batavia (Jakarta) was John Shillaber, who the following year became the brother-in-law of Dr Thomas Richardson Colledge through his sister Caroline (see 94, 95 and 96), and was advocating a similar policy in the Far East. Added to Roberts's commission were negotiations first with Siam (Thailand) and Cochin-China (southern Vietnam), and subsequently with Japan.

His visit to Muscat was successful and he sailed on the U.S. sloop *Peacock* to Cochin-China by way of Manila, Canton and Macao, taking John Robert Morrison (143) on board as interpreter and translator for his further negotiations. His mission in Cochin-China failed, but in Siam, in spite of delay and difficulties caused by triple interpretations from English into Portuguese, Portuguese into Chinese, and Chinese into Siamese, he had such success that he returned straight home, delaying his mission in Japan for a further visit, when he might also exchange treaties in Muscat and make a second attempt in Cochin-China. He undertook this second voyage in March 1835, also on board the *Peacock*

ERECTED TO THE MEMORY
of
EDMUND ROBERTS ESQ OF PORTSMOUTH NEW HAMPSHIRE
by the
citizens of the United States resident
at CANTON
1836

and this time accompanied by the schooner *Enterprise* with Captain Archibald Campbell (89) in command. In Siam, a form of Asiatic cholera broke out on his ship and Roberts himself became too ill for the negotiations. Preceded by the *Enterprise*, the *Peacock* left near the end of May for Macao, where the epidemic killed Campbell, nine days before it killed Roberts.

The flags of all foreign consuls at Canton were hoisted half-mast in his honour. He commanded respect and regard, it was reported locally, for his 'intelligence, discernment, and good sense, decision of purpose and kindness of heart, dignity of person and gentleness of manners, firmness of principle and purity of feeling, equanimity of disposition and delightful cheerfulness'.

Readily recognized by its extensively fractured table-top, his granite chest-tomb lies immediately to the east of 87, its head-end to the north and its long axis (like the rest in this line) north-south. In form it is much like the others in the cemetery, except that the table-top has curved edges and a moulded top and the inscription surface is raised about 1.3 cm above the rest. The fractures have been repaired with cement, in which missing pieces of the inscription have been successfully impressed. Roberts's tomb, 89, 92 and one other were the only memorials in this line when Fitch Taylor visited the cemetery in 1839.

OTHER OBSERVERS: HSPH: Numbered 48.
REFER TO: DAB; Morse iv p 326; Morrison ii p 469; Ruschenberger i pp 79ff and 195ff; Canton R of 31/5 and 14/6/ 1836 and 21/11/1837; Burial R 11,218 p 349; Taylor ii.

89.   ARCHIBALD S. CAMPBELL   *American*

CAPTAIN CAMPBELL succeeded to the command of the schooner *Enterprise* in April 1834, and was with her when she accompanied the sloop *Peacock* on the secret missions of American agent Edmund Roberts (88) to Muscat, Cochin-China, Siam and Japan. The sloop was 'the smallest of her class', and sometimes derided as just the tender to the *Enterprise*. The *Peacock* flew the pennant of Commodore Eward P. Kennedy, commander of the American East India squadron. Both Roberts and Campbell died in Macao from cholera.

Campbell's chest-tomb is similar in design and measurements to Roberts's, lying parallel to it. The inscription is well cut and well preserved, but it is clear that there was nobody ashore from Campbell's ship who was responsible for supervising its wording: the ship's name was the 'Enterprise' and its log assigns him the rank of Lieutenant Commander. The reports of the date of his death vary from the 3rd to the 6th. Rev G.H. Vachell conducted the burial service in Macao; at Canton, flags of the foreign consulates were at half-mast.

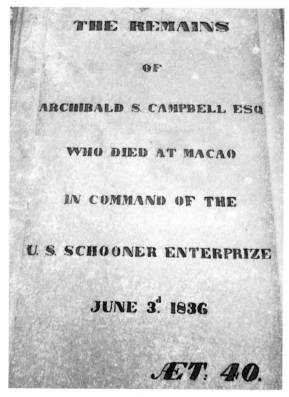

THE REMAINS

OF

ARCHIBALD S. CAMPBELL ESQ

WHO DIED AT MACAO

IN COMMAND OF THE

U. S. SCHOONER ENTERPRIZE

JUNE 3^d 1836

ÆT. 40.

Top

ERECTED TO THE MEMORY
OF
LIEUTENANT COMMANDANT ARCHIBALD S CAMPBELL
by the
officers of the U S Ship Peacock and Schooner
ENTERPRIZE
1836.

Inscription on east side

OTHER OBSERVERS: HSPH: Numbered 49.
REFER TO: Loomis; Ruschenberger i p 3 and ii pp 181ff; Canton R of 7, 14/6, and 5/7/1836; Burial R 11,218 p 349; Dodge pp 44 and 142.

90.   EDWARD G. LARKIN   *American*

IN MEMORY
OF
EDWARD G. LARKINS
of Portsmouth N.H.
who died on board the
U.S.S. "JOHN ADAMS"
June 15th 1839
AGED 28 YEARS.

Inscription on top

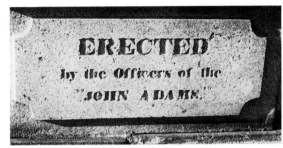

South end

THE FAMILY NAME was Larkin, as the log of the *John Adams* has it, not Larkins. Larkin was born on 11 October 1809, making his age at death 29, not 28 as shown. He was one of the 22 children of Ann Jeffrey (née Wentworth) and Major Samuel Larkin, who became a comfortably well-off auctioneer of prizes and cargoes captured by privateers in the waters of Portsmouth. Edward was a captain's clerk, a civilian appointment in the American Navy made by the naval captain. He died aboard his ship while it lay off Tung Koo Island at the north end of the Pearl River estuary. Buried on one of the small delta islands close by, his body was later moved to Macao for re-interment.

The *John Adams* was first designed as a frigate, then elongated by the builder, and in 1829 rebuilt again as a sail-propelled sloop-of-war; she was in the East Indies from 1838 to 1840, arriving off Macao under Captain Wyman with the frigate *Columbia* at the beginning of May 1839, both ships then sailing for the Sandwich Islands early in August: it was during this visit that Larkin died.

His granite chest-tomb lies about 30 cm to the east of 89, to which it is parallel and similar in design and size; rectangular tablets with incised corners are carved in high relief on its sides and ends. The edges of the table-top are rounded, ending in mouldings which form a rectangular frame for the main inscription. All the lettering is well cut and well preserved, in a pleasing general lay-out.

OTHER OBSERVERS: HSPH: Numbered 50.
REFER TO: US Navy; Wentworth i p 560; Taylor ii; Canton R of 30/4, 14/5, and 13/8/1839; Canton P of 4/4/1840.

91.   EMILY MILNER   *British*

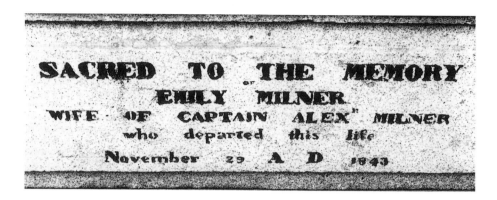

CAPTAIN MILNER may have been, like some others, a former captain in the 'country trade' who had turned to actual trading in opium, while his wife lived in Macao. They may have been American: but without evidence of their nationality, she is here listed as British.

Her granite chest-tomb follows closely the size and design of its neighbours in this line, except that the table-top lacks over-mould and inscription, has vertical edges, and is supported on a thick bed-mould. The meagre epitaph is cut on the west side of the box, and its poor quality has given rise to some doubt of the identity of the occupant and of the surname, whether of the wife or of the husband. There can be no doubt, however, that it is the grave of Alexander Milner's wife Emily, and not, as the Church List records, of Alexander Milner himself.

OTHER OBSERVERS: PCL: ALEXR. MILLINER; JMB and HSPH: MILLINER; HSPH: Numbered 51.

92.   ELIZABETH McDOUGAL GILLESPIE   *American*

BURIAL RECORDS show that she died in 1836, aged 22, and her interment service was conducted by the chaplain to the Superintendent of Trade, Rev G.H. Vachell, on 7 December. When two ships of the American East India Squadron, the *John Adams* and the *Columbia*, were anchored off Macao, the chaplain of the squadron, Fitch Taylor, visited the cemetery and among other general comments said he had heard of the 'sweet qualities of her amiable character'. He went on: 'I saw her

IN MEMORY
OF
Elizabeth McDougal Gillespie.
Born at New York June 6. AD 1814.
Died at Macao. Dec 6. AD 1837.

West side

once, just previous to her leaving America for Canton with her guardian, in hopes that the voyage would contribute to her restoration to health. It was otherwise ...' Taylor sentimentally expressed the feelings the cemetery roused in him with verses which clearly refer to Elizabeth:

She sleeps – but not beneath the deep
That mourns the sea-dirge for its dead,
While low among the tides they sweep
Or rock upon their coral bed.
She sleeps – but not beneath the ground
Where kindred dead lie near and deep,
And friends oft gather at the mound
To think, and love, and newly weep.
She sleeps – a gem from western land,
That shone as ray of diamond light;
But soon was lost on foreign strand,
A setting star in earliest night.
She sleeps – where strangers stop to trace
The story of the early dead;
And one far-voyager seeks her place
His tribute tear o'er worth to shed.

The dimensions of this granite chest-tomb are almost identical with those of 91, and its design

with that of 90. The table-top has rounded edges and upper mouldings that frame a rectangular surface devoid of inscription. Its perpendicular sides and ends are mounted on the usual podium, supported by the usual moulded plinth, and each has a rectangular panel with incised corners carved in recess on the surface. The lettering of the inscriptions is well cut and clear.

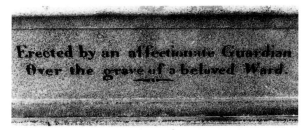

Erected by an affectionate Guardian
Over the grave of a beloved Ward.

East side

OTHER OBSERVERS: HSPH: Numbered 52.
REFER TO: Genealy Mag viii/6 of June 1939 p 327; Burial R 11,218 p 350; Taylor ii.

93.   RICHARD TURNER   *British*

RICHARD TURNER was registered in 1822 as a merchant in Bengal, and by 1826 had moved from India to Canton, to establish his own agency, principally trading in opium. He was a partner of A.P. Boyd in the firm of Turner & Co, which was housed in the Spanish factory, and he became a central figure in both the General Chamber of Commerce and the Society for the Diffusion of Useful Knowledge in China.

SACRED

TO THE MEMORY OF

RICHARD TURNER ESQ^RE MERCHANT

OF CANTON WHO DIED AT MACAO

MARCH THE 28TH A.D. 1839.

AGED 53 YEARS.

Mary Croft Turner. The Turners were friends of the diarist Harriet Low. He died 'after several weeks of suffering'.

Last in the line, his granite chest-tomb stands three metres east of 92, its head to the north. It differs from the others in that the table-top has rounded edges and a well-proportioned moulding round the inscription surface; and the sides and ends of its box are slightly splayed, with trapezoid moats 4 cm wide forming their panels.

He was one of the group, with William Jardine in the chair, appointed at a public meeting to organize a British floating hospital for seamen at Whampoa, and when he died he had become a life member of the Medical Missionary Society in China. He also kept a house in Macao, where three children were born during 1826–30 to his wife,

The initials cut on the south end are very large. The marks on the granite podium offer evidence that iron railings once surrounded the tomb.

OTHER OBSERVERS: HSPH: Numbered 53.
REFER TO: EIR&D for 1822; Morse iv pp 128, 205, and 254; ACK for 1835-9; Canton R of 16/6/1835 and 2/4/1839; FInd of 4/7/1839; Canton P of 13/10, 13 and 30/11/1838, 6/4 and 30/11/1839, and 8 and 15/8 and 19/12/1840; Braga 1940 p 30n; Bapt R 11,218 pp 331–3; Loines p 72.

THE COLLEDGE CORNER

THE FATHER OF the three infants buried here (94, 95, and 96), Dr T.R. Colledge, joined the Company in 1819, and sailed east in 1821 to take up duties as surgeon to the British factory at Canton. In 1827 he opened an eye clinic in Macao, for which he rented accommodation; some six years later he transferred it to a new building specially constructed to house it. Like Dr Colledge, his colleague Dr Peter Parker, the American surgeon who became its director, contrived to divide his time between duties in Macao and at Canton, which included the training of assistants.

Chinnery drew an aquarelle of the new hospital building and, in an oil, depicts Colledge standing at work in his clinic, with his Chinese assistants and two Chinese patients. In March 1833 Colledge, one of Macao's most eligible bachelors, married Caroline (née Shillaber), a close friend and confidante of the diarist Harriet Low, at a ceremony

Chinnery: Dr and Mrs Colledge

conducted by Rev Charles Wimberley, followed by a reception which Hunter called 'a brilliant affair'.

Drs Colledge and Parker, supported by the Rev E.C. Bridgman, founded the Medical Missionary Society of China, but by the time it was formally inaugurated Colledge had already left China for home, in May 1838. He had seen both Dr Robert Morrison and Lord Napier through their fatal illnesses while he practised in Macao. Caroline did not leave China until about eight months after her husband, sailing for England in February 1839 with their one remaining child and the Rev G.H. Vachell and his family on board the *Inglis*.

REFER TO: DNB; Hardy pp 352, S10, S26, S38, 155; Morse iv pp 145–6 and 346; Crawford p 624; Canton R of 20/3/1833, 15/5/1838, and 9/2/1839; Canton P of 8/12/1838 and 19/2/1839; Loines pp 46–7, 113, 145–66, 168–70, 173, 178, etc; Hunter p 127; Marriage R 11,218 p 329; Ch Rep for May 1838 pp 32–44; Conner plates 96 (p 232) and 146 (p224).

94. LANCELOT DENT COLLEDGE *British*

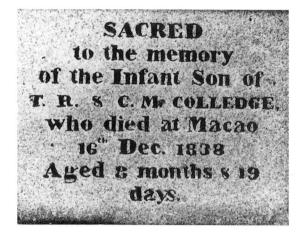

SACRED
to the memory
of the Infant Son of
T. R. & C. M. COLLEDGE,
who died at Macao
16th Dec. 1838
Aged 8 months & 19
days.

South end

THE INSCRIPTION lacks a name. The infant's parents, Caroline Matilda (née Shillaber), Harriet Low's American friend, and Dr Thomas Richardson Colledge, lie in the Shurdington churchyard near Cheltenham, England, in a grave beneath a cross-top ledger on whose sides are cut lines commemorating the whole family, and it is from one of these that the full name of this eight-month-old infant has been derived. He was called after Lancelot Dent, head of one of the oldest of the merchant companies in the Orient, Dent & Co, and a friend of his father. It seems that none of the three Colledge memorials was erected until after both parents had left Macao. This infant, their fourth, was born on 26 March, and his father left Macao a month later. The newspaper report of his death, giving it as 15 December, differs from that in the inscription and

is wrong. His mother left for England six weeks after he died.

The small, neat, chest-tomb stands many metres from 99, the next in the line, and close to the northwest corner of 87. Immediately to the north in the next line are buried two of the brothers of infant Lancelot Dent (95 and 96), and their tombs are all so similar that one description must suffice for the three. Each stands head to the north on a granite podium, and from a simple moulded plinth its sides and ends rise perpendicularly 46 cm to a moulding under a table-top, on which the quotation is deeply cut. In reverse of the general pattern, the south ends carry the main inscriptions.

I know that whatsoever God doeth, it shall be for ever nothing can be put to it nor any thing taken from it; and God doeth it that men should fear before him.

Top

OTHER OBSERVERS: HSPH: Numbered 54.
REFER TO: Canton R of 3/4/1838; Canton P of 22/12/1838; Burial R 11,218 p 360; Loines.

95.   WILLIAM SHILLABER COLLEDGE   *British*

South end

THIS IS ONE of the three tombs commemorating sons of Dr and Mrs Colledge, all dying in their infancy. Burial records state that the Rev G.H. Vachell, then chaplain to the Superintendent of Trade, performed both baptismal and burial services, and that this infant was 'said to be born' on 24 February 1837; a newspaper gives the date of birth as the 20th. His middle name was intended to continue his mother's maiden name into succeeding generations.

The memorial lies at the western end of the fifth line of the Crockett group, its long axis running north-south and its head against the northern cemetery wall a couple of metres north of 94 and west of 96.

The biblical text, not a full verse, is an extract from the gospel of St Matthew 10:18, which begins: 'Take heed that ye despise not one of these little ones; for ...' and follows on as in the inscription. Both inscriptions are easily legible.

Top

OTHER OBSERVERS: HSPH: WILLIAM SHILLERER COLLEDGE, Numbered 55.
REFER TO: Canton R of 7/3/1837 and 30/10/1838; Canton P of 27/10/1838; Bapt R 11,218 p 355.

96. THOMAS RICHARDSON COLLEDGE *British*

South end

THE QUOTATION ON the table-top of this chest-tomb is from Coleridge's *Epitaph to an Infant*, a poem first published in the *Morning Chronicle* of 24 September 1794. The original version of the second line ran 'Death came with friendly care' and has been amended, probably from a version more favoured in those religious circles unwilling to give Death any credit for anything.

The memorial is the last of the three in the Colledge Corner and lies parallel with and alongside to the east of 95, its head also under the north wall. The inscriptions are well cut and very easily read, except that the '26th' has been inked in by mistake for the '27th' during preparation to photograph the south-end inscription.

ERE SIN COULD BLIGHT OR SORROW FADE

GOD WITH A FATHER'S CARE,

THE OPENING BUD TO HEAVEN CONVEYED

AND BADE IT BLOSSOM THERE

Top

OTHER OBSERVERS: HSPH: Numbered 56.
REFER TO: Braga 1940 p 28; Canton R of 2/2/1836; Bapt R 11,218 p 347; Burial R 11,218 p 353; Samuel Taylor Coleridge: Complete Poetical Works (ed. Hartley Coleridge 1912) p 68.

97.   EDMOND MURRAY DANIELL   *British*

ANTHONY STEWART Daniell, the younger of two brothers in Macao and Canton in the 1830s, was the father of this infant. The elder brother James had been a Chinese-language pupil of Dr Morrison (141). There is no record of the parents having married in Macao, and it is likely that they were already wed when they sailed for China. Anthony travelled out to set up in business with James as Daniell & Co, after James had been thrust out on his own devices when the Company, on the Select Committee of which he had served, closed down in 1834.

A third Daniell who visited in 1837 appears to have been at the Bengal end of the business. After taking a walk with Anthony and James and with Mr J.F. Davis (later Sir John, Governor of Hong Kong) and his wife, Harriet Low wrote that she could not 'imagine a greater contrast than these two brothers. One all fun and life, the other so languishing, so romantic, that the sound of anything gross or commonplace shocks him'. Anthony, the sensitive brother, was shocked at the barbarisms of Davis, who was 'very blunt, and sometimes not so nice in his observations'. The brothers' firm failed and was closed in June 1841.

The burial register records that the infant son of Anthony was 'said to have been born on the 12th September' to Harriett (with a double t) Daniell, and the service was conducted by the Rev G.H. Vachell on 16 May. Harriet (with one t) Daniell also gave birth to a daughter Gertrude at Macao on 30 June 1838. A portrait of a young woman sitting by an open piano painted by Chinnery (40) may be either of Harriett or of her sister-in-law, one of whom had, according to Harriet Low, possessed a piano, or of Julia Baynes, wife of a Company supercargo. There is a great deal less information available about Anthony than about James Daniell, who was married to Jane Le Goyt at Macao, and six children were born to them there. The subject of

179

one of Chinnery's portraits was Harriet May, the young daughter of one of the two Daniell brothers.

This small, granite chest-tomb, of sturdy design, stands close to the north cemetery wall some 2.5 metres east from the corner where the three Colledge infants lie buried. Its table-top, 10 cm thick with square edges and a substantial bed-mould, is surmounted by a closed funeral urn. The inscription is on the south face of the box and is well cut and very clear.

OTHER OBSERVERS: PCL: EDMOND MURRAY HARRIEL; JMB: EDMUND MURRAY DANIELL; HSPH: EDMUND MURRAY DANIELL, Numbered 57.
REFER TO: Loines pp 118–9, 138, 150, and 177–8; Marriage R 11,218 p 327; Bapt R 11,218 pp 331a, 332, 334, 335, 336, and 357; Burial R 11,218 p 348; FInd of 25/10/1838; Canton R of 18/6/1839; Morse iii pp 229 and 327 and iv pp 97, 110, 164, 230, 241, 254, and 324; Eitel pp 68 and 189; Nye Morning p 29; SFP&MA of 19/10/37 and 21/7/1841; Canton P of 12 and 19/10, 7 and 21/12/1839 and 4/7/1840; Waley p 78, 82, and 93; Blake p 36; Conner pp 218–9 and plates 91 (p 222) and 92 (p 223).

98.   CAROLINE REBECCA CROCKETT   *British*

LITTLE CAROLINE Crockett was born in Macao on 21 October 1830 to the wife of Captain Crockett (87), and baptized on 2 January following by the Rev G.H. Vachell, the Company chaplain, 'in the chapel of the British Factory in Macao'. The occupation of her father was recorded as 'free mariner' and his residence as Macao. She survived her infant sister (100) by just four months. The Rev Vachell conducted her burial service the day after she had died on board 'the British ship *Jane Lintin*', on which the family was living.

A small, pleasing, chest-tomb of coarse-grained granite, this memorial stands close to and to the east of 97, its head to the north.

SACRED
to the memory
of
CAROLINE REBECCA
eldest daughter of
Capt & Mrs Crockett
who died at LINTIN
NOVEMBER 21ST 1835
IN THE Sixth YEAR OF HER AGE

The podium is covered with turf but the plinth remains visible and, rising vertically from it, the sides and ends of the box have rectangular panels in high relief without lettering. The mason was not provided with her age until he was well ahead with the cutting of the inscription: the space left for 'Sixth' was not enough to allow the carving of letters of the same size as the rest of the last line.

OTHER OBSERVERS: HSPH: Numbered 58.
REFER TO: Canton R of 15/11/1830; Bapt R 11,218 p 333; Burial R 11,218 p 344.

99.   HUGO RUDOLPH JACOBUS SENN VAN BASEL   *Dutch*

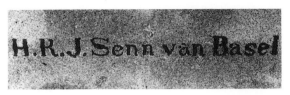

West side

THIS IS THE memorial of a two-days-old child 'born the 18th. Died the 20th June 1839 at Macao'. The archives at The Hague fill out the initials in the name: Hugo Rudolph Jacobus, the fourth child of Magdalenus Jacobus and his cousin Maria Elizabeth Senn van Basel, whom he married in September 1834. Had Hugo survived he would have been one of a family of four sons and four daughters. The others were long-lived. Their father was from a family with a distinguished record of both home and colonial service in the 18th and 19th centuries. He was in business at Canton and Macao from about 1826 and was also acting as the Dutch Consul at Canton from 1830; he left Canton in 1839 after closing the consulate. He returned later to continue his business, re-opening the consulate in 1844 as the full Consul and trading until early in 1847. He was replaced as Consul in March 1848, shortly before sailing from Hong Kong to take up the appointment as collector-general of taxes in Semarang, where he remained until he was dismissed in mid-1851 for complaining to the King about the Dutch East Indies government. He died in 1863 and his wife, full of years, in 1884.

This small chest-tomb, lying 4.5 metres east of 94 and directly south-east of 98, its long axis running north-south, is of simple but severe design. The sides and ends of the box have carved recesses. The lettering is difficult to read.

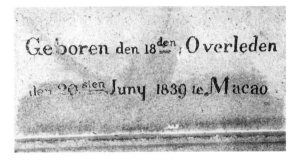

East side

OTHER OBSERVERS: JMB: H.R.J. SENN VAN BASAL; HSPH: SENN VAN BASEL, Numbered 59.
REFER TO: Nederlands 1945 pp 257–8; Bapt R 11,218 pp 341 and 356; Canton R of 3/7/1830, 15/11/1833, and 2/4 and 24/12/1839; Canton P of 5/12/1838, 6/4, 14/9, and 21/12/1839; Dutch Archives 1544, 1545, 1562, and 2660; CM of 5/3 and 17/12/1846, 28/1 and 4/3/1847, and 30/3 and 25/5/1848; FC&HKG of 11/12/1847, 8/3/1848, and 9/8/1851; ACK for 1836, 1837, and 1838; Monroe lxxxvii pp 118 and 125.

100. ANN CROCKETT *British*

SACRED
TO
THE MEMORY
OF
ANN, the Infant Daughter of
CAPT. & MRS. CROCKETT.
who died at MACAO JULY 21st 1835.
——— Aged 21 Days ———

IN A SAD SEASON for the Crockett family (see 87), within two months of their return to Lintin after the birth and death of Ann at Macao they had also lost their elder daughter Caroline (98). The age and the date both pose problems, as they are at variance with the records made and signed by the Rev G.H. Vachell after officiating at both baptism and death.

The infant was 'said to be born on 1 Sept.', baptized on the 20th, and buried on the 23rd. She probably died on the 21st, in which case the mason has carved the wrong month.

Her small, granite chest-tomb lies immediately to the east of its slightly larger neighbour, her sister's, which it closely resembles in design. They lie alongside, heads to the north cemetery wall. Cut on the table-top, the inscription is more artistically set out than that of 98 and easy to read, though the stone itself is fractured.

OTHER OBSERVERS: HSPH: Numbered 60.
REFER TO: Bapt R 11,218 p 341; Burial R 11,218 p 343.

101.   T [rest unknown]   *Nationality unknown*

APART FROM THE inscription, 'T 6 May', none of the cemetery records gives an inkling of what infant it was who was laid to rest below what is the cemetery's smallest memorial. It may have been put into place in the same period as the others that surround it, at some time between the late 1830s and the early 1840s. An intensive search of the local papers of the period revealed nothing, except that in one dated 6 May 1843 is announced the birth 'at Macao on the 22nd April [to] the lady of P. Tiedman Jr. Esq. of a son'. This is the sole birth of a European child recorded about then whose surname began with a T. There is no evidence, however, that this was the one who died two weeks later, nor that he was buried in the cemetery. The Dutch family of Tiedman was for many years associated with the foreign trade of Canton and Macao.

The memorial lies alongside and east of 100, its head under the north cemetery wall. It is cut from a single block of grey, medium-grained granite, to form five low-tiered steps, the top step forming the lettering surface. If the block rests on any foundation, that foundation lies hidden in the soil. The steps measure 85 x 47 cm, 72 x 37 cm, 66 x 29 cm, 59 x 22 cm, and 51 x 15 cm. If there was an inscription, all that can now be recognized is the one large letter on one line and the day and month of an unknown year on the next. Below is some indication of more letters, but so indistinct as to be indecipherable, though not through weathering.

OTHER OBSERVERS: PCL: no name given; JMB and HSPH: not listed.
REFER TO: Canton P of 6/5/1843.

102.   JOHN FRANCIS HIGHT   *British*

HIGHT WAS ONE of the small, confident group of merchants who started trading in Hong Kong very soon after the Colony was founded. He visited Macao briefly in September 1843: there is no record of this subsequent visit except for the notice of his death of 'Hong Kong fever'. Nor is there any evidence, beyond their uncommon family name, that he was related to 118.

This full-sized, granite chest-tomb is 64 cm in height to its top, from a podium 249 cm long, 157 cm wide and 28 cm high, and stands in line with 94 and 99, about a metre to the east of 99 and head-end to the north. Above a moulded plinth 15 cm high, the vertical sides and end of the box rise 41 cm to a moulding, which supports a somewhat severe table-top with vertical edges. On the sides and ends are simple rectangular panels carved in relief. The inscription is on the top, and strikingly well cut.

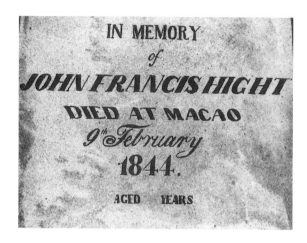

OTHER OBSERVERS: HSPH: Numbered 61.
REFER TO: FC&HKG of 14/9/1843; Canton P of 8/10/1842 and 17/2/1844.

103.   GEORGE W. HARRISON   *American*

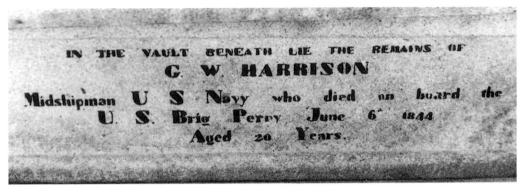

East side

NO INFORMATION about the family of this young man has been found, nor of the circumstances leading to his death, which the ship's log confirms, assigning to him the Christian name of George. The US naval brig *Perry* was of 280 tons and launched from Norfolk in May 1843, and it was her first commission that brought her to Macao.

His chest-tomb of coarse granite lies parallel to and 1.2 metres east of 102. A moulded plinth stands on a podium; the vertical sides and ends of the box are recessed with rectangular tablets with incised corners, and the box supports a polished, 20 cm-thick table-top with rounded edges and heavy mouldings.

The text of the inscription on the west side, poorly planned and spaced, is an extract from Byron: *Childe Harold* canto 3, stanza 57, but omits the second of the stanza's first four lines.

OTHER OBSERVERS: HSPH: Numbered 62.

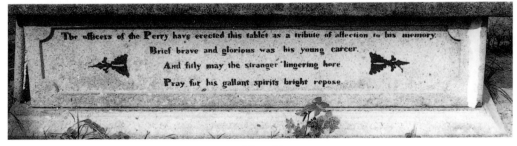

West side

RICHARD MARKWICK *British*

THERE WERE TWO Markwicks at Canton and Macao about this time: Richard and Charles. Hopkinson gives Richard's age at death as 45, Braga states that he was 'born on the 31st day of December 1791', which would make him 44.

In about 1825 Richard resigned his employment as steward in the Company's factory at Canton, and from 1826 to 1833 is listed among the private merchants there, as a shopkeeper. In 1830 he was a partner in Markwick & Lane, Co, a company that advertised itself as agent for the schooner *Sylph*, which carried passengers between Canton and Macao at a direct-route fare equivalent to HK$30. By 1833 he had his own firm, Markwick & Co, through which he also ran the European bazaar and a hotel at Canton, and the European warehouse and a hotel, Markwick's Tavern, in Macao. In 1836, C. Toogood Downing stayed at both hotels and left short descriptions of each. A small river-boat, an adjunct to his Canton hotel, was caught carrying contraband goods between his shop at Canton and the receiving ships off Lintin:

14 cases of silk goods and four containing a miscellany, in all worth over $5,000. The cases were confiscated while in transit. Markwick died in Macao at 8 am on Saturday 30 January 1836, after a lingering illness. His younger brother Charles was murdered in April 1857 at the age of 63, and lies buried in the Hong Kong Colonial Cemetery.

His grey granite chest-tomb is severe; its base, half a metre east of 103, supports a moulded plinth 15 cm high, 287 cm long and 183 cm wide, the box rising vertically 47 cm to a massive table-top, which has no bed-mould. The ends have recessed, rectangular tablets with incised corners. The table-top is 13 cm thick, has rounded edges, and carries no lettering.

OTHER OBSERVERS: HSPH: Numbered 63.
REFER TO: Hopkinson; Braga 1940; Morse iv pp 110, 128, 351, 356, and 358; Canton R of 16/2/1833 and 2/2/1836; Downing; Williamson; FC&HKG of 4/4/1857.

105. MARGARET BOVET *British-Swiss*

MARGARET – 'as universally loved, esteemed, and respected during her life as regretted after her death, which took place at Macao on 6 January 1837 at the age of 23 years and 23 days' – was the young English wife of the Swiss merchant Charles Henri Bovet, the youngest of five brothers in a family of watchmakers from Fleurier in the canton of Neuchâtel. Watches, clocks and musical boxes were among the goods most in demand in China; they were also more readily available to the independent foreign merchant than was opium. James Cox was the first merchant to focus specially on the mechanical instruments trade. His son, John Henry Cox, took over the business and was later in partnership at Canton with Daniel Beale (160).

In 1815, three of the Bovet brothers set up their business in London to supply the British market, and Beale's colleague, Charles Magniac, started dealing with them, to such effect that in 1818 Edouard, one of the London brothers, joined him. The business flourished; in 1834 another brother, Charles Henri, and in September 1836 a nephew, Louis, joined them from Switzerland. Louis thought Charles Henri's wife Margaret a merry girl and 'perhaps the one from among all the English families here whose company one would desire most', but she was beginning to suffer the problems in breast-feeding the couple's infant son Gustave that seem to have led a few months later to her death. The bereaved Charles, 'no longer the person he was', left his partnership in Bovet Brothers & Co in 1839 to return to Switzerland, the firm being well on the way to achieving a near-monopoly of the import into China of the 'montre chinoise' and musical boxes.

Fritz Bovet, who travelled out to joined the firm in 1848, was chiefly responsible for the growing popularity of the musical box among the Chinese. An accomplished musician, he studied, memorized, and wrote down popular Chinese tunes and sent his transcriptions back to the factories in Switzerland, where they were incorporated into musical boxes for the China trade.

Margaret's chest-tomb, of medium-grained grey granite, lies 1.5 metres further to the east than tomb 104. It is narrower, has a bed-mould, and is daintier than its neighbour. Its podium and moulded plinth, 145 cm wide and 229 cm long, support the 28 cm-high, vertical ends and sides of the box, and these are recessed and rise to a polished slab with rounded edges, and a well-proportioned over-moulding that frames the main inscription surface, which is in relief.

It carries the only French inscription in the cemetery. The surname AUSSI as it appears in the church list is due to faulty translation. A newspaper report assigns her death to 'Sunday night 8th January', but the date inscribed on the table-top, the 6th, is confirmed in a letter by Louis.

OTHER OBSERVERS: PCL: MARGARET BOVET AUSSI; HSPH: Numbered 64.
REFER TO: Neuchâtel (Louis's letters home); Bonnant; Canton R of 17/1/1837; Canton P of 8/9/1838; CM of 30/11/1848.

106. CLAZINA VAN VALKENBURG REYNVAAN *Dutch*

VOOR CLAZINA VAN VALKENBURG ECHTEGENOOT VAN H.G.J. REYNVAAN GEBOREN TE GRONINGEN 25 MAART 1822 OVERLEDEN TE MACAO 9 NOVEMBER 1846
Inscription

THE DATE OF '22 Maart' was inked in for a photograph, and was a deciphering error of the inksman. Clazina van Valkenburg (née Vietor) – the 'faithful wife of H.G.J. Reynvaan' – was born at Groningen in Holland on 25 March 1822, came out to Macao as a young girl, and there married Henry Gérard Jean Reynvaan on 24 August 1843. A son was born to them in Macao on 30 October the following year and christened Jacobus Marinus after his paternal grandfather. Her husband, seventh in a family of eight survivors, was born in Amsterdam in 1815, and joined the family firm of tea importers at Rotterdam. By 1840 he was already established as a merchant and as Netherlands commercial agent at Canton. He was associated with Senn van Basel (99) and journeyed a great deal between Batavia and Canton. His wedding to Clazina was conducted by the Rev W.M. Lowrie on 24 August 1843 in Macao. Less than a month after her death, he moved his firm from Macao to Canton, and that year almost lost his life in an attack by pirates, suffering 'two severe spear wounds in the neck, contusion on the head, shoulders, and thighs'; his Swiss companion was drowned. He liquidated his firm in May 1850 and moved to Hong Kong. By 1855 he had returned to Holland, where he died early in 1875.

Badly damaged and of grey, medium-grained granite, his wife's chest-tomb lies east-west, at right angles to all its neighbours and close to the north wall in the rear line of the group. Its base is underground, but most of a 15 cm-high plinth is visible, supporting a box with vertical sides and ends, each with a raised rectangular tablet surface surrounded by a moulded moat, with a 10 cm-thick under-moulded table-top with vertical edges.

The tablet on the south side carries the single inscription. The inscription is well cut, but repairs to three fractures on the surface have produced such distortion that its wording had to be sought from other records.

OTHER OBSERVERS: PCL: VAN H.C.I. REYNVAAN; HSPH: CLAZINA VAN VAI KINBURY, Numbered 65.
REFER TO: Nederlands 1949; Canton R of 6/10/1840 and 8/6/1841; Canton P of 19/6/1841 and 2/9/1843; CM of 7/1/1847, 12/8/1847, and 20/6/1850; Dixson HKG of 17/6/1850.

107. PETER KEY *British*

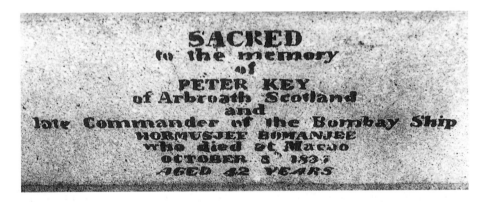

CAPTAIN PETER KEY of Arbroath was in command of other country ships before joining this, his last: the *Cornwallis* in 1833, the *Futty Salam* in 1834, whose agent at Canton was Framjee Pestonjee, and the *Hormusjee Bomanjee*, a ship of 759 tons which he sailed from Bombay to Canton for Dent & Co.

It was announced on 22 September 1835 that the *Hormusjee Bomanjee* would leave Whampoa for Bombay on 15 October under his command, but before it could set sail, he had died in Macao. When the ship's departure was again advertised on 13 October, the name of her captain was blank. The *Cornwallis* was the ship on board which the Treaty of Nanking was signed in 1842.

His grey, medium-grained granite chest-tomb lies north and south, end-on to the cemetery wall, with a podium and grooved plinth 251 cm long and 152 cm high, from which a box rises 25 cm vertically, its polished sides and ends grooved to form raised tablet surfaces. The table-top has a rounded moulding along its edges and is without lettering or carving. The inscription is deeply cut in very small lettering on the west side, not artistically crafted, and far from easy to read.

OTHER OBSERVERS: HSPH: Numbered 66; ship HOBMUSJEE.
REFER TO: Canton R of 16/9, 24/10/1833, 22/7/1834, and 22/9/1835; ACK for 1835.

108.   HENRY GARDNER BRIDGES   *American*

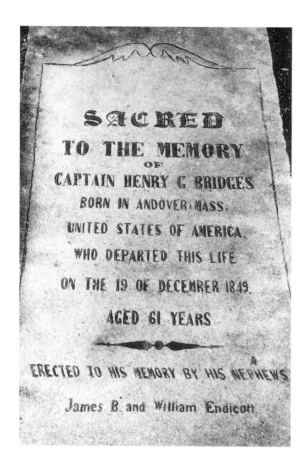

SACRED
TO THE MEMORY
OF
CAPTAIN HENRY G BRIDGES
BORN IN ANDOVER MASS.
UNITED STATES OF AMERICA
WHO DEPARTED THIS LIFE
ON THE 19 OF DECEMBER 1849
AGED 61 YEARS

ERECTED TO HIS MEMORY BY HIS NEPHEWS
James B. and William Endicott

BORN IN ANDOVER on 11 May 1791 into the two old maritime Salem families of Bridges and Gardner, Henry first went to sea when barely 15 and in a ship noted for its speed, the *Hazard*, of which John Gardner was captain. His own commands included the brig *Cambrian*, the ship *Janus* in 1829, and in 1839 the *Navigator*, which he sailed to Hong Kong just after British trade with Canton was stopped, before the British fleet blockaded Whampoa, and at a time when hostilities had become unavoidable. Because they were no longer permitted to ply up-river, British ships were being sold to Americans, and British merchants were chartering foreign ships, so that they might shift the goods then piling up before the blockade was enforced – cotton in Hong Kong and tea and silks at Canton (see Chapter 3, pages 22–3, for eyewitness descriptions).

It is not known precisely when it was that Captain Bridges decided to stop sailing: perhaps his nephews, James Bridges Endicott (166) and William Endicott, persuaded him. He may then have been stationed on a receiving ship up-river when taken ill, and had been sent to Macao to recover when he died. He married Eliza (née Chadwick) in 1824, and she bore him five children, each of whom died in its infancy. She died at Salem in March 1850, and it is doubtful if she had by then heard of her husband's death. It was through his sister Fidelia that he was related to the Endicotts (see also 33 and 34).

The date of his death is recorded as 'the evening of the 21st', both in the reports of local newspapers and in records of the Peabody Museum at Salem, Mass. The records in the museum, where an oil of Bridges hangs, painted by Henry Cheeves Pratt in 1834, state Whampoa to be the place of his death. The notes connected to copies of his portrait record the year of his birth as 1789.

His chest-tomb, of grey, medium-grained granite, lies in the extreme northeast corner of the cemetery, its head close to the north wall, its mitred podium almost touching that of 107. Not well-proportioned, the sides of the box, 254 cm long, and the ends, 147 cm wide, rise vertically 28 cm from a moulded plinth and are carved with raised tablets but carry no lettering. The inscription is well cut on a 10 cm-thick table-top, which has vertical edges, no moulding either below or above, and a grooved rectangle that frames the inscription area. The upper end of this frame is replaced by a simple, arched design, very similar to that of 6. The first word is in old English script.

OTHER OBSERVERS: HSPH: Numbered 67.
REFER TO: Cutler pp 36 and 396; Forbes p 152; FC&HKG of 26/12/1849; CM of 27/12/1849.

109. MARIA REES *British*

NO INFORMATION HAS come to light about Maria other than what is in the inscription, except that her death followed a short illness. Her husband, Thomas Rees, first arrived at Canton in July 1833 in command of the *Lord Amherst*, a barque of 328 tons, less than two months before the agents offered it for sale. One local newspaper mistakenly gives August as the month the ship arrived.

It was not sold, however, and Rees was on the high seas bound for Australia in May the next year, again as its master. Soon after returning, she was chartered by Dent & Co, anchoring at Lintin as an opium store-ship, and Rees was listed as living aboard her during the two years from 1836. There, he engaged in sharp practices for the agent's greater profit, and incurred the wrath of Jardine, Matheson & Co when he crippled a price agreement reached between the two opium rivals, by covertly offering a refund on shore of part of the price being settled by customers when they came on board. The subterfuge discovered, by 1838 he was back in command at sea, first on the *Emily Jane* and then the *Psyche*. He finally left in 1842 for England as a passenger, and died there the next year. He was a

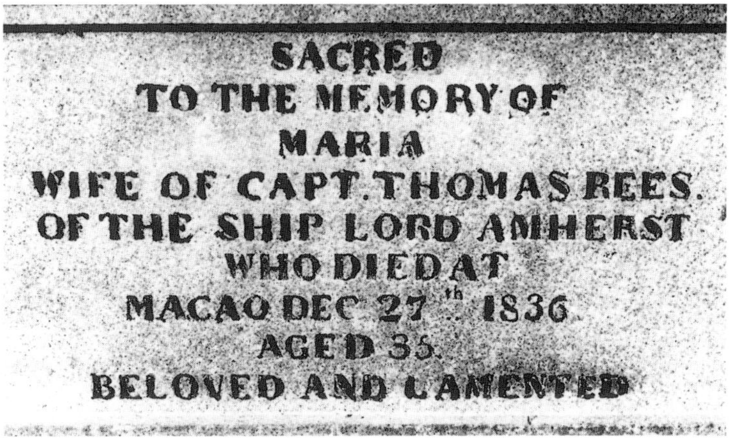

SACRED
TO THE MEMORY OF
MARIA
WIFE OF CAPT. THOMAS REES.
OF THE SHIP LORD AMHERST
WHO DIED AT
MACAO DEC 27 th 1836
AGED 35
BELOVED AND LAMENTED

brother of George Rees (127).

This grey granite chest-tomb stands about nine metres east of 105 and just south of 107. It has a massive, mitred podium 25 cm high, 249 cm long and 157 cm wide, and a polished and moulded plinth 257 cm long, 157 cm wide and 46 cm high, which supports the vertical sides and ends of a 25 cm-high box, each with a recessed panel. The inscription is deeply incised, well preserved, and easy to read.

OTHER OBSERVERS: HSPH: Numbered 68.
REFER TO: Canton R of 5/8 and 13/9/1833; FInd of 17/8/1837; Canton P of 8 and 28/9/1838 and 15/7/1843.

110. FREDERICK ILBERY *British*

TO THE MEMORY
OF
FRED^CK ILBERY
WHO DIED AT MACAO
23RD NOV^R 1833
AGED 19 YEARS
Inscription

THE NAME Ilbery or Ilberry (both spellings are used in the Company records and elsewhere) was not then uncommon at Canton. One of them was the husband of 57. An Ilbery was in partnership with Christopher Fearon (see 84). Nothing is known about the youth Frederick, however.

His is the most northerly of the four chest-tombs that lie along the eastern cemetery wall, in the last line of the Crockett group. Severe in design, it is of grey, medium-grain, polished granite, and stands on a podium and a vertical 15 cm-high plinth without moulding 203 cm long and 135 cm wide. The vertical, butt-jointed sides of the box, its sides and ends lacking edge-rolls or panels, rise 46 cm to a 10 cm-thick square-edged table-top without bed-mould, which supports a rectangular granite slab 124 cm long, 60 cm wide and 8 cm thick of similar design, which carries the inscription, framed by two rectangular grooves. The same inscription is also cut on the west end, but less artistically.

OTHER OBSERVERS: HSPH: Numbered 69.
REFER TO: Morse iv p 254.

111.　　EUPHEMIA DURANT　　*British*

SACRED
To THE MEMORY
OF
Mʀˢ EUPHEMIA DURANT
departed this life
JULY 13ᵗʰ 1834　　Aged 26

MRS DURANT frequently travelled on her husband's ship the *Good Success*, her name often on its passenger lists in the Canton papers of the early 1830s. It was a 'country ship' of 544 tons, plying between China and India and served locally by Jardine, Matheson & Co, its agents. Mrs Durant is first recorded as having arrived on board in March 1831 from Calcutta.

On one unusual occasion, Captain N. Durant was required by the Chinese Custom House on Macao's Praya Grande to get an official permit for his wife to board the boat that was to carry them to his ship, which was anchored in the Macao Roads. A tip would have been enough, but he refused to pay. A violent fracas broke out and he and his comprador were badly beaten. Local journalists took the Customs officers to task for their 'rapacity and insolence'; and the Company lodged so strong a protest with the Viceroy that he was constrained to order the mandarins in Macao to see to it that the Custom House ceased extorting money from foreigners. Captain Durant continued to sail in the *Good Success* on these voyages after his wife died, until he himself died at Cirgaum in April 1838, during an outbreak of cholera, aged 34. Mrs Durant's sister lies buried nearby in tomb 113.

Conner has suggested that Euphemia may have been the wife of Chinnery's friend of the 1840s, the French seafarer and opium dealer attached to Dent & Co, J.A. Durran (or Durant or Durand or Duran), and assigns to him the story of the refusal to bribe customs officers, but the evidence supports neither the suggestion nor his participation in the incident.

Euphemia's chest-tomb, of grey, medium-grained granite, is very much larger than its neighbour 110. The upper part of a polished, mitred podium stands some 10 cm above ground; the plinth, its ends 152 cm wide and sides 257 cm long, has a wide moulding which adds 15 cm more to the height, with the box rising 51 cm more. Each of the ends and sides of the box has a rectangular recessed tablet with concave corners; the table-top is polished and has no bed-mould. The inscription is cut on the south side, and is well preserved and easy to read.

OTHER OBSERVERS: HSPH: Numbered 70.
REFER TO: Canton R of 3/4, 13/5, and 15/10/1831, 16/2, 17/6, and 30/7/1833, 17/3/1835, and 12/6/1838; Morse iv p 337; Conner pp 252–4 and 283.

112.   NATHANIEL KINSMAN   *American*

NATHANIEL KINSMAN
of Salem Mass U.S.A.
Inscription on north side

NATHANIEL KINSMAN was born on 6 February 1798 into an old and eminent Massachusetts family. In six generations, the family produced 13 sea-captains and ship's masters; at the age of 20, Nathaniel went to sea himself on several voyages to Batavia (Jakarta), seeking to secure his fortune from his 'venture' cargo and, more importantly, to make contacts in the Far East for his future as a ship's master, one of them with his countryman John Shillaber (see 88, 95). Among his exploits, he freed a Malay slave in the East Indies; and in Calcutta he swopped portraits of American presidents for two elephants. The freedman, John Alley, whom he took back to Salem with him, lived out the remaining 67 years of his life with the Kinsman family, visiting Macao at least once in 1843. Of the tricky shipment of elephants, Kinsman said ruefully that 'they must have room to turn around, as they always tack ship with the vessel and stand athwart ships'.

At Salem on 9 June 1835, Kinsman married Rebecca (née Hamilton), who also came from an old Salem family: her maternal grandfather was one of George Washington's revolutionary gener-

SACRED
TO THE MEMORY
OF
NATHANIEL KINSMAN
SALEM MASS. U. S. A.

Died at Macao Ap. 30, 1817.

Aged 18 Years.

Top

als and a founder of the Order of the Cincinnati. Kinsman made his first voyage to China without her, and she accompanied him on his second, when he was to join the merchant firm of Wetmore & Co. With them on this journey went two of their three children, a niece, the Malay servant John Alley, and a cow. They arrived in Macao on 13 October 1843, and settled in a large house on the Praya Grande, where Rebecca precipitated herself into the social life of the foreign community, making a particularly effective hostess during the visit of the American plenipotentiary, Caleb Cushing. Nathaniel so prospered that by 1847 he expected to leave for home with his family to retire, had he not been stricken a second time by 'thickening of the pylorus', which carried him off. He was buried the day he died, in 'the most lovely spot that can be imagined', and the Rev. Dr William Speer (see 140) conducted the service at the graveside. His wife sailed for America some three week later. Their youngest son Abbot, who was born in Macao, visited his father's grave in 1863 when he was 19.

His wife was most diligent in writing up her diaries during her sojourn in Macao, and much can be gleaned from them now about the daily life of foreigners then living there.

Kinsman's chest-tomb of dressed granite lies close to and alongside 111, its mitred podium supporting a moulded plinth 254 cm long and 163 cm wide, rising 28 cm to the box and a substantial bed-mould, on which is a table-top with square corners and vertical edges 8 cm thick. Each of the sides and ends of the box has a rectangular tablet in relief 2.5 cm high, with concave corners.

OTHER OBSERVERS: HSPH: Numbered 71.
REFER TO: Kinsman; Monroe; Monroe Mary passim; Canton P of 21/10/1843 and 30/3/1844; FC&HKG of 8/5/1844 and 4/5/1847.

113.　ISABELLA RACHEL SUTHERLAND　*British*

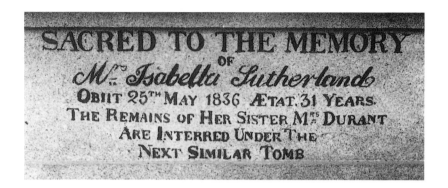

SACRED TO THE MEMORY
OF
Mrs Isabella Sutherland
OBIIT 25TH MAY 1836 ÆTAT. 31 YEARS.
THE REMAINS OF HER SISTER MRS DURANT
ARE INTERRED UNDER THE
NEXT SIMILAR TOMB

MRS SUTHERLAND was a sister of Euphemia Durant (111). She lived at Calcutta with her husband, James Sutherland, and it seems safe to assume that he was associated with his brother-in-law Captain Durant in the country trade between India and China. She and her family arrived in Macao as passengers on the *Cowasjee Family* only three days before she died. She was buried on 27 May in a ceremony conducted by the Rev G.H. Vachell, then chaplain to the Superintendent of Trade. James left Macao on Captain Durant's ship the *Good Success* on 1 September bound for Bombay.

Her grey, medium-grained granite chest-tomb is exactly similar in size and design to that of her sister (111), but they no longer lie next to one another, 112 having since been – for some inscrutable reason and quite contrary to the stated intention – inserted between them. It is the most southerly in this last line of the group.

OTHER OBSERVERS: HSPH: Numbered 72.
REFER TO: Canton R of 24/5, 7/6, and 6/9/1836; Burial R 11,218 p 348.

114.　JOHANNES PHILIPPAS ('BERNARDUS') ZEEMAN　*Dutch*

BERNARDUS ZEEMAN (as he was known in Macao) was, as the inscription shows, second-in-command of the Dutch factory at Canton, having been an 'assistant' from 1792 until the

death of John Rabinel (43) in 1816, when he was promoted second supercargo to replace J. H. Bletterman, who became chief. Zeeman was not himself replaced as assistant. By the time he died, the Dutch proportion of the trade of Canton had much reduced.

His wife was Maria Santa (née da Crusa), who bore him two children in Macao, Elizabeth in 1803 and Thomas Johannes in about 1806. In 1816 or thereabouts, the two children were painted together in Holland by the English painter Charles Howard Hodges (1774–1837).

The head of Zeeman's medium-grained granite chest-tomb is close to the south wall, parallel to and alongside 66. A mitred podium supports a moulded plinth 15 cm high, the vertical sides and ends of a box 46 cm high with recessed rectangular tablets, and a table-top with square edges resting on a bed-mould and carrying the inscription, in which the spacing of the letters shows that the mason was unused to the Dutch language.

TER GEDACHTENIS
VAN
DEN WEL EDELE HEER
BERNARDUS ZEEMAN
TWEEDE DER NEDERLANDSCHE
FACTORY TE CANTON IN CHINA
GEBOOREN AMSTERDAM
DEN 6 APRIL 1767
OVERLEEDEN MACAO
DEN 22 JULY 1821

OTHER OBSERVERS: PCL: BERNARDUS ZEEMAN TWEEDE; JMB and HSPH: ZUMAN; HSPH: Numbered 73.

REFER TO: Dutch Archives; Morse iii pp 348 and 176 and iv pp 6 and 72; Gent Mag for January 1846 p 110; Bakker.

The Zeeman (right) and Urmston tombs

197

115. GEORGE B. URMSTON *British*

IN MEMORY
OF
GEORGE B. URMSTON
WHO DIED THE 20th: MAY, 1813.
AGED EIGHT MONTHS & TWO DAYS.
Inscription

THE FATHER OF the infant George was James Brabazon Urmston, a senior member of the Company, which he joined in 1799. His grandfather was a sea-going member of the Company from 1763, and by 1795 became commodore of a fleet of 30 East Indiamen. By 1812 James was one of the supercargoes below the Select Committee at Canton. His principal responsibility was the weighing of tea, for which he drew a net annual commission of over two thousand pounds. Within seven years he succeeded as the Company's chief, a position he held until retirement. George was born in Macao on 18 September 1812 and baptized in the Company house on the 26th by the then chief of the Company, J.F. Elphinstone. Urmston was closely involved in the H.M.S. *Topaze* events that led in 1822 to the evacuation of the British factory at Canton and a threatened suspension of trade (see also Chapter 2 pages 17–19). In November 1826 he left on retirement, to be succeeded as chief of the select committee by Sir William Fraser (62). In 1833 Urmston published his *Observations on the China Trade*, arguing the advantages of removing it entirely from Canton to Chusan. Nothing further has come to light about the family. The name should not be confused with that of Urmson (37).

Its head close to the convent wall, George's granite chest-tomb is 30 cm east of 114. Its podium supports a moulded plinth 13 cm high, and each of the vertical ends and sides of the box carries a recessed rectangular tablet, below a substantial bed-mould and an 8 cm-thick table-top with vertical edges and square corners. The lettering is well preserved, well cut, and easy to read.

OTHER OBSERVERS: HSPH: GEORGE G. URMSTON, Numbered 74.
REFER TO: EIR&D for 1815, 1817, and 1822; Chatterton p 172; Morse iii pp 177–8, 209, 242, 307, and 346, and iv pp 38, 40–1, 87 and 122.

116.   CAWTHORNE CAPPER   *British*

NO RECORD HAS been found either about Captain Capper or about his father Jasper in London.

The memorial lies at the foot of 115, its head to the east. A mitred podium and moulded plinth support a box with 46 cm vertical sides and ends, on which are carved rectangular raised tablets with inverted quirk corners, a bed-mould, and a 5 cm-thick table-top, which has vertical edges and square corners. The inscription, which is on the table-top, has no moulding frame, and the lettering is well-preserved. Braga, however, records a 'st' after '31', and Hopkinson reads the figure as '30'.

OTHER OBSERVERS: HSPH: CAPt CAMTHORNS CAPPER, Numbered 75.

117.   JOHN KEY WISHART   *British*

NO RECORD HAS been found of this captain of the barque *Countess of Minto*, beyond what is shown here.

His chest-tomb is one of three (117, 118 and 119) which stand close together, their heads towards the east and some 4.5 metres north of 116, all similar in size and design to 116 except for the inscriptions, each of which is cut in the tablet on its south side. The lettering on this tomb is deeply incised, but small and not easy to read. A local report of his death gives his name as 'John R. Wishart'.

OTHER OBSERVERS: HSPH: JOHN KEY WHISHART, Numbered 76.
REFER TO: FC&HKG of 9/11/1843.

118.   MATTHEW JAMES HIGHT   *British*

SACRED TO THE MEMORY OF
MATTHEW JAMES HIGHT
Late Commander of the Antares,
who departed this life on the 6th September 1843.
Aged 27 years
Inscription

HIS IS A most uncommon name, yet there are two such in the cemetery: the other being 102. There was a Captain Hight in command of the *Roxburgh Castle*, a British ship of 1,200 tons, when it arrived in November 1854 from Whampoa. A Mary H. Hight died at Hong Kong in 1868 and lies buried in the Colonial Cemetery, Happy Valley. They are all likely to be of one and the same family based in the region in the 19th century. Captain Hight died at Taipa, where his ship was probably lying in the Roads. On a previous run, the *Antares* left the estuary waters on 5 February 1841 for Calcutta by way of Singapore. He is recorded above as British because he was with a British schooner in the India-China trade,

The middle one in the trio of chest-tombs, his granite memorial is slightly taller than its neighbours, the sides and ends of the box being 51 cm high. Their podia are almost touching, and leave very little room. Like the others, Hight's inscription is cut on the south side.

OTHER OBSERVERS: HSPH: MATHEW JAMES HIGHT, Numbered 77.
REFER TO: Canton P of 9/9/1843; Dixson HKG for 1854; FInd of 1/5/1841.

119.   ROBERT McCARTHY   *British*

THERE WERE MANY ships with the name *Eliza* trading in India and China. Captain McCarthy's ship belonged to the Company's country service, in which he was an officer of many years standing. On his previous trip, he had arrived at Hong Kong on 15 March 1843 from Calcutta, sailing up to Whampoa on the 17th, and seems then to have been moving to and fro regularly: on 25 May he made for Whampoa, and must have been in Macao early in August, where his death took place after a sickness of only a few days. The local newspaper report states that he died in his 38th year.

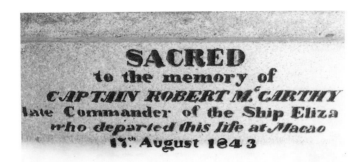

The last and most northerly of this trio, his granite chest-tomb is identical in design and measurements to 117, and lies with its podium touching the north side of that of 118. The inscription is cut in the tablet on the south side of the box. Its deep but small letters are so close together as to be difficult to read.

OTHER OBSERVERS: HSPH: CAPTAIN ROBERT McCHARTHY, Numbered 78.

120. WILLIAM MORGAN *British*

SACRED TO THE MEMORY OF
CAPTAIN WILLIAM MORGAN
late Commanding the British Ship General Wood
who died in Macao on the 14th July 1843.

Inscription

CAPTAIN MORGAN was in the service of Jardine, Matheson & Co as a captain of their ships carrying freight between Bombay, the Straits, Manila and China from about 1833 to 1840, first on the *Pascoa*, then on the *Scaleby Castle*, a ship the firm had bought from the Company after its monopoly ceased in 1833, and on which in July 1839 Morgan's wife joined him for the journey from India to China. She returned to England in January the next year to see her mother, and must have sailed back again, for she gave birth to a son at Hong Kong only five months before Captain Morgan died in Macao. By June 1840 his active seafaring life had reached its end, and he was appointed as his firm's agent at Hong Kong, living on board the barque *General Wood*, their depot ship. Settling down to a new life

SACRED TO THE MEMORY OF
CAPTAIN WILLIAM MORGAN
late Commanding the British Ship General Wood
who died in Macao on the 11 July 1843

ashore as a trading agent, he bought Lot 50 for $207. His firm sold the *Scaleby Castle* in 1841. At the time he was made Justice of the Peace in June 1843, he was living in a bungalow on Caroline Hill, Hong Kong.

Separated from 119 by a gap of 10 metres, this polished, grey granite chest-tomb continues the west line northwards; its mitred podium and the plinth, 254 cm long, 157 cm wide and 28 cm high, are of the usual design, as are the ends and sides of the box, with their rectangular tablets carved in high relief, with incised corners.

A thick bed-mould with square corners and vertical edges supports the table-top. The inscription is cut in deep lettering on the south side tablet.

OTHER OBSERVERS: HSPH: Numbered 79.
REFER TO: Williamson; Canton P of 8/9 and 27/10/1838, 20/7/1839, 18/1/1840, 3/7/1841, and 4/3 and 15/7//1843; SFP&MA of 14/12/1837 and 25/6/1840; Canton R of 28/2/1843; FC&HKG of 30/6/1843 and 7/6/1845; Morse iv pp 373ff.

121.   JAMES BATEMAN   *British*

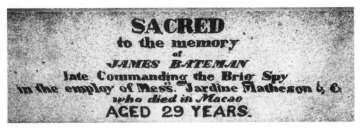

South side

**ERECTED
AS A MARK OF ESTEEM AND AFFECTION
by his Brother Officers.**

Inscription on north side

CAPTAIN JAMES BATEMAN died at some time after 1833, when the firm of Jardine, Matheson & Co was first established. Nothing beyond what is in the inscriptions has been discovered.

His granite chest-tomb is like 120 in measurement and design and lies immediately to its north, the two podia almost touching. The lower-case letters of the south side inscription are very small and difficult to read.

OTHER OBSERVERS: HSPH: Numbered 80.

122.   JOHN HENRY LARKINS   *American*

**SACRED TO THE MEMORY OF
JOHN HENRY LARKINS
who died in Macao on the 30th March 1943
Aged   Years**

Inscription

LARKINS WAS A member of the firm of Fletcher, Larkins & Co in Macao, and died there of smallpox on 30 March 1843, after only a few days' sickness. There is no evidence that the 'Larkins' of 90 was related to him. Standing three metres further north than 121 and similar in measurements to it and to 120, this polished, fine-grain, grey granite chest-tomb is readily distinguished from them by the closed funeral urn, 81 cm high and 33 cm in diameter, which surmounts its table-top. The urn stands on its own podium carved from one piece of stone, with base 132 cm long, 61 cm wide and 13 cm high, and three rectangular steps, the lowest 6 cm, the middle 5 cm and the uppermost 2.5 cm high. The podium of the tomb itself is mitred, the moulded plinth 254 cm long, 127 cm wide and 30 cm high supports its box, and the table-top has a bed-mould. The inscription is carved on the south-side tablet in lettering easy to read, and lacks an age at death.

OTHER OBSERVERS: HSPH: Numbered 81.
REFER TO: Canton R of 4/4/1843; FC&HKG of 6/4/1843.

---

123.   ANDREW FORREST   *British*

SACRED TO THE MEMORY OF
ANDREW FORREST MARINER
for many years in the employment of
Messrs Jardine Matheson & Co in China
who died in Macao 19th January 1843
Aged 43 Years

Inscription on south side

ERECTED
as a tribute of esteem and affection
by his friends and brother officers.

Inscription on north side

AT THE TIME OF Forrest's death, he was described as the second officer on the *Lady Hayes*. He died while the ship was in the Taipa Roads. He appears among those working on a storeship at Lintin in 1838. The *Lady Hayes* was a country ship operated by Jardine, Matheson & Co (see also 82).

Lying alongside 122, this chest-tomb is very similar to it, but has no urn, its plinth is 15 cm high, and its table-top is somewhat thicker. The lower-case lettering of the inscription on the south side is deeply cut, but small and difficult to read, a problem increased by the closeness of the tomb to its neighbour. The absence of punctuation accounts for the wrong surname of 'Mariner' in the church list. Some accounts spell his name with one 'r'.

OTHER OBSERVERS: PCL: ANDREW FOREST MARINER; HSPH: Numbered 82.
REFER TO: Canton R of 24/1/1843; ACK for 1838.

WILLIAM MARQUIS *British*

SACRED TO THE MEMORY OF
CAPTAIN WILLIAM MARQUIS
Honble East India Companys service
who died in Macao 4th December 1842
Aged 42 Years

CAPTAIN WILLIAM MARQUIS was in the Orient for many years. He was present at an unusual meeting held in Canton by commanders and officers in the service of the Company on 7 November 1833, to plan an expression of gratitude to William Jardine, a leading free trader. The British ship *Thames*, a 'fine, handsome ship' of about 1,400 tons, was one of the fastest of the East Indiamen, and Marquis was her master when she set out from London for Bombay in July 1841. He was probably commanding her when he visited Canton in 1833, for she was in China late that year. She had completed 11 trips to China under the Company's flag by the time its China operations ceased. It is not clear who bought her, but she was sold for $10,700.

Captain Marquis was still her master when he died on board on a Sunday at 2 pm in Macao, after a lingering illness.

His granite chest-tomb, north of a gap of 4.5 metres, lies in line with and parallel to 123, to which it is similar in size and design. The inscription is cut on the tablet on the south side in deep lettering, too small to be easily read.

OTHER OBSERVERS: HSPH: Numbered 83.
REFER TO: Canton R of 15/11/1833 and 6/12/1842; FInd of 18/11/1841; Morse iv p 382; Chatterton; Canton P of 10/12/1842.

125.   J. FERDINAND DAVID   *American*

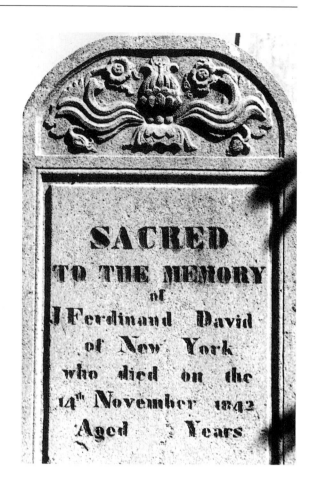

NO INFORMATION HAS been found of David's family, his age at death, and career. His record in the inscription is meagre, and probably he had no relatives or close friends in Macao.

His headstone is of medium-grained, dressed granite and in line with trees growing between the west line of the group and the chest-tombs of the Riddles Row. Rough-hewn at the back, top and sides, it measures 156 cm high, 75 cm wide and 14 cm thick, and stands facing west behind a coarse-grained, granite step 112 cm long and 43 cm wide. Its top is a flat curve springing directly from the sides. The surface is carved in two parts: an inscription surface framed by a rectangular moat 2.5 cm wide and 1.3 cm deep, and above it a recessed segment filled with an elaborate device in high relief. The inscription is handsomely cut and well preserved.

OTHER OBSERVERS: HSPH: Numbered 84.

SACRED
TO THE MEMORY
of
J Ferdinand David
of New York
who died on the
14th November 1842
Aged   Years

126.   ROBERT FRANCIS MARTIN   *British*

OF CAPTAIN MARTIN no information has been found other than that in the inscription itself.

Some nine metres north of 124, his memorial and 127 are a very similar pair of grey, fine-grained, polished granite chest-tombs lying close together, long axes east-west, mitred podia almost touching, but separate from the others in the line. Each moulded plinth, 249 cm long and 157 cm wide, supports the vertical sides of a box 28 cm high, on which are carved in high relief rectangular tablets with deeply incised corners. The bed-mould and table-top of each tomb are carved from one piece of granite 15 cm thick, the table-top having square corners and vertical edges and lacking surface moulding and inscription.

The inscription is deeply cut on the south-side tablet and the lower-case lettering is far from easy to decipher. The spelling of the ship's name is in the old form Buccleugh (modern Buccleuch). The Hopkinson list gives the name of the ship simply as the *Duke*, a typographical error.

OTHER OBSERVERS: HSPH: Numbered 85.

GEORGE REES *British*

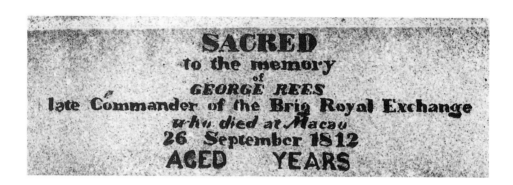

OF CAPTAIN George Rees's seafaring life and family there is little information. He was in command of the ship *Austen* in 1838, when it was lying at Lintin, possibly a storeship or, more probably, a country ship discharging a cargo of opium from India. In August-September 1840, he sailed from Mauritius to Calcutta as master of the English barque *Milford*, and in December 1841 was reported as in command of the brig *Royal Exchange*, then at Canton and operated by Jardine, Matheson & Co. Maria, the wife of his brother, Captain Thomas Rees, was buried in the cemetery (109) in 1836. The lack of George's date of birth and of his age at death in 1842 suggests that he no longer had any relatives or close friends living in Macao.

His chest-tomb lies north of and very nearly touching 126, the north-east corner of its podium almost touching the base of 133 in the east line. For a description of the tomb, see its fellow, 126. The inscription, which is cut on the north-side tablet, is in extremely small lettering and very difficult to read. The inking is in error, as it shows the date of death as 1812; both Braga and Hopkinson have read it accurately as 1842.

OTHER OBSERVERS: HSPH: Numbered 86.
REFER TO: Canton P of 8/9/1838 and 18/12/1841; FInd of 24/9/1840; Williamson.

128. NATHANIEL SIMPSON *American*

NOTHING BEYOND WHAT is in this inscription has been discovered of Nathaniel Simpson. The *Constellation* was on a mission in the Far East between 1840 and 1844.

Rough-hewn at the back, his grey, medium-grained granite headstone measures 104 cm high, 51 cm wide and 13 cm thick, its top a flat arch springing from the inside edge of two shoulders, which a groove 2.5 cm from the top edge converts into scrolls ending in coils. It stands facing west, north of 126, its back in line with 125, and behind a coarse-grained, granite step 89 cm long and 36 cm wide, rough-hewn on sides, back, and top. Its foot-stone is also of grey, medium-grained, dressed granite, 48 cm high, 28 cm wide and 9 cm thick, and is unusually carved in the same shape as its headstone. The inscription is poorly cut, has a spelling mistake in 'Remains', and is wearing badly. It is so similar to 76 and 77 that all three are almost certainly cut by the same mason. Other observers give the year of death as 1849, but the ship's log places it as 1842 and the date as 25 August.

OTHER OBSERVERS: HSPH: Numbered 87.

Sacred to the Memory
of
NATHANIEL SIMPSON
late a Seaman of the U.S.S. Constellation
WHO DIED AUGUST 24th 1842
This Stone Was Placed over his Remans
BY HIS SHIPMATES

129.   JAMES McDOUALL   *British*

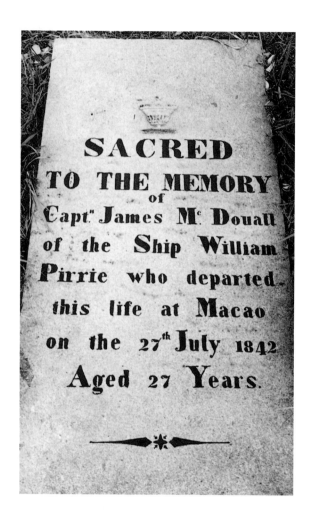

THE NAME IS given by other observers as McDonald, which may be either correct or a typographical error copied from one another. There is record of a Captain Macdonald (or N.M. McDonnal) in command of a British ship *William Pirrie*, which arrived from Bombay in south China waters in June 1842, its cargo consigned to W. & T. Gemmel & Co in Macao. She lay at Whampoa from late that month to early September, ready for freight or charter from its agent, J.M. Bull. She departed for London on the 9th. There was also a ship called the *William Perrie*, built in 1839 for Perrie & Co of Belfast. Of Captain McDouall (if that was his name) or his ship the *William Pirrie* (if that was her name), there is no adequate information.

On the ground, about nine metres north of 127 and in line with it and 126, lies this grey, fine-grained, rectangular, polished granite slab, 170 cm long, 76 cm wide and 15 cm thick, its head towards the east. The inscription is well cut and excellently preserved: the contrast with the work on 128 could hardly be greater. Above the word 'SACRED' is carved a closed, fluted urn in low relief; and below the last line, a simple linear decoration.

OTHER OBSERVERS: JMB and HSPH: JAMES McDONALD; HSPH: Numbered 88.
REFER TO: Peabody; Canton P of 11/6/1842, weekly advertisements from 25/6 to 3/9/1842, and 10/9/1842.

JOSEPH DAVIES *British*

OF OFFICER DAVIES nothing beyond what is in the inscription has been found, and only one reference to his ship. In 1839, a barque named *Crest* was built in Sunderland for a Hull owner, to be commissioned for the London-Calcutta trade.

On the ground in line with 125 and 128 and to the northwest of 129, from which it is separated by a tall bauhinia tree, lies this grey, fine-grained, rectangular, polished granite slab, 147 cm long, 81 cm wide and 15 cm thick, its head to the east, and similar in layout and lettering to 129. Above and below the inscription, well cut with broad lettering and well preserved, are simple linear designs.

OTHER OBSERVERS: HSPH: Numbered 89.
REFER TO: Peabody.

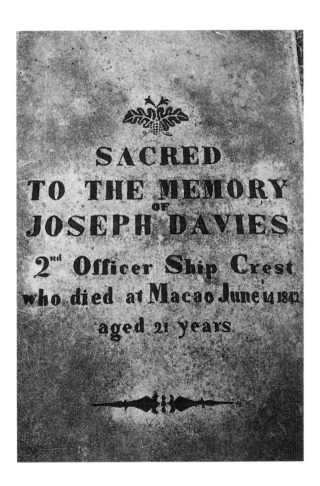

SACRED
TO THE MEMORY
OF
JOSEPH DAVIES
2nd Officer Ship Crest
who died at Macao June 14 1842
aged 21 years

131.   JOHN ASTELL   *British*

JOHN ASTELL DIED of dysentery while serving on HMS *Alligator*. The newspaper report spelled his name 'Astle', gave the year of his death as 1841, and stated that he died at the Naval Hospital in Macao, where there was no permanent naval hospital. He should not be confused with John Harvey Astell, a writer with the Company in the early 1820s, who stayed on with Lord Napier and succeeded Sir George Best Robinson as deputy to the Superintendent of Trade.

Lying 3.7 metres directly east of the slab 130, this large, grey, fine-grained, polished granite chest-tomb stands on a mitred podium and a moulded plinth 10 cm high, head to the east, the sides of its box 254 cm long and the ends 157 cm, rising 28 cm to a bed-mould and an 8 cm-thick, medium-grained, granite table-top, which bears the inscription, well cut, well preserved, and easy to read.

OTHER OBSERVERS: HSPH: JOHN ANSTELL, Numbered 90.
REFER TO: Canton R of 9/11/1841.

132.   EDWARD FITZGERALD   *British*

AS REPORTED IN the press of 26 June 1841, Lieutenant FitzGerald was wounded in the leg during an action off Canton on 24 May 1841 and died on board his ship. He was buried the next day, the service attended by the British Commander-in-Chief Sir Hugh Gough (whose name Mount Gough on Hong Kong Island commemorates) and his staff, many of his brother officers and several Macao residents. Sixty-three of his friends and shipmates subscribed a total of $273 for the memorial. Six months after he had died, one friend supplied the local press with a verse and some detail of the monument's chaste design, its 'proportions beautiful', and the construction, which had been 'left to the vigilant care of Dr Allan [Allen], at present of the naval hospital in Macao'. Dr Allen's ministrations produced a monument 'as pleasing to the eye of taste as any other in the cemetery':

SACRED
to the
MEMORY
of
LIEUTENANT
ED. FITZGERALD
late
belonging to
H.M.S. MODESTE
who died at
MACAO
on the 22nd. June 1841
from the effects
of a wound received
while gallantly storming
the enemy's battery at
CANTON.
Inscription on west side

THIS MONUMENT
was erected
by
his numerous friends
and shipmates
in the Squadron in which
he has served
as a tribute of respect to his
MEMORY
Inscription on east side

There is a tear for all that die;
A mourner o'er the humblest grave;
But nations swell the funeral cry
And triumph weeps above the brave.

His ship, a sloop of 568 tons, was built in 1837 with an armament of 19 guns; she carried a complement of 120 men. Her commission for China,

under the command of Harry Eyres, brought her into the Macao Roads five kilometres offshore in July 1840, together with the *Melville* and the *Columbine*. From there they joined the main body of a fleet assembling under Admiral Elliot in Tung Koo Bay on the eastern side of the Pearl River estuary. As part of the fleet's light division, she took part in all the hostilities in north China off Chusan and returned to be in the action at Canton in 1841. The *Modeste* was much in demand, fighting off Chinese fire-rafts and putting landing parties ashore for the shallow-water operations along the Pearl River.

It was in a landing action against a battery between the Dutch and French Follies near Canton that FitzGerald received his fatal wound. In his journal for 11 June 1841, Surgeon Cree records that while ashore from his ship, at anchor in the Macao Roads, he 'went to see poor Lord Edward Clinton who is staying at this hotel [Smith's in Macao] having been wounded in the knee at Canton. He is a lieutenant of the *Modeste*. I had known him before, in the Mediterranean. The ball had lodged in the knee joint, but had been extracted. There was great inflammation. I saw him with Allen, the Surgeon of Macao Hospital, who is attending him and wished to consult with me about him. There is no doubt amputation ought to have been performed, but I believe he would not consent to it. He has much fever and is labouring under great nervous shock. The poor fellow died two days after I saw him.'

This can hardly be coincidence: both FitzGerald and Clinton were wounded in the leg during an action near Canton, both were lieutenants and both aboard the *Modeste*. FitzGerald received his wound on 24 May 1841, dying from its effects a month later, on 22 June. Meantime, Surgeon Cree was called in to consult Dr Allen about 'Clinton's' condition, and 'Clinton' died two days later, apparently on 13 June, possibly Cree's error made at a later date. The dates vary, so do the name and the place of death; otherwise, the circumstances of both coincide. Searches in Burke's Peerages have revealed nothing directly. FitzGerald may have been a younger son of the 2nd Duke of Leinster, which would account for the title Cree gave him and the family name on the monument; the FitzGeralds were not infrequently christened 'Edward'. If Edward was a son of the 2nd Duke, then the Irish revolutionary, the Lord Edward FitzGerald who was fatally wounded in 1798 as he was being arrested on a charge of treason, and who is generally credited with causing the abolition of the Irish parliament in 1801, was his uncle; but there is no direct evidence.

FitzGerald's naval monument, just south of 131 and even closer to the east of slab 129, is a grey, medium-grained, polished granite column, square in section, surmounted by an overlapping, square bed-mould and table cut in one piece and carrying a closed urn, the height of these rising to 254 cm. The column is on a moulded plinth, 15 cm high and 67 cm square, mounted on a podium of two granite steps, of which the upper is 109 cm square, formed by two slabs lying north-south, and the lower by bonded slabs measuring 173 cm square. Carved on the sides of the column are recessed rectangular surfaces with concave corners. The urn is carved in relief, oak leaves below and a linked chain above, emblems fitting a naval officer.

There is, however, a memorial (No. 328) to Lord Edward Pelham Clinton in the Hong Kong Cemetery, which states that he died on 12 May 1842 'on board H.B.M.S. Harlequjin ... his body was committed to the deep of the Gulf of Siam'. Cree created the discrepancies: he might have known both of them and confused the two.

OTHER OBSERVERS: JMB: Ed. Fitz Gerald; HSPH: Ed. FitzGerald, Numbered 91.
REFER TO: Canton P of 26/6 and 18/12/1841; Cree p 88; Burke 1976, 1980.

133.   LORD HENRY JOHN SPENCER CHURCHILL   *British*

SACRED
To the Memory of
THE RIGHT HON^{BLE}
LORD HENRY JOHN SPENCER CHURCHILL
4TH SON OF
GEORGE 5TH DUKE OF MARLBORUGH
Inscription on north face

THIS MONUMENT
IS ERECTED BY
HIS OFFICERS AND PETTY OFFICERS
IN TESTIMONY OF THEIR
ESTEEM AND AFFECTION
Inscription on east face

LORD JOHN WAS a son of the illustrious English family of Spencers, of which his father was a notoriously profligate member, 'the spendthrift, spend-all fifth Duke, the Regency buck who had undermined the family finances', we are told by A.L. Rowse. It was he who revived the old family name of Churchill to be joined with that of Spencer. Lord John was born on 22 September 1797 to the Duke's wife, Lady Susan Stewart, daughter of the 8th Earl of Galloway. He entered the Royal Navy and was promoted to Captain in 1826, and from 1839 he assumed command of the *Druid* on service in the East Indies. The *Druid* arrived in Macao from Sydney in January 1840, to join the fleet which was then assembling in the Pearl River for operations with the expeditionary force in China. (For further notes on the expedition see 132, 136 and 138, and Chapter 3 pages 24–7.)

While the fleet was in the Capsuimoon Strait,

South side

Churchill's death, at 10 am on Wednesday 3 June, followed a week of severe sickness and was attributed to congestion of the brain complicated by an attack of dysentery. His body was taken to Macao and buried early in the morning of the 5th. In a large funeral procession, almost as large as that accompanying the coffin of Sir Humphrey Senhouse (136), preceded by a Portuguese band playing the funeral march, were the Governor of Macao and a detachment from the local garrison, Captain Elliot, Captain Smith and Captain Warren of the Royal Navy, many of the officers of the three warships in port, some 80 sailors and 30 marines, and practically all the foreign residents. Captain Elliot read the service. Lord John's death was reported as casting a deep gloom over the whole of the British community, services and civilians alike.

One of three naval memorials standing together in the line (132, 133 and 136), Churchill's is the largest and most imposing monument in this part of the cemetery. Of grey, medium-grained, polished granite, it comprises a base, a two-stepped podium, and a cube box with bonded sides capped by a table 15 cm thick with a bed-mould, surmounted by a closed funeral urn. The base is 368 cm long and 279 wide, each step of the podium is 10 cm high, the lower 290 x 224 cm, the upper 221 x 160 cm. On the podium stands the monument proper, the cube, its base surrounded by a bonded, moulded plinth 133 cm long, 97 cm wide and 18 cm high. The east and west faces of the cube are supported laterally by consoles, whose lower scrolls rest on the upper step and upper scrolls against the plinth sides, all carved with simple grooves running parallel to the console edges.

The north and south faces of the cube carry the main inscriptions cut on granite squares; the west face carries the crests of the Churchills and the Spencers carved side by side in low relief. The urn crowning the monument has two naval designs in relief, oak-leaves and a linked chain similar to those on the urn of 132. There are several errors in the inscriptions, including the title of the 5th Duke of Marlborough, to correct which an unsuccessful attempt was made.

OTHER OBSERVERS: HSPH: Numbered 92.
REFER TO: Gregory; Canton P of 18/3 and 6/6/1840; Canton R of 31/3 and 6/6/1840.

134.   SAMUEL BURGE RAWLE   *American*

SAMUEL RAWLE, from an American Quaker family, formed and dissolved several partnerships during his life in the Far East, which seems to have started with his arrival from New York at Canton in October 1836 on the *Plymouth*. The initial H given in a local notice of his arrival, was probably a misprint for his name as reported when he left for Philadelphia on the same ship the following February, and when he returned in March 1838 on the *Chandler Price*. He was listed among Canton's foreign residents during the next three years. In 1839, he and all the other foreigners who had stayed on were besieged in the factories by the Chinese.

The evenings of confinement were lightened with singing, Rawle and Gideon Nye among the leaders. After release he returned to America and, when the hostilities of 1841–2 had ended, took passage back to China on the *Talbot* in June 1843, and entered into successive partnerships at Canton, first with T.C. Lewis, with Wetmore & Co in 1844, with N. Duus in 1845, and with Sandwith Drinker (39) in 1848. Rawle and Drinker parted company in 1853, to carry on business each on his own. The lorca *Mary*, lost in a typhoon off Lintin on its way from Whampoa to Macao, was jointly owned by Rawle and Duus.

Mrs Rawle was also from a Quaker family. She arrived to join Samuel between May and August 1844 accompanied by a daughter, Mary, and a granddaughter aged 13, Amelia. They kept a house in Macao, where she became a 'judicious and sympathizing and at the same time experienced friend' of Mrs Kinsman the diarist (see 112). Their move to Hong Kong in 1846 was greatly regretted by

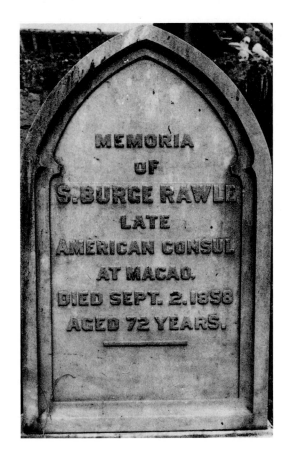

Mrs Kinsman, who 'wished more than I can express that she and her daughter were living at Macao, instead of Hong Kong' and received them with pleasure when they visited Macao to stay with the Kinsmans. Amelia married merchant Charles Delano Williams in 1852 at the Anglican Cathedral in Hong Kong. Later that year, her sister Ann Isabel Rawle arrived to stay, and married the Rev Walter Henry Medhurst at Gideon Nye's Macao house in February 1854 – their infant daughter, a great-grandchild of Samuel Rawle born later in the year, lies buried in the Old Cemetery (35), and her mother died a few months later at Singapore. It is not clear how many members of the family were in the region; a Miss Rawle, possibly another daughter, sailed from Hong Kong in 1857 for Singapore. Rawle himself passed his remaining years in semi-retirement as the American Consul in Macao.

One of the most pleasing memorials in the cemetery, his headstone faces west and almost touches the southeast corner of 133's base. It stands on a moulded plinth of grey, medium-grained, dressed granite. The headstone is of Carara marble, polished on all sides and edges. On the plinth it stands 71 cm high, including a pointed arch of 24 cm rising directly from its sides; it is 44 cm wide and 13 cm thick, and simply and carefully carved. The edges of the stone, including its arch, are continuous, raised mouldings, and form a recessed inscription surface. The lettering is cut in relief. The word MEMORIA may have been intended to read MEMORIAL.

OTHER OBSERVERS: PCL: S. HURGE RAWLE; HSPH: Numbered 93.
REFER TO: Canton R of 4/10/1836, 14/2/1837, and 13/3/1838; ACK for 1837, 1838, and 1839; Nye Peking; Canton P of 1/7/1843; FC&HKG of 5/10/1844, 31/5/1845, 8/10/1845, 14/10/1848, 2/6/1852, 31/8/1853, 18/2/1854, and 11/9/1858; CM of 5/6/1845, 9/11/1848, 26/4/1849, 16/9/1852, 25/8/1853, 23/2/1854, 8/3/1855 and 30/11/1857; Monroe lxxxvi pp 171 and 320 and lxxxvii pp 390, 403 and 408; SFP&MA of 22/2/1855.

135.   FREDERICK SMITH   *British*

ONE GEORGE FREDERICK SMITH, mariner, was married to Mary de Rozario at Calcutta on 22 January 1792, and they may have been Frederick Smith's parents. After 18 months of service with the Hong Kong Government, Frederick was appointed deputy registrar of the Supreme Court of Hong Kong in June 1845, drawing a salary of $350 made up of contributions from the parliamentary grant and the local revenues. In 1850, having been in poor health for some time, he went to Macao 'for a change of air'. His friends, it was reported, 'scarcely expected that he would ever return – of his perfect recovery they had no hope'.

He died there on 16 June 1850 – in the local papers the 17th, as in the inscription – aged 39 years, leaving a widow and young family. One daughter had been born in Hong Kong in August 1848. Contributions towards the widow's expenses and the cost of their passage home were made by many liberal firms and friends in Hong Kong.

Smith's headstone of pinkish grey, coarse-grained, dressed granite stands 1.2 metres south of and in line with 134, faces west, and is readily recognized by its steep gable top, which rises 34 cm from a narrow shoulder at each side to the stone's full height of 105 cm; it is 67 cm wide and 11 cm thick. Its surface, recessed by a moulded frame cut round the edge, is divided into the gable area above and the main inscription area below: the upper gable area is adorned with a simple floral design cut in low relief and separated from the lower by a moulded segmental arch spanning the width of the stone, and beneath this are carved five smaller arches. The surface is rough and has flaked and pitted so badly that less than 10 words of the inscription are legible. Cut in the same type of granite but unadorned, its footstone lies a few feet to the east of 126.

Braga examined it some 70 years ago and was able to read more than is now possible: the following is his reading:

FREDERICK SMITH
WHO DIED AT MACAO
17th June 1850

OTHER OBSERVERS: HSPH: Numbered 94.
REFER TO: Bengal P&P xvi p 42; HKBlBk CO133/4 pp 64 and 100; Kyshe; FC&HKG of 22/6/1850 and 23/8/1848; CM of 20/6/1850.

136. SIR HUMPHREY LE FLEMING SENHOUSE *British*

SACRED

to the memory

of

CAPTAIN SIR HUMPHREY LE FLEMING SENHOUSE

RN CB & KCH

of Seascale in the County of Cumberland

Senior Officer in Command of the British fleet

in the China Seas

who died on board H.M.S. Blenheim

at Hong kong

on the 13 June 1841

AGED 66 YEARS.

From the Effects of fever contracted during the zealous

performance of his arduous duties at the Capture of the

Heights of Canton in May 1841.

Inscription on south face

THIS MONUMENT

was erected in testimony

of

esteem and respect

for their distinguished and lamented Chief

by the Officers of the Army & Navy

composing the China Expedition in 1841.

Inscription on north face

HUMPHREY SENHOUSE was born in 1781 in Barbados, where his father became surveyor-general. This would make him 60 at death, a date confirmed by Braga and Hopkinson, not 66 as the inscription seems now to read. Another record puts his year of birth at 1788, which does not fit the dates of his Royal Naval service, which started in 1797 in the West Indies. He visited England for the first time as the century was drawing to its close. The reference to Seascale in the inscription marks his descent from an ancient Saxon family from Cumberland. In 1810 he married a Miss Manley, the daughter of a vice-admiral.

His battle record is impressive, and includes several occasions when he volunteered for dangerous duties. He took part in the Battle of Trafalgar

North face

as a lieutenant on board the *Conqueror*, where the 'heroic conduct, the judgment, the activity, the zeal' he evinced earned him special commendation. He was in the action at Corunna in 1809. During 1812–4 he commanded a naval sloop in the American war. In 1815, when Napoleon landed from Elba, he was there for the renewed action that brought the final defeat of the French, and as flag captain of the *Superb* received Napoleon's personal surrender as a prisoner on board. In 1832 he

was appointed knight commander in the Royal Guelphic Order of Hanover (KCH), an honour which ceased to be conferred by the British Crown after 1837.

It was the trouble brewing in China that brought him to the Far East in 1840 in command of the *Blenheim*, a warship of 74 guns, to join the expedition of some 48 vessels assembling under the fleet command of Rear-Admiral George Elliot, his flagship the *Melville*, with the same armament (see also 132 and 133). The main force of the fleet sailed from Calcutta to the Macao Roads and then Hong Kong. The joint plenipotentiaries, Admiral George Elliot and Captain Charles Elliot, had concluded that operations would be more successful if undertaken nearer the seat of government and, leaving a small blockading force in the Pearl River, moved the force north to Chusan. After initial success, they gave way to Chinese pressure to negotiate in South China, where Admiral Elliot suffered a heart attack and sailed for home, leaving Captain Elliot as the sole plenipotentiary. Elliot reopened hostilities against Canton. After successes in the Pearl River, he agreed a cease-fire with the Chinese Commissioner, which was then repudiated by Peking, whereupon Elliot decided to capture Canton. Senhouse had meanwhile succeeded to temporary command of all the naval forces, with General Sir Hugh Gough remaining in command of the military. A short action took place in May 1841. After a series of swift operations, the Canton Governor yielded, just as Senhouse and Gough, both ashore in the thick of the fighting, were about to invest the city, and Elliot halted the action. (An account of these actions and negotiations is in Chapter 3 pages 24–7.)

When Elliot halted the action, an appalled Senhouse was reported as saying that 'he would rather have died and be buried under the walls of Canton than have signed the terms'. It was said that 'the ruin of his country's honour and interests in China' caused him to die of a broken heart. In a state of exhaustion 'heightened by anxiety, grief and vexation', he developed the sickness then known as 'Hong Kong fever'. Carried downriver by the *Blenheim*, he died as she anchored at Hong Kong.

All off-duty officers were bidden to attend the funeral, and black crêpe was ordered to be worn. Having little faith in the permanence of Hong Kong as a British settlement, Senhouse had expressed the wish to be buried in Macao; and his body was transferred to the *Nemesis* for the short voyage. On the day following his death, a large funeral procession formed at Captain Elliot's house and moved off to the strains of the Governor's band, followed by a contingent of Portuguese troops, a junior naval officer as chief mourner, the captain of the *Columbine* bearing his decorations, the coffin borne by 12 naval ratings from the *Blenheim*, three naval captains and three senior military officers as pall-bearers, the Governor and his staff, General Gough and his staff, the fleet's senior officer and the senior officer of the military contingent, about 70 other naval and military officers, and almost all the British and other foreign community of Macao. The service was conducted by the *Blenheim*'s naval chaplain.

Senhouse's monument was erected early in 1842. Of fine-grained, polished grey granite, it stands in total nearly four metres high, and comprises a two-tiered bonded podium, a cube box without plinth,

a table with bed-mould, and a slab bearing a two-metre-tall obelisk. The sides of the box have grooves 2.5 cm wide and 1.3 cm deep cut about 5 cm from the edges; and on the square tablets so formed are carved the inscriptions and, in low relief, Senhouse's coat-of-arms. The inscriptions are mostly in small letters and difficult to read.

OTHER OBSERVERS: HSPH: HUMPHREY LE FLEMING SENHOUES, Numbered 95.
REFER TO: DNB; Gent Mag for June 1841 p 654, July 1841 p 84, and December 1841 p 654; Canton R of 1 and 8/12/1840 and 13/4, 25/5, 1, 14, 15 and 29/6/1841; Canton P of 19/6/1841 and 12/3/1842.

JAMES INNES *British*

JAMES INNES arrived in China either late in 1825 or early in 1826, at what was then an unusually advanced age for a new beginning. Disillusioned by trouble over the lease of Scottish property belonging to the Dukes of Queensberry, and by the eviction of his family, he was driven to seek a new life in the Orient. He took much advice before setting out, and was well aware of the difficulties he would encounter as an independent merchant without the immunity from expulsion enjoyed by those employed by the Company. Some time after his arrival, his independence was challenged by the Company's Select Committee, and he revealed his contumaceous nature in a threat, that if it expelled him, he would make sure that some 200 Parsees and 40 other Britishers, who were also trading independently, would quit Canton with him. He appears to have made his point, as he stayed on as a 'free-trader' without further challenge.

A busy life thereafter was punctuated by incidents which all too clearly revealed the depth of his loathing for privilege and vested interest, conditions which he attacked frontally wherever he met them, often championing the cause of personal liberty even in the face of properly constituted authority and the jurisdiction of the courts.

In one such rumpus at Canton, having found firewood stored on the pavement near his house and his demands that it must be removed not being met, he set fire to the house of one of the Chinese officials. The committee simply recorded its disapproval on that occasion, and the trouble faded; but one writer later pointed out that in British law the punishment for arson was death. On another

occasion, when his coolies were unloading boxes consigned to him as containing silver coin – a very heavy commodity – the customs officers noticed them carrying two boxes at a time and had them opened, to discover that they contained opium and not silver. Tortured to reveal the source, the coolies implicated Robert Forbes (see 163), as consignee of the American ship *Thomas Perkins*, hoping to protect

Innes. Foreign merchants and their compradors were unjustly accused of being implicated and arrested, the transport of all cargo was stopped, and Innes was ordered to leave Canton. The 'irate Scotch gentleman', as Nye described him, refused to obey; the local Mandarins stopped all foreign trade, arrested some traders, and threatened the Hong merchants with the *k'ang* (a wooden collar, somewhat akin to the stocks). Innes was forced to give in, wrote a vindication of the coolies and the captain of the *Thomas Perkins*, and was allowed to leave for Macao. The Chinese refused to reopen trade, and the British Superintendent of Trade, Captain Charles Elliot, wrote seeking advance indulgence from Lord Palmerston, then Secretary of State for Colonies, should he need to place Innes under arrest in Macao if he continued to defy Mandarin authority. When Innes got wind of this letter a year or so later, he wrote to the press not only denying Elliot's right to arrest him in Macao, just as he had denied the right of the Chinese to touch him at Canton, but warning that the leader of any party sent to arrest him would be shot 'through the head, or heart by a well practised rifle'. In the meantime, he had brought a case into the Macao courts accusing another Scottish merchant of robbing the schooner *Bombay* of eight chests of opium, valued at $4,000, a case quoted some 10 years later in the famous Summers case challenging the jurisdiction of the Hong Kong courts over Britishers in Macao.

West face

Nonetheless, Innes was a friend to all in need. When Lord Napier (164) fell sick at Canton in September 1834, it was Innes who took him from the superintendent's house to his own, which was far more airy, to be looked after until he left on his last journey to Macao. Innes was for some time partner of a Mr Fletcher, and when he himself died in 1841, his partnership was taken over by John Henry Larkins (122) in a newly named company. Innes's last illness was long and painful, and he died at home in Macao on Thursday 1 July (not, as his inscription predicted, in June). He was buried the next day; at his last rites were the plenipotentiary Captain Elliot, all his fellow countrymen living in Macao, and many Portuguese and other foreign residents.

A metre south of 136, his grey stele stands, square in section, resting on a moulded, granite plinth rising from a two-stepped bonded podium; on the podium a square table with bed-mould supports a small step which in turn carries a closed fluted urn with a square base. All is in granite, the stele and plinth polished, very grainy, and of poor quality. On the four faces of the column, about 5 cm from the edges, are cut grooves 2.5 cm wide and 1.3 cm deep, forming rectangular tablets with incised corners. The inscription is cut on the west face; above it is the Innes family coat-of-arms with a five-point star as crest, and below it, in full flight and low relief, a large eagle (perhaps, rather, the stormy petrel).

Much of the lower-case lettering in the inscription is difficult to read; with its personal references to his knightly origins and the litigious vexations he suffered on land and at sea, in a life spent where he knew he would die – 'not far from the shore' – it is so wryly apt that the libertarian Innes probably composed it himself: the Latin date, too, was in an unusual and 'uncivilized' form, and the 'Junii' of his death turned out to be a bad prediction. The word 'esto' seems to be a mason's error for 'estu', tide. We are indebted to Professor Alan Green, then of the University of Hong Kong, and the late Kenneth Maidment, then Vice-Chancellor of the

University of Auckland, for their help over the oddities of this Latin epitaph. Of the devices that are cut above and below it: the family escutcheon was matriculated in the Lyon Register in 1753; the bird may have been an Innes design.

OTHER OBSERVERS: HSPH: Numbered 96.
REFER TO: Canton R of 21/10/1834 and 6/7/1841; Morse iv pp 130, 164, 236 and 352; Gent Mag for July 1835 p 137; Forbes p 346; Canton P of 15 and 22/12/1838, 31/10/1840, 3/7/1841 and 20/8/1842; FC&HKG of 18/7/1849; SFP&MA of 14/8/1841.

138.   DANIEL DUFF   *British*

North side

CAPTAIN DUFF reached China in command of his regiment and played a leading part in the joint military-naval actions to reduce the defences around the Bogue in January 1841, capturing the islands of north and south Wantung, and fighting on the heights to the north of Canton in hot, sultry May weather that wrought havoc among his troops. When the forces were withdrawn from Canton, he returned to Hong Kong in very poor health, and had not yet recovered when he sailed to Macao to

THIS TOMB WAS ERECTED
by his Brother Officers 37" Reg. M. N. I.
in token of their respect and esteem.

South side

attend the funeral of Sir Humphrey Senhouse (136). On his way back from the cemetery, he was handed a letter with news that his wife had died at Vizagapatnam, India, on 22 April, and he never got over the shock. On 7 July a fever, still unabated, carried him off, and he was buried the next day with full military honours.

The Madras Light Infantry was a section of the military forces first recruited by the Company. The 37th Regiment of native infantry from Madras formed part of General Gough's expeditionary force sent to China in 1840. It suffered extremely heavy casualties, not only in actions in the Chusan and Canton campaigns, but at sea on the voyage from India, and from malaria and dysentery in China and in Hong Kong, where the troops were kept on board transports to avoid unnecessary contact. Duff's regiment left for Madras in March 1842, so prized in the fighting round Canton the previous May that it was renamed the 37th Madras Grenadiers: clearly this news had not reached Macao by the time Duff's stone was cut. The regiment was disbanded in 1882.

Duff's chest-tomb, of fine-grained, polished grey granite, supports an urn. A plinth 15 cm high with a broad moulding rests on a substantial, mitred podium 254 cm long and 163 cm at base, supporting a box with rectangular tablets in raised relief cut on the rounded ends and sides. The table-top has a bed-mould and square corners and vertical edges but no upper moulding, and is 5 cm thick. The urn stands on the table-top, closed with fluted sides on a rectangular, three-stepped podium, all cut from a single block of stone, and is 58 cm high and 33 cm in diameter; the lowest of the steps below is 6 cm, the middle 5 cm and the uppermost 4 cm high. The inscription is in two parts; both are deeply cut, and the lower-case lettering is not easy to read.

OTHER OBSERVERS: HSPH: Numbered 97.
REFER TO: Canton P of 10/7/1841 and 19/3/1842; FInd of 14/10/1841; Canton R of 13/7/1841; Gent Mag for February 1842 p 229.

JAMES HOOKER *British*

AFTER AN ATTACK of fever lasting only three days, James Hooker died at his hotel in Macao at six o'clock on a Sunday morning. The newspapers described his passing as a great loss to the British community in China. His death was also reported in the Calcutta papers, from which it may be concluded that he was previously settled there and perhaps that he or his family had been connected either with the Company's marine service or with one of the Company's 'country ships'. It is not known when he arrived in the Far East. He became a partner in the firm of Hooker, Lane & Co, which owned the British Hotel in Macao.

Presented with the bright prospect of the colonization of Hong Kong and the altered foreign relations with China, he had hardly set up business as a marine storekeeper and ship's chandler when death intervened.

His tomb is a fine-grained, polished, grey granite slab measuring 178 cm x 81 cm, lying last in the south end of the east line of the group, about 30 cm from 138, its head to the east. The brief inscription is artistically set out and well cut.

OTHER OBSERVERS: HSPH: JAMES HOCKER, Numbered 98.
REFER TO: Canton R of 13/7/1841; Canton P of 17/7/1841; FInd of 14/10/1841.

> SACRED
> To The Memory of
> JAMES HOOKER
> who departed this Life
> 15th July 1841
> AGED 42 YEARS

140.   CORNELIA BRACKENRIDGE SPEER   *Americans*
and MARY CORNELIA SPEER

CORNELIA SPEER was the daughter of Alexander Brackenridge of Pittsburgh, near where a town is named after the family; her grandfather achieved prominence in 1794 in the American 'Whiskey Ring' conspiracy against the tax on whiskey. The Rev Dr William Speer, a trained physician, was ordained minister and, after marrying his 24-year-old wife, appointed to serve the Presbyterian mission in China. They arrived in Macao on Boxing Day 1846, with the Rev John French (father of Maria French, 26), as their fellow-passenger. Cornelia was already pregnant when they set out, and already during the voyage the symptoms of a fatal disease made their first appearance. Her decline was rapid.

She was prevented 'from using her vocal powers by the state of her lungs', as Rebecca Kinsman noted in her diary, though she joined her husband and Mr French in singing with taste and feeling at church services, and she became 'very feeble and her cough very troublesome – we fear for her'. Her end, sped by the birth of her daughter, 'a pretty creature, left motherless in a land of strangers', she contemplated 'without alarm and even with joy'. Another missionary, Dr William Dean, has written that 'the last words she uttered were "I am going home"'. Her infant daughter Mary, deprived of her mother, survived her by less than three months, and was buried under the same memorial.

In 1849, after a time at Canton, Dr Speer returned to America, where from 1851 he worked among the Chinese residents in San Francisco, and for many years published a newspaper in Chinese and English. He returned to China in 1876, in

search of material for a book on the question of Chinese emigration.

This pleasant monument to the mother and infant daughter is close to the convent wall and in line with the last memorials in the east line of the Churchill row. A column of marble 102 cm high, its bottom 66 cm square in section, tapers towards its top to 60 cm, on which is an overhanging cap with a large cavetto bed-mould, all standing on a moulded plinth and base of granite. The base, on which rest two steps to the plinth, is 30 cm high and 104 cm square, and the plinth 85 cm square; the upper step has a shallow moulding at the top. The column cap is a table and a slab, together 32 cm high. The table is 81 cm square and has a cavetto bed-mould, vertical edges, and square corners; the slab is a flat, shallow pyramid, slightly smaller at base than the column top. The marble of the column was quarried just north of Canton, a hornblende syenite known as 'Canton marble' and not true marble; it has two diagonal cracks, the upper crack spreading across the inscription on the west face, but with no serious damage to the lettering. The last line of the inscription, 'They shall walk with me in white', is from Revelation 3:4.

OTHER OBSERVERS: PCL: Mary is not listed; HSPH: CORNELIA BRACKENRIDGE, Numbered 99.
REFER TO: Schoyer; Davis; Monroe lxxxviii pp 71–7; Dean p 373.

---

141. ROBERT MORRISON *British*

FOR THE CELEBRATIONS connected with the centenary in 1934 of Robert Morrison's death, a plaque of white marble with a commemorative inscription in Chinese was set up on the cemetery wall, alongside his tomb. This and the inscriptions in English on the top of the tomb itself and in Chinese on the west end, together offer a concise and general résumé of his life and work.

At the end of the tomb (translation)

It is said that man can achieve immortality in this world only through his immortal sayings and deeds. Mr Robert Morrison of Great Britain is an example of such an immortal man. When he came to China in his youth he studied diligently and worked hard, so that he completely mastered the Chinese language in its spoken and written forms. After he became proficient in his studies, he made use of his knowledge to compile a Chinese-English dictionary and other books, so that those who wished to learn the Chinese language could use them as guides for their study and achieve better results with less effort. This is why the British people admired the tirelessness with which he pursued his studies and the indefatigability with which he taught others, and praised him as a British scholar of virtue. In order not to forget his contribution to the world, we set up this tablet to commemorate him:

Robert Morrison, of Great Britain, was born on the 5th day of the 1st moon, in the 46th year of the reign of Ch'ien-lung, and died in his 52nd year, on the 26th day of the 6th moon, in the 14th year of the reign of Tao-kuang, and by the 13th year of Chia-ch'ing he began to manage the business of his company. In the 3rd moon of the 14th year of Tao-kuang, his company was dissolved, and he turned to work for the government. A few months later he died. Fortunately he left behind him his

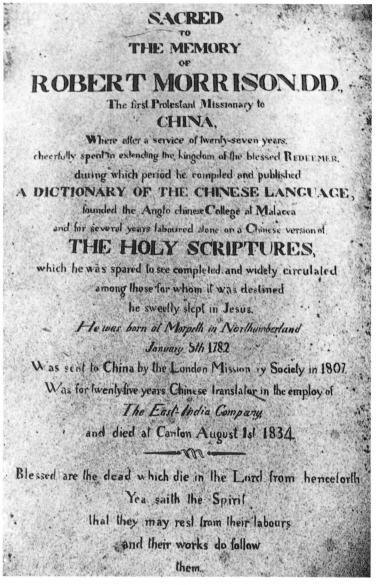

SACRED
TO
THE MEMORY
OF
ROBERT MORRISON, D.D.,
The first Protestant Missionary to
CHINA,
Where after a service of twenty-seven years,
cheerfully spent in extending the kingdom of the blessed REDEEMER,
during which period he compiled and published
A DICTIONARY OF THE CHINESE LANGUAGE,
founded the Anglo chinese College at Malacca
and for several years laboured alone on a Chinese version of
THE HOLY SCRIPTURES,
which he was spared to see completed and widely circulated
among those for whom it was destined
he sweetly slept in Jesus.
He was born at Morpeth in Northumberland
January 5th 1782
Was sent to China by the London Mission ry Society in 1807,
Was for twenty-five years Chinese Translator in the employ of
The East-India Company
and died at Canton August 1st 1834

Blessed are the dead which die in the Lord from henceforth
Yea, saith the Spirit
that they may rest from their labours
and their works do follow
them.

Top

wide and his contribution made ever-lasting. Truly such a man is rarely seen in this modern age. Tao-kuang 23rd year, 8th moon, 15th day. A.D. 1843, 10th month, 8th day. Tablet set up by friends from all countries.

Commemorative plaque alongside the tomb (translation)

The preaching of the Reformed Christian Church in China started with Robert Morrison. Before coming to China Mr Morrison prepared himself by studying astronomy, medicine and Chinese. In 1807 after a voyage of 222 days by way of America, he arrived safely at Canton. Nominally a merchant, he secretly preached religion, though preaching was strictly forbidden by the Manchu government and his work to be obstructed. He set up a printing press in Macao to publish, one after another, his translations of the Bible, prayers, psalms, hymns and religious tracts. He also established the Anglo-Chinese College in Malacca for educating the young generation. Working in this dark and tyrannical age, he showed himself second to none in courage and faced dangers bravely. All this could not have been accomplished without the help of God.

Mr Morrison was delicate in health but kept himself busy in his work. His environment was adverse and sinister. With the exception of his eldest son who was with him, his family was far away from him in their native country. Of the 200 and more letters that he sent home,

son, John Morrison, who, although not able to inherit all his distinguished qualities, was a man of great merits, so that today his knowledge can be spread far and only two reached his family. Bad as his environment was, he still worked hard without lapse. Thus he succeeded in laying the foundation of the Chinese Christian Church, which was indeed a great achievement.

On 1 August 1834, he was seriously ill. When he was dying, a gathering of Christians wept bitterly beside his bed. But Mr Morrison still comforted them and said that after one hundred years the number of Christians would have increased by ten thousand times. The strength of his faith and the depth of his insight were certainly not possessed by common people.

Now that it is the hundredth anniversary of Mr Morrison's death, the Kwangtung branch of the Chinese Christian Church commemorated the occasion. They deeply admired his virtues and sincerely mourned his death. Thus they set up this tablet to show their respect for him.

Great is Mr Morrison who devoted himself to Christ
Preaching the Gospel according to the Will of God;
Guided by the Holy Ghost he risked himself in coming to us,
And brought abundant blessing to the descendants of the
  Yellow Emperor.
Suffering much hardship, he set up a good example in his
  preaching,
And worked without lapse from the beginning even to his
  death.
His faith and love were without equal in the past or present,
And his virtues were high as the sky and deep as the sea.

The rules of the Company controlling the entry of the British into China prohibited unofficial clergy and missionaries from entering and working in any of the territories within its monopoly, so that only the Company's own official chaplains were admitted. Morrison entered by subterfuge: he journeyed first to New York, transshipped to an American vessel, and sailed to Macao and on to Canton,

welcome in neither place. When forced to leave Canton, he was befriended by Americans living in Macao. To continue the study of Chinese was one of

Chinnery: Robert Morrison

his main problems: since the Chinese were forbidden on pain of death to teach the language to foreigners he was forced to pursue his studies clandestinely. His presence at Canton was in due course accepted by the Chinese.

In 1809 he married Mary (née Morton), then a 17-year-old visiting China with her parents and brother. On the day of the wedding, the Company offered him an appointment as Chinese secretary and translator to the British factory at Canton – and with it permission to work at Canton officially – and, even prepared to encourage his work of translating the New Testament and compiling a dictionary and a Chinese grammar, agreed to fund the printing of the last two, despite the knowledge that such activities constituted a capital crime.

In 1816 he joined Lord Amherst's embassy to the Chinese Emperor as translator and interpreter. In June 1821 Mary died of cholera (142). Returning to England in 1823, Morrison was acknowledged widely as one of Europe's leading sinologues, and taught Chinese for a time. Among his students were Thomas Smith, brother-in-law of Eliza Wedderburn (145), his own son John Robert (143) and Samuel Dyer (146). He married again in 1824 while in England, and in 1825 was elected a Fellow

of the Royal Society. With his new wife Eliza (née Armstrong), he left for China again in 1826 and, and during their voyage on the Company ship *Orwell*, a mutiny broke out on board: it was Morrison who succeeded in reasoning with the mutineers and having their grievances met. On this second visit he was largely responsible for the first appearance in China of American Protestant missionaries, some of whom were to become famous for their

contributions to sinological study and to diplomacy.

When the Company lost its monopoly of British trade in China, Morrison was appointed Chinese secretary to Lord Napier (164), who replaced the Company chief as official Superintendent of Trade; he was already ailing, and died at Canton only a fortnight after meeting Napier in Macao.

Napier, with all the Europeans and Americans in Canton and a large number of Chinese, accompanied his remains to the ship bound for Macao. The service, which was attended by all the foreigners in Macao, was conducted by the American Rev Edwin Stevens, who, with John Robert and another American friend, the Rev S. Wells Williams, had sailed with the body from Canton. He lies buried next to his first wife and John Robert.

In February 1835, his son John and a group of Morrison's friends at Canton, including Sir George Robinson, William Jardine, D.W.C. Olyphant, Lancelot Dent and the American Rev E.C. Bridgman, established a commemorative Morrison Education Society in China, which engaged in educational works until about 1857. At the University of Hong Kong, his name is commemorated in Morrison Hall, founded by the London Missionary Society in 1913, and in the Morrison Collection, which contains his European books; his Chinese books are in the School of Oriental and African Studies at the University of London. In 1957 Mr and Mrs B.F. Wong donated their villa in Macao for use as a Morrison Memorial Centre.

East of 140 and close to the wall, its head to the west, Morrison's chest-tomb is of fine-grained, polished, local grey granite, similar in design to 142 and 143. Of all the memorials it is the most frequented by visitors to the cemetery. A moulded plinth 279 x 160 cm at base rising 29 cm to 197 x 104 cm, rests on a mitred podium and encases the bottom of the vertical sides and ends of a box 38 cm high, which supports a 5 cm-thick table-top with bed-mould. An inscription in English is on the top; the other is in Chinese, beautifully cut on a Belgian black marble tablet inset into the westernmost of the four rectangular panels, which are carved in relief on the ends and sides of the box.

The inscriptions are of unusual length, clearly cut, and well preserved.

The commemorative plaque on the wall (pictured opposite) is a rectangle of 132 x 64 cm with a shallow gabled top, which increases the height by 13 cm and under which is carved in relief the symbol of a scholar: an encircled open book; the emblem is flanked by two simple, different floral designs in relief, decorative rather than emblematic. The rest of the surface is devoted to its long inscription, in the calligraphy of the late Rev Chung Chak-ling, for many years Minister of the Hop Yat Church in Hong Kong.

OTHER OBSERVERS: HSPH: Numbered 100.
REFER TO: Morrison passim; Ride passim; Gent Mag iii for April 1835 p 436 and January–June 1835 p 435; Morse iii p 178; Ellis p 58; FInd of 23/4/1835; Canton R of 10/10/1837; Canton P of 8/9/1838; Ballot; Drake.

142.   MARY MORRISON   *British*

MARY MORRISON was the eldest daughter in a family of six children. Their father was Dr John Morton, and her mother, Rebecca, née Ingram, was related to Winnington Ingram, later Bishop of London. They journeyed to China in 1808, taking their large family with them, for a long holiday before he took up a new appointment as Surgeon-in-Chief to the army in Northern Ireland. Their stay of some months in Macao was long enough to see the 17-year-old Mary married to Robert Morrison (141) on 20 February 1809. The climate

soon brought nervous symptoms which, when she became pregnant, her doctor, Dr John Livingstone (see 41), viewed with some misgiving.

In her letters, which she often made 'wet with my tears', she repeatedly referred to being weak, helpless, and low in spirits. Her first child, James, died the day he was born and, as usual at the time for Protestants, he was buried on Meesenberg Hill near the northern extremity of the Macao peninsula – a hill called after a former member of the local Dutch community. The hill has long since been demolished to provide in-fill for a reclamation scheme. The graves that could be identified were moved later to the New Protestant Cemetery, where there still stands an unmarked, almost completely covered memorial in the form of a small, rectangular headstone that bears a simple inscription to the infant James Morrison.

Their second and third children, Mary Rebecca and John Robert (143), were born in 1812 and 1814, and in 1815 Mrs Morrison took them with her to England and Ireland, where she went in an attempt to regain her health. By 1820 she was well enough to return to Macao, after more than five years' absence, but in June the next year she succumbed to cholera, while pregnant once more with a baby which, Dr Morrison mourned, 'found a grave in its mother's womb'. His attempts to fulfil his promise to lay her body to rest in the same grave as James on Meesenberg Hill were harrowing. 'The Chinese would not let me even open the same grave. I disliked burying under the two walls, but was obliged to resolve on doing so, as the Papists refuse their burying ground to Protestants. The want of

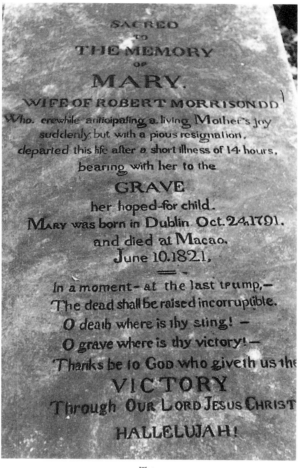

Top

a Protestant burying ground has long been felt in Macao'. The Company's Select Committee offered to buy ground for a new cemetery which, as Morrison later recalled, 'enabled me to lay the remains of my beloved wife in a place appropriate to the sepulture of Protestant Christians denied a place of interment by the Romanists'.

The burial service was conducted by the Rev Harding, chaplain to the Company, attended by the family and most of the foreigners in Macao, including Sir Andrew Ljungstedt (60), one of the Morrisons' oldest friends in Macao. The pall-bearers were Dr Livingstone and Dr Pearson, the chief and members of the Select Committee, J.B. Urmston (see 115) and Sir William Fraser (62). Thus opened the history of what is now known as the Old Cemetery.

Since Morrison's work kept him at Canton for months each year, where he was not permitted to take them, his children were sent to live with his brother in England.

Mary Morrison's chest-tomb is of practically the same dimensions and design as that of her husband,

234

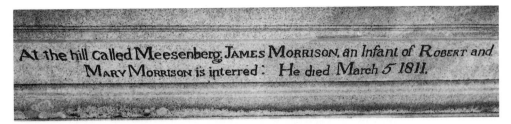

North side

but lacks an inscription in Chinese on the west end, and has a tablet on the north side carrying information about their first-born, James. An error in the lettering of the north-side inscription offers 'Al the Inll' for 'At the hill".

OTHER OBSERVERS: HSPH: Numbered 101.
REFER TO: Morrison passim; Gent Mag for January-June 1835 p 435.

143. JOHN ROBERT MORRISON *British*

Inscription on the top

BORN ON 17 April 1814, J.R. Morrison accompanied his mother, Mary Morrison (142), when she went to England for her health from 1815 to 1820, and was present with his sister Rebecca at their mother's interment the following year. His father, Dr Robert Morrison, sent John back home to school, just as he was about to turn eight. Morrison returned to England on long furlough in 1823 and took John back to Macao with him in 1826, taking him on to Canton when only 12, 'to learn Cantonese'. Morrison hoped that when he grew up John would become a good enough Chinese scholar to revise his father's translation of the New Testament, and kept a close eye on young

John's progress with this in view. He showed early signs of fulfilling his father's aspiration, and was only 16 when he was appointed Chinese translator to the British traders in China. He visited Cochin China (southern Vietnam) and Siam (Thailand) as a member of the mission of Edmund Roberts (88), in which Chinese was one of the intermediary languages used. He was one of a trio with Dr Colledge (see 94, 95 and 96) and the Rev Charles Gutzlaff who were active in the monthly production of *The Chinese Repository*. He became just as valuable to the new British authorities in south China as had been his father to the Company: in 1840 he was selected to join the China expedition led by Admiral George Elliot, and the next year he acted as secretary and treasurer to the Company's successor, the new Superintendent of British Trade. Both Chinese and British opinions of his ability were high: during hostilities in the Pearl River, the huge sum of $50,000 was offered by the Chinese authorities for his capture alive – the same as for the capture of Admiral Elliot, the naval commander, and of Commodore Sir James J.G. Bremer, the military commander. In the peace negotiations of 1842 at Nanking, the Chinese side instanced him and Gutzlaff as showing the level of the intellect and linguistic ability confronting them, while the British regarded him as 'one of the outstanding figures on the English side'.

Appointed Chinese Secretary in 1843, he moved to Hong Kong to become the new Colony's first chief administrator; in June he had been in the first list of Justices of the Peace; in August he was among the first members of the new Executive and Legislative Councils.

That summer was his last. The Governor, Sir Henry Pottinger, had given him the Treaty of Nanking to translate, and he was in the middle of it when he fell sick with 'Hong Kong fever', and was sent to Macao for a change of air and a rest. Pottinger was to follow him a few days later. That same day the official announcement of his appointment as Colonial Secretary and as a member of both Councils appeared, but he died four days later on 29 August.

Pottinger publicly declared his death 'an irreparable national calamity, and he doubts not but as such it will be received and viewed by his Sovereign and country'. His funeral was attended by a very large gathering, with his half-brother Robert as chief mourner, supported by Pottinger. The pall-bearers included Patrick Stewart (44).

The granite chest-tomb lies just to the north of 142, to which, and to 141, it is similar in size and design. In marked contrast to the tombs of his parents, the table-top bears only his name: in view of his distinction and popularity, the lack of an English inscription must have been his personal wish.

The Chinese inscription is cut on a Belgian black marble tablet let into the west end of the box, and offers information about his career and character.

Translation

It is said that a man renowned for his virtue will beget outstanding offspring. Is not the late British scholar John Morrison an example of such an outstanding offspring? Born in Macao, China, he followed the career of his father and fulfilled his own wishes. The more excellent his learning became, the harder he worked, and the more cultivated his virtue, the more thorough his understanding, so that the Chinese essays and poetry written by him differed in no way from those written by Chinese people. As for his ability to speak the Chinese language both in its standard form and its various dialects, that was but a minor accomplishment.

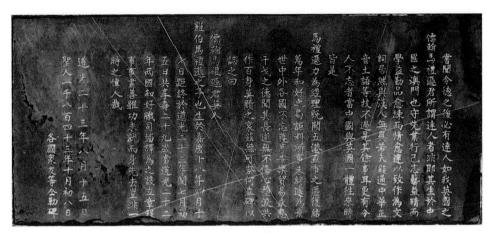

West end

Moreover, what should not be forgotten are his efforts in promoting communications between China and Britain. He helped to bring about the opening of the five Treaty Ports, and laid the foundation for friendship between these two countries for generations to come.

Unfortunately he died without having completed his work, but both the East and the West will remember with gratitude what they owe to him for their trading and peaceful relations. When the sad news of his death was announced, none could help shedding tears. They could do nothing but commemorate him in the following inscription:

John Morrison, the son of Robert Morrison, of Great Britain, was born on the 17th day of the 4th moon in the 18th year of the reign of Chia Ch'ing, and died in his 29th year, on the 5th day of the intercalary 7th moon in the 23rd year of the reign of Tao Kuang. He was a translator during the peaceful period in the 22nd year of the reign of Tao Kuang, and helped to lay down the terms of peace between the two countries. He tried his best in everything he did, but did not live to see the fruits of his labour. Is he not a great man of his age?

OTHER OBSERVERS: HSPH: Numbered 102.
REFER TO: Canton R of 15/11/1830, 31/5/1833, 23 and 30/6/1840, and 27/4 and 4/5/1841; ACK for 1835–9; Fairbank i p 98; Waley p 162; HKR of 4/7 and 22/8/1843; FC&HKG of 30/6/1843; Canton P of 26/8 and 2/9/1843; Drake; Conner plate 154 .

144.   CHRISTIAN CATHRO WALKER   *British*

HERE LIE THE REMAINS OF
CHRISTIAN CATHRO
Spouse of **JOHN WALKER** (Bombay Country Service).
She died at Macao on the 18. October 1838.
at the early age of twenty four

Inscription on north side

South side

West end

NO INFORMATION of Christian Walker has come to hand beyond what is in the inscriptions. The 'country service' consisted of British firms licensed by the Company to trade between India and elsewhere in the East, but not with England. The captain of a ship was allowed to take his wife with him as a passenger, a privilege reserved to ship's masters: it is likely that John Walker was in command of a ship, and his wife may have died while his ship was anchored either in Macao or at Whampoa. He died at sea in January 1845, while on board the *Hindustan*.

Christian's chest-tomb of fine-grained, polished, grey granite lies parallel to 141, 142 and 143, slightly out of alignment north-west. While it is similar to them in size, on its podium a larger moulded plinth of 279 x 157 x 28 cm supports the box, with vertical sides and ends that are recessed about 1 cm to form the rectangular surfaces with concave corners which carry the four inscriptions. The table-top, 201 x 104 cm with its rounded edges and an over-mould, is somewhat cumbersome.

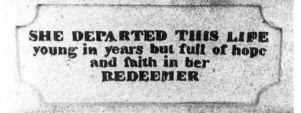

East end

OTHER OBSERVERS: HSPH: CHRISTIAN CATHRO SPOUSE, Numbered 103.
REFER TO: Canton P of 27/10/1838; FC&HKG of 30/4/1845.

145.   ELIZA SCRYMGEOUR WEDDERBURN   *British*

WHEN SHE DIED, Eliza Wedderburn seems to have been paying a visit to one of her sisters (née Mary Turner Scrymgeour Wedderburn), who was married to Thomas Charles Smith. Eliza was the third daughter of Henry Scrymgeour Wedderburn of Fife, descended from the hereditary Standard Bearers of Scotland and the Wedderburns of Wedderburn in Berwickshire, and her mother Mary (née Maitland) was granddaughter of the 6th Earl of Dundee, both from old and distinguished Scottish families. Thomas Smith, her brother-in-law, had joined the Company as a writer, probably in 1815, and applied himself to learning Chinese so well that Dr Robert Morrison (141) recorded his progress with satisfaction two years later. Smith worked in the Company's service until he became supercargo in 1828, and was the fourth member of the Company's Select Committee from 1830. He returned to England after some indiscretion in 1831, making his way back to China as a private merchant when the Company had ceased operating there in about 1834.

Eliza's fine-grained, polished, grey granite chest-tomb, head close to the convent wall at the foot of 141 and 142, is the only memorial in this corner with a long axis north-south. It measurements and design are the same as the others in the group, except that the raised tablets on the sides and ends of the box have no lettering.

The inscription, of a form unique in this cemetery, begins with the initials cut directly into the granite of the table-top, the rest of it following on a white Carara marble plaque 51 x 61 cm let into a rectangular recess. It is so well cut and neatly

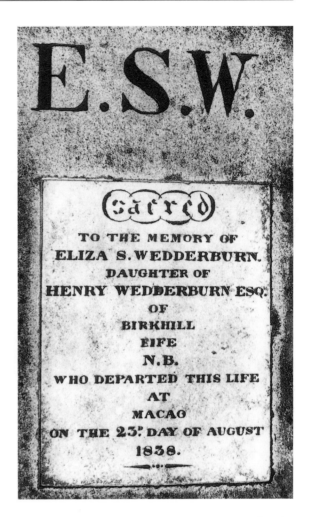

spaced that it is almost certainly the work of a Calcutta mason. The initials 'N.B.' stand for North Britain, often used then to mean Scotland.

OTHER OBSERVERS: HSPH: Numbered 104.
REFER TO: Morse iii pp 164, 251, 256, 327, 343 and 377.

146.   SAMUEL DYER   *British*

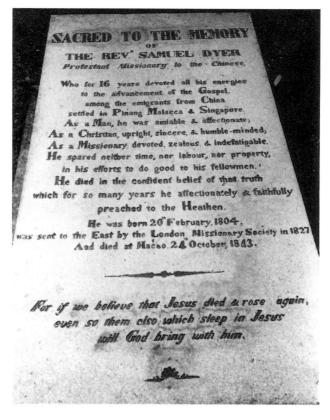

SACRED TO THE MEMORY
OF
THE REV.ᵈ SAMUEL DYER
Protestant Missionary to the Chinese.

Who for 16 years devoted all his energies
to the advancement of the Gospel
among the emigrants from China
settled in Pinang Malacca & Singapore.
As a Man, he was amiable & affectionate,
As a Christian, upright, sincere, & humble-minded,
As a Missionary devoted, zealous, & indefatigable.
He spared neither time, nor labour, nor property,
in his efforts to do good to his fellowmen.'
He died in the confident belief of that truth
which for so many years he affectionately & faithfully
preached to the Heathen.

He was born 20ᵗʰ February, 1804,
was sent to the East by the London Missionary Society in 1827
And died at Macao, 24 October, 1843.

For if we believe that Jesus died & rose again,
even so them also which sleep in Jesus
will God bring with him.

ONE IN A FAMILY of 10 children, Samuel Dyer was the son of John Dyer, secretary of the Seamen's Hospital at Greenwich. Robert Morrison (141) had lived at Greenwich as a student, and became acquainted with John, in whose quarters at the Hospital he met Samuel, later one of his intimates. Samuel joined the Inner Temple as a student and then read law, classics and mathematics at Trinity Hall in Cambridge, leaving (for sectarian reasons) for the seminary at Gosport, after only five terms. The family moved north of the Thames in 1820 into the parish of Paddington Chapel, where Samuel preached and taught. His teaching there was so effective that when he was sent to Penang in 1827 on his first mission for the London Missionary Society a tablet, now no longer in place, was erected in the schoolroom with a long inscription to remember him by.

When Morrison was in England on furlough from China, he had embarked Samuel on the study of the Chinese language, to help when he took charge of the Anglo-Chinese College which Morrison had founded at Penang. Before leaving, Samuel married the eldest daughter of Joseph Tarn, one of the London Missionary Society's directors. In 1835 the Society moved them to the headquarters of its China mission at Malacca. After a furlough taken between 1839 and 1841 in England, he and his family returned east to work in Singapore.

The most lasting element in his renown was his devotion to the improvement of printing in Chinese, and the substitution of movable, metal-cast type to replace the traditional wood-blocks. Statistical sampling showed him that most purposes would be served from a type font of 5,000 Chinese characters, for which he designed the punches. He had the punches cut in England and sent back for the casting of type. Taking advantage of the manner in which many characters are built from a limited number of common elements, he was able after a time to reduce the number of punches and the cost of printing.

With the signing of the first peace treaty after the Sino-British war and the opening of the Treaty Ports to British trade, Dyer's London Missionary Society arranged for a conference in Hong Kong in August 1843, to discuss its mission to China. Dyer went as conference secretary, and when the conference ended he paid a visit to Canton, where he was stricken with a bout of Hong Kong fever, recovering enough by 9 October to embark on the *Charlotte* bound for Singapore. After four days at anchor in Hong Kong harbour, the ship called at Macao to take on more cargo, and Dyer was seized by a virulent attack on board; on the evening of the 19th he was taken ashore and given into the care of Dr Peter Young (see 150) in a state of delirium, and died on the 24th. He was buried the next day next to his former friend and teacher Morrison, and not far from the new grave of Morrison's son, John Robert (143).

Last in the group, his coarse-grained, polished, grey granite chest-tomb, like that of his mentor, lies east-west but with its head to the east. Its podium stands less than a foot to the east of 143, which it closely resembles in almost every detail. The inscription is on its table-top. 'Pinang', for Penang, was frequently so spelt. Some observers, including Hopkinson, have misread the year of death as 1813, when Dyer would have been only 13 years old. Two historians and his biographer give the month of his birth as January.

OTHER OBSERVERS: HSPH: Numbered 105.
REFER TO: Davies passim; Wylie p 52; Dean p 246.

---

147. SAMUEL SMITH *American*

A 'SAMUEL SMITH, seaman, unemployed, found asleep near the Post Office' in Hong Kong was charged with being 'a rogue and a vagabond' in June 1847, too lazy to work though repeatedly offered employment, convicted for the second time, and jailed for two months. It is not known if this was the same Samuel Smith buried two years later in Macao, nor if he was dozing on the yard-arm while furling sails when he plunged to his death. Three in the cemetery from the same ship died, two after falling from aloft (Smith and 64), but not at the same time.

The American ship *Plymouth* first arrived at Macao in the latter part of 1848 and plied in the China waters for more than a year.

Samuel Smith's memorial is a low headstone of coarse-grained, polished, off-white granite badly pitted due to unequal expansion. It stands behind a step about two metres to the northeast of 146, with its back a metre from the cemetery's eastern wall. The top forms a semi-elliptical arch with a 10 cm rise, giving a total height of only 86 cm, width 58 cm and thickness 17 cm. A border 2.5 cm wide at the sides and 5 cm at the top surrounds a recessed surface, which carries the inscription below a simple design carved in low relief. The step of rough granite at its front is 94 cm wide and 38 cm deep. It is almost certain that this and the stones of the two other crewmembers of the same ship were from the same mason's workshop: they are nearly identical in all aspects of material, design, size and deterioration.

OTHER OBSERVERS: HSPH: Numbered 106.
REFER TO: CM of 10/6/1847; Loomis.

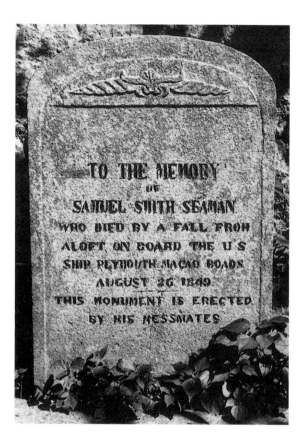

148. ARTHUR HAMILTON McCALLY *American*

NO DETAIL HAS come to hand about McCally's nationality or trade. The nationality given is a guess, for the sole reason that his headstone is so much like those of 1, 3, 5, 45 to 49, 125 and 147, all known to refer to Americans. In the Dutch cemetery at Chinsurah in India is a memorial to one L.C. McCally, who died on 8 April 1838 at the age of 29, erected by his friends in Assam: there is, however, no evidence of any relationship.

His medium-grained, polished, off-white granite headstone stands half a metre to the north of 147, its rough-hewn back against the east wall, its top a semi-elliptical arch giving a total height of 157 cm to the stone, its width 81 cm and thickness

18 cm. The inscription surface is recessed and rectangular, below a floral design in high relief on the arched part. The stone stands on a moulded plinth 94 x 27 cm, its podium now underground. The lettering has lost its definition.

OTHER OBSERVERS: HSPH: ARTHUR HAMILTON CALLY, Numbered 107.
REFER TO: Bengal P&P xvi p 207.

SACRED
to the memory
of
ARTHUR HAMILTON M^CCALLY
who died at Macao
after a painful and
lingering Illness
SEPTEMBER 25th 1835

AGED 27 YEARS
Inscription

---

149.   JANE HOWARD   *British*

THE NAME OF Thomas Howard, mariner, is in the lists of European residents of Calcutta kept by the Company from 1817 for eight years or so. If Jane was his wife, he was probably the master of one of the Company's country ships and his wife accompanied him when he paid his trading visits to China.

Of Jane Howard no record has been found. In the Colonial Cemetery at Hong Kong a Sarah Howard lies buried, but there is no evidence of any relationship.

A metre or so north of 148 and about three metres out from the wall, this is another low, rectangular headstone. A slab of fine-grained, polished, off-white granite, rough-hewn at the back, it is 89 cm wide, 84 cm high and 15 cm thick, supported by neither step nor base, and devoid of ornamentation.

On its west face is inlaid a rectangular, Belgian black marble plaque 64 x 46 cm, on which an experienced mason in the Calcutta firm of Simpson and Llewelyn has cut the inscription, in V-grooved lettering

OTHER OBSERVERS: HSPH: Numbered 108.

SACRED
To the Memory of
JANE HOWARD
The Wife of
CAPTAIN THOMAS HOWARD
Who died at MACAO
23rd February 1823
Aged 22 Years.

Simpson and Llewelyn Sri Calcutta

150.   MARGARET HUTCHISON YOUNG   *British*

THE YOUNGEST daughter of Andrew Hutchison of Sytherum in Fifeshire, Margaret was married to Dr James H. Young by the Rev Vincent J. Stanton, the first colonial chaplain of Hong Kong (see Chapter 3 page 24) on 25 November 1847 at the new Colonial Chapel in Hong Kong. No information of the purpose of her being in either Hong Kong or Macao nor of the circumstances of her death has been found. It seems likely that she was visiting Macao to recover her health. Her husband had arrived in Hong Kong in 1846, and conducted a medical practice there for three or four years.

At the same time, a Dr Peter Young was practising in Macao as a physician (see 146), and he was a witness at their wedding. Nothing has come to light to establish any relationship between the two Scottish doctors Young, however.

After Margaret died, the widower joined a Presbyterian mission and took up work at Canton; he moved in 1851 to Amoy, where he remarried, and after his second wife's death and his own illness in 1854, he returned to England and died early the following year.

Margaret's chest-tomb lies some distance from the east wall of the cemetery and level with 141, 142 and 143. It is of a medium-grained, polished light-grey granite. Its podium supports a moulded plinth 249 cm long and 155 cm wide rising 25 cm to 193 x 102 cm; on the plinth rest the sides and ends of the box, which meet in rounded corners and carry rectangular tablets devoid of lettering. The

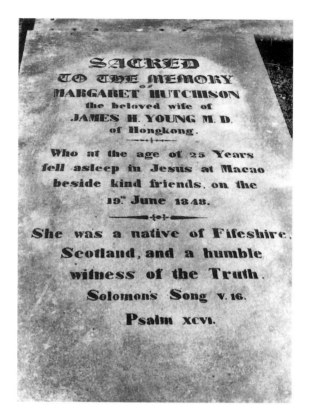

table-top has a bed-mould and carries the inscription, in a good state of preservation.

OTHER OBSERVERS: HSPH: MARGARET HUTCHSON YOUNG, Numbered 109.
REFER TO: FC&HKG of 1/12/1847; Wylie; Monroe lxxxvi p 19; CM of 29/9 and 22/12/1853.

151.   GEORGE CRUTTENDEN   *British*

THE NAME OF Cruttenden was well known at Calcutta during the latter half of the Company's operations, the earliest from 1753 with Edward Holden Cruttenden, who was a Director of the Company in London from 1765 to 1771. George was either his son or nephew. V.C.P. Hodson differs from the inscription in the year of birth (1767), and records his baptism in London as in January 1768. Since the minimum age for a cadet in the Company's service abroad was 15, he falsified his year of birth when he entered in April 1781, and later admitted it. He served in the Bengal Native Infantry, in which he reached the rank of brevet major before retiring from the Company in 1809. He was listed as a resident of Calcutta and partner in a trading firm until 1822, by when he had left India to trade from China. George Chinnery (40) painted a portrait of him in India in his major's uniform, no longer extant. He is commemorated on the southern wall of St John's Church in Calcutta (the 'Old Cathedral') by a sculpture carved in white marble by Sir Richard Westmacott, R.A. (1775–1856), a pupil of Canova and among England's most prolific monumental sculptors.

Standing back against the wall east of 150, this unusual monument is a cylindrical column supported by three large granite steps, above its top a circular cap with a closed urn. To the west side of the upper half is attached a rectangular, marble tablet with the inscription, well cut by Simpson and Llewelyn, the Calcutta monumental masons, in an effective but simple design. On the lowest

step are marks that show how the memorial was once surrounded by railings, with a gate in the middle of their west side.

OTHER OBSERVERS: HSPH: Numbered 110.
REFER TO: Bengal P&P xxv p 113; Hodson; EIR&D for 1815, 1817 and 1822; Phillips p 277; Conner pp 93 and 295fn17; Gunnis.

152.   CHARLES JOHN WHELER   *British*

THERE IS NO information of Charles Wheler beyond what is on his headstone, except that his middle name was John and his rank in the Bombay civil service was that of writer. He bears a name well known in the Company during the second half of the 18th century, in particular that of Edward Wheler, who was a Director for the 12 years from 1765, and the Company Chairman in 1773 and 1774. At a ball held at Calcutta in 1777 given in honour of his fashionable wife Harriet (née Chicheley Plowden – see 158 and 161), she had 'astounded all the ladies by the size of her hoop'.

Wheler's rude headstone stands at the north-west corner of the steps, on a level with 149, of very rough, coarse-grained granite without visible base or plinth. Rough-hewn at its back, it is 69 cm wide, 11 cm thick and 109 cm high at the centre of its arched top. Above the top line of the inscription there may once have been a design, but only one or two lines can now be discerned, too regular to be due to weathering. It is very difficult to read.

OTHER OBSERVERS: HSPH: Numbered 111.
REFER TO: EIR&D for 1824; Bengal P&P viii p 160.

153.   ISABELLA ANNE TEMPLETON   *British*

LITTLE INFORMATION has been found of Isabella other than what is in the inscription. A press notice gives a different age at death, which occurred at William Jardine's house, only four days after her arrival from England. Captain John Templeton, her husband, was probably then employed by Jardine as master of one of his ships. He was listed as an independent merchant in 1826 and 1829, among the foreign residents at Canton. Since his name is among those inscribed on a piece of plate presented to William Jardine in 1835, he may once have been in the service of the Company. In 1836 his firm of merchants and agents, John Templeton & Co of Canton, appears as agent for Lloyds.

Isabella's chest-tomb, lying east-west and with its west end in line with 152, follows much the usual design of podium, moulded plinth and box with vertical sides and ends with rectangular tablets in relief, except that the tablets have right-angled corners. The top mouldings of the box carry a table-top, on which three granite steps, cut from one block, support a closed urn with fluted bowl. The inscriptions have irregular spacings and show

Inscription on south side

weathering surfaces, but are easy to read. 'Mathew' is misspelt.

OTHER OBSERVERS: HSPH: Numbered 112.
REFER TO: Canton R of 15/11/1833 and 1/12 and 4/8/1835; Morse iv pp 128 and 187; ACK for 1836.

WHO ON THE 29TH JULY 1835, DEPARTED THIS LIFE
IN THE FERVENT HOPE OF A HAPPY RESURRECTION.
AGED 24 YEARS.
WATCH THEREFORE FOR YE KNOW NEITHER THE DAY NOR THE
HOUR WHEREIN THE SON OF MAN COMETH — MATHEW...
Inscription on north side

BUTTIVANT SAILED from Portsmouth on 8 June 1813 as third officer in the *Phoenix*. There is no information about his transfer to the *Royal George*. It was on her seventh voyage to China in 1817 that the incident took place in which Frederick Wintle (155) was wounded, and on her ninth that Buttivant lost his life in the Macao Roads; she was consumed by fire on her 10th voyage. For her trips to the Far East she was chartered by the Company from her owner, John F. Timmins. The Company had more than one ship in its service bearing this name.

To the north and in line with 153, head to the east, stands Buttivant's discoloured, coarse-grained, granite chest-tomb; the box on its podium and plinth has sides and ends that are not marked with design or lettering, and the inscription is cut on the table-top.

OTHER OBSERVERS: HSPH: Numbered 113.
REFER TO: EIR&D for 1815 and 1817; Morse iii p 95 and iv p 113.

To the Memory
OF
JOHN HENRY BUTTIVANT.
LATE
Chief Officer of H.C.S. Royal George.
THIS
Monument is erected by his
Commander and other Friends,
AS A
Testimony of his Worth
AND
THEIR REGRET.
He died in Macao Roads,
September 9th 1823,
Aged 30 years.

155. FREDERICK B. WINTLE *British*

THERE IS NO record of Lieutenant Wintle's service in the Royal Navy other than this reference to the cause of his death on board the Company's ship *Royal George* (see also 154). An attempt to carry his body to his grave provoked an incident which, had not Dr Morrison (141) intervened, could have been internationally serious. Wintle had died shortly after his ship put into Lintin during its seventh voyage in China; the next day his brother officers took his body to Macao 'for burial in the place set apart for dead Protestants', which at the time was on a hillside and for which formal permission was unnecessary. But in a few cases Company officials and their families were interred in the garden (now the Camoens Garden) attached to the Company's house (now the Camoens Museo), and the Governor gave permission for the burial to take place there instead. The incident, of which there is an account in Chapter 7 pages 60–1, occurred at the landing-stage outside the Chinese Customs House. Wintle's body was duly interred on the hillside set apart and in due course a headstone was placed over his grave. The stone was transferred from its hillside plot to the cemetery at some time after 1821, when it was first opened; and this would account for its being now without a plot and incorporated into the wall. The remains themselves are likely to be still in the hillside or among the spoil taken from it.

The Wintle headstone, set into the wall slightly north of 154, is of rough, coarse-grained granite and comprises two parts: the inscription rectangle, 135 cm high and 93 cm wide, topped by a segment, 100 cm wide and 28 cm high, bearing a

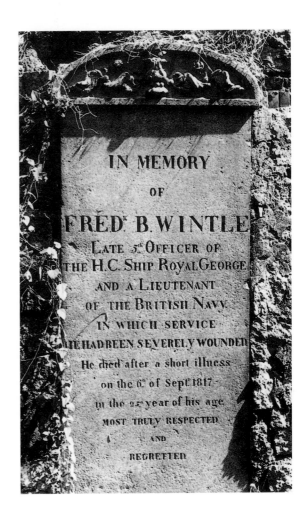

IN MEMORY
OF
FRED. B. WINTLE
LATE 5th OFFICER OF
THE H.C. SHIP ROYAL GEORGE
AND A LIEUTENANT
OF THE BRITISH NAVY
IN WHICH SERVICE
HE HAD BEEN SEVERELY WOUNDED
He died after a short illness
on the 6th of Sept. 1817
in the 25th year of his age
MOST TRULY RESPECTED
AND
REGRETTED

device in high relief. The inscription is cut in very clear letters, well spaced and well preserved.

OTHER OBSERVERS: HSPH: Numbered 114.
REFER TO: EIR&D for 1817; Morse iii p 317.

156.   [UNKNOWN]

THIS MEMORIAL, a miniature, granite chest-tomb, its long axis east-west near the wall just north of 154, is one of the cemetery's gems. A podium supports its plinth, which has a very wide moulding; on the vertical sides and ends of its box are moats, which surround raised, unadorned, rectangular, tablet surfaces; a substantial bed-mould supports an 8 cm-thick table-top. No sign or mark offers a clue to the identity of the deceased. Since it is in the part of the cemetery where the Company's members predominate, it was probably intended to mark the last resting place of a member of one of the Company families living in Macao.

OTHER OBSERVERS: Not listed by any.

157.   JAMES THOMAS ROBARTS   *British*

BORN ABOUT 1784, Robarts joined the Company in 1801. While still a junior member in 1806, he set up Baring & Co, a private commercial agency, in partnership with James Molony and George Baring, dealing in cotton and opium, and associated with Thomas Beale (159) and Charles Magniac, founder of the firm that became Jardine, Matheson & Co. By 1812, he was in the list of supercargoes with Molony, George Urmston (115) and William Fraser (62), his duties to 'copy the general books and weigh Teas'.

In 1816, he was one of three – with Molony and Magniac – appointed to look into the repayment of debts following Thomas Beale's (159) business failure. Between 1819 and 1821, he was in England for health reasons, and on his return to duty he continued up the Company ladder until he was second supercargo on its Select Committee, and by then so ill that he had soon to be invalided out of the service. He died on the day he was due to embark from Macao for England. Other observers have misread his surname as Roberts, and he is not to be confused with his contemporary in the Company, John William Roberts, who became its President in 1806, died in the Company house in 1813, and was buried in its garden (now the Camoens Garden).

A full-sized, granite chest-tomb, his memorial lies further along the wall in line with 156, head towards the east. A moulded plinth rests on its podium, the sides and ends of the box have raised tablet surfaces, and mouldings on the heavy tabletop, which has rounded sides and ends, surround an inscription with well-cut, nicely spaced lettering, reasonably easy to read.

TO THE MEMORY
OF
JAMES THOMAS ROBARTS ESQ.RE
MANY YEARS IN THE CIVIL SERVICE
OF
THE HONOURABLE
EAST INDIA COMPANY.
AT CANTON,
IN THE EMPIRE OF CHINA
WHO DIED AT MACAO
JANUARY 28TH 1825.
IN THE 41ST YEAR OF HIS AGE

OTHER OBSERVERS: PCL, HSPH, and JMB: JAMES THOMAS ROBERTS: HSPH: Numbered 115.
REFER TO: EIR&D for 1817; Morse iii pp 177 and 249 and iv pp 52 and 88; Molony.

158.   R. CHICHELEY PLOWDEN   *British*

THE CHICHELEY PLOWDENS were family members of the Company, and though the name was seldom absent from the Company's active list during the last century of its operations, no certain information is to hand about the Chicheley Plowden of the Bengal civil service who is buried here, nor about his status on the *General Kyd* at the time he died in the Macao Roads. One authority has it that he was a son of W.H. Chicheley Plowden and his wife Catherine (161): but it is inconceivable that they had a son in 1804. James Molony, who in 1819 married Catherine's sister, gives the impression that they were not married before 1817 or 1818, recording that for years neither sister showed any sign of bearing children. A Richard Chicheley Plowden was in India with Edward Wheler (see 152) as a writer in the Company's service from 1777, and he was a Director in London from 1803 almost until his death in 1830. None of his four sons bore a name starting with the initial R.

Plowden's coarse-grained, granite chest-tomb is plain in design. No podium can be seen; a simple moulded plinth supports the box, on the vertical sides and ends of which are carved rectangular tablets with incised corners, devoid of design and lettering. The table-top is 8 cm thick, rests on a substantial bed-mould, and carries the inscription, neatly cut and well preserved. The 'lay' is a grammatical error, and the 'interr'd' of its final line was first cut as 'entered' and the error then corrected.

OTHER OBSERVERS: HSPH: Numbered 116.
REFER TO: Molony; Bengal P&P xxvi p 152 and xxviii p 216; EIR&D for 1814; Braga Jack.

THOMAS BEALE *British*

SACRED TO THE MEMORY
OF
THOMAS BEALE

THOMAS WAS the uncle of Daniel junior (160), brother of his father, Daniel senior. Much confusion attends the record of the lives and activities of the brothers and their sons in China. Not only do news reports of the time often fail to give a Christian name or initials, but Thomas senior had a son Thomas Chaye, so that even where a report does give a Christian name, it is not always clear which one of the two fathers or which of the two sons is the subject. The two cousins were also friends and business associates.

Thomas is first found among the five unofficial foreign residents at Canton in 1796, then secretary to his elder brother, who was the Prussian Consul. Thomas himself succeeded as Prussian Consul, from 1798 to at least 1814; Charles Magniac (see 105) was his Vice-Consul from 1802, and both were partners in the firm Beale Magniac & Co, commercial agents with Indian interests. Their main business appears to have been the import of opium and cotton and the export of tea. 'Mr Beale resided constantly at Macao and Mr Magniac ... conducted their business at Canton; a great deal of the Indian Agency was however conducted by Parsees.' The Prussian consulship eventually devolved upon Jardine, Matheson & Co through Magniac, that firm's founder.

The Prussian consular flag afforded a measure of protection, but not enough to shield Thomas Beale from the ruin following his tangled, large-scale speculations. He offered opium futures as security for huge loans in a falling market; invested over a million dollars in shaky and illicit dealings with Brazil, in collusion with 'a man of the most rapacious unprincipled character', a corrupt Judge of Macao who was also its Customs Master and Public Treasurer, and who double-crossed him and then died. Beale failed to extract payments from the other major debtors, was declared insolvent in 1816, and appeared little in the public eye until January 1841, when his body was discovered in a shallow grave above the water-mark on the shore of Casilha Bay. The cause of death, though not established, was generally assumed to have been suicide.

His remains were buried alongside those of his nephew Daniel, and the Rev E.C. Bridgman conducted the service, which was attended by many of the English and Portuguese community. The committee appointed to wind up his estate comprised James Molony, J.T. Robarts (157), and Charles Magniac.

Beale's largest claims to local fame were his garden, 'literally filled with plants and trees of the rarest kinds', and his aviary, 'filled with the most choice collection of birds', including a rare male Bird of Paradise. The collection was supported by portfolios of 'beautiful and correct drawings by Chinese artists, from nature, of birds, fish, plants, &c. indigenous to China and the eastern islands'.

His chest-tomb is very similar to 158 in design and dimensions, and differs only in that the inscription is cut lengthways on the table-top, and not across it. The one other memorial with an inscription cut in this way is 44.

OTHER OBSERVERS: HSPH:: Numbered 117.
REFER TO: Molony; Morse ii pp 285, 311, 322, 366 and 390, iii pp 81, 176, 208, and 239 and iv pp 128 and 189; Canton R of 18/12/1841 and 18/1/1842; Canton P of 25/12/1841 and 15/1/1842; Loines p 114; Downing i p 38; Monroe lxxxvi pp 25–6; Bennett.

160.   DANIEL BEALE   *British*

Inscription on south side

**BENEATH
THIS SARCOPHAGUS ARE
DEPOSITED
THE REMAINS OF
DANIEL BEALE ESQR.**

Inscription on north side

DANIEL BEALE junior was the son of Daniel senior and nephew of Thomas Beale (159). His name and that of his cousin Thomas Chaye first appear in the Company records in 1826, as members of the firm of Magniac & Co. His father was in the Company service until he became one of the only two independent merchants at Canton, and by 1787 had also, as a trading protection, secured appointment as the Prussian Consul.

By 1796 Daniel senior's younger brother Thomas (159) had joined him as secretary, and was himself appointed Consul in 1798, when Daniel senior seems to have left China. Daniel senior died in 1842 at the advanced age of 84, far outlasting both his son and his brother.

Daniel junior's white marble memorial is the only sarcophagus in the cemetery, and the only memorial still surrounded by iron railings. The podium supports a plinth, on which rests the main bulk of the sarcophagus. Its corners are fluted columns, and at the ends and sides between them are tablets, the north and south sides bearing the two inscriptions. The pyramidal top rests on a 5 cm-thick table and has an upward-projecting wing at each corner.

OTHER OBSERVERS: HSPH: Numbered 118.
REFER TO: Morse ii pp 150, 175, 187, 285 and 390 and iv pp 109 and 128; Canton R of 14/4/1835, 9/8/1836 and 23/6/1842.

The tombs of 161 and 160

161.   CATHERINE PLOWDEN   *British*

Inscription
SACRED
TO THE MEMORY OF
CATHERINE
THE WIFE OF W.H.C. PLOWDEN ESQ[R].
SUPER-CARGO IN THE SERVICE OF
THE HON[BLE]. EAST INDIA COMPANY
IN CHINA.
AFTER MANY YEARS PASSED AT MACAO,
RESPECTED AND LOVED BY ALL
FOR HER INESTIMABLE WORTH,
SHE DEPARTED THIS LIFE
ON THE 18TH. OF JANUARY 1827
AGED 35 YEARS.
THIS MARBLE
IS PLACED OVER HER REMAINS
BY HER DISCONSOLATE HUSBAND
AS A LAST AND SAD TRIBUTE TO THE MEMORY
OF A WIFE DEEPLY LAMENTED AND
MOST AFFECTIONATELY BELOVED.

CATHERINE (née Harding) was the eldest daughter in a family of 12 children. The third daughter married James Molony, also of the Company, and the two sisters shared a house in Macao for a short period after they were married. It was they who offered to take care of Rebecca Morrison when her mother (142) died in 1821: when the Molonys left China for England the next year, they took Rebecca with them. Catherine married William Henry Chicheley Plowden in England, some time between 1816 and August 1818, when she returned to China with him after sick leave.

Her husband was born at Calcutta in 1787, one of the sons of Richard Chicheley Plowden, a Company factor who sailed to India in 1777 with his sister Harriet and her husband Edward Wheler (see 152) and was later a Director in London. William entered the Company's service in 1804, and left England direct for China in the *Neptune*, arriving at Canton in January 1807. On his way back to England in 1816 during a sea voyage for health reasons, he had an interview with Napoleon on the island of St Helena, as did many English tourists of the time. As he ascended the rungs of the Company ladder, Catherine must have expected him to become its chief, but she was already dead when he did succeed Sir William Fraser (62) in December 1827. The cause of her death is not known, but it may have been in connection with the birth of their daughter six weeks previously.

Chicheley Plowden held the highest Company

post in China until he returned to England in February 1830 after a particularly difficult time, in which he found himself at variance with the other members of the Select Committee over the ban imposed on British ships going upriver to Whampoa. His view proved to be correct and their's wrong, and the Court of Directors in London removed them, but not before he had already left China. In August 1832 he returned, again in the office of President, leaving finally in 1834, to attend to circumstances that 'urgently require his presence in England', and handing over to John Francis Davis, a future Governor of Hong Kong (1844–8). When the Company closed its operations in China that year, Lord Napier (164) was despatched to China as Superintendent of British Trade, with Davis as his second superintendent and, when Napier died, Davis followed him in the office. Had Chicheley Plowden remained a little

longer, he himself would have occupied it. He died at 93 in 1880, after 53 years as a widower.

Catherine's marble chest-tomb lies close up against the granite base that carries the north railings of 160, its long axis east-west, head to the east. On the podium, a marble pedestal moulded in its upper aspects supports the box, the vertical sides and ends of which are so carved that the one stone forms four steps in ascending relief leading to a central tablet. A moulding on the top of these sides and ends expands to carry an 8 cm-thick table, where the inscription is cut.

OTHER OBSERVERS: HSPH: Numbered 119.
REFER TO: Clark; Morrison ii p 103; Bengal P&P xxvi p 152, xxviii p 216, and xxx pp 83, 90, and 98; EIR&D for 1814, 1817, 1822, and 1823; Morse iii pp 30, 229, and 343 and iv pp 126, 144, 242, 324, 342, and 367–8.

---

162. JAMES CANNING *British*

HERE LIES
THE BODY OF JAMES CANNING
LATE STEWARD TO THE BRITISH FACTORY
Ob: 28ᵗ April 1832
Aged 48 years.

JAMES CANNING appears in the staff list of the Company at Canton in 1827 as 'butler', and in 1828 and 1829 as 'steward' drawing a small extra allowance as Clerk to the Chapel. Appointment as steward to the British factory would almost certainly be made from among the stewards serving on board the Company's ships.

William Hunter offers the following portrait of 'Jeems' Canning when in attentive action at a large dinner party in the factory, assisted by Apong, 'a

Chinaman known as Bacchus', whose sole duty was to pour out the wine:

CANNING:
Not the great George. he rules at home the State.
Oh no! 'tis Jeems, whose duty 'tis to wait,
And from behind the Tai-Pan's chair,
With napkin wand, with hand and eye
Directs celestial flunkeys with demon-iac air!

APONG:
While corkscrew Bacchus, son of Han,
In joss-like silence walks the table round,
Nor asks each guest, 'Spose can, no can?'
But armed with bottle, swift as eagle's glance
He sees — and fills each empty glass.

The most northerly in the group and the last in the cemetery (except for those re-sited in the 1970s from the New Protestant Cemetery), the steward's coarse-grained, granite chest-tomb is much the same as the others — with podium and moulded plinth, a box with vertical sides and ends carrying rectangular tablets with concave corners carved in relief about 1.3 cm high, and a bed-mould supporting an 8-cm-thick table-top. The inscription is on the north-side tablet, deeply cut and well preserved.

OTHER OBSERVERS: HSPH: JAMES CAWNING, Numbered 120.
REFER TO: Morse iv pp 146 and 187; Hunter p 230.

---

163. THOMAS T. FORBES *American*

BORN IN 1803, Thomas Forbes became a close companion of his brother Robert Bennet Forbes, 18 months younger, who worshipped Thomas as a hero. Their father was Ralph Bennet Forbes; their mother, Margaret (née Perkins), the sister of James and Thomas H. Perkins, who had built up a prosperous Far East trade. When only in their mid-teens, the brothers used a large gift of cash as 'adventure money' to invest in the export of silks from China. A canny businessman, Robert was known to the Chinese as 'Old Foxy'. Thomas succeeded as head of Perkins & Co of Canton, the business in opium and other goods opened by his uncles, and was US consul there when he died.

He met his end in violent weather. Against all advice, he had set out from Macao aboard his yacht the *Haidee*, with Samuel Monson (56) and others, in an unsuccessful attempt to reach Lintin Island to pick up the mail. Returning during a typhoon, they were swept overboard and drowned off Macao; his remains were recovered and interred four days later, the day before Monson's. He is recorded in the burial records at London as having been buried in the cemetery by 'George Vachell, the Company's chaplain' on 13 August 1829.

On a visit to Macao, Robert wrote to their mother from there in January 1837, describing the tragedy, the cemetery, and Thomas' grave. The letter was published in his *Reminiscences* (1876), in which he confirmed that Thomas' remains had been moved and laid to rest in the family vault at Forest Hills, the cemetery near Boston, Mass., a fact also confirmed in a letter from Harriet Low when in Manila, to her sister in Brooklyn, written some five weeks after Forbes' death, in which she set out the names of the victims.

Other than the space of 2.4 metres between 53 and 56, the rest of the memorials along the wall in the north section (51, 53, 56, 58 and 59) form so compact a row, their podia almost touching, that the space is most unlikely to have been a vacant lot, and must have been the site of the temporary burial

of Thomas Forbes, next to his friend Monson.

The following inscription is cut on the west of an obelisk that marks the family vault, where his remains were re-interred on the 16th December 1853:

THOMAS T. FORBES
Born April 11, 1803, Died Aug 9, 1829

OTHER OBSERVERS: Not recorded by other observers.
REFER TO: Burial R 11.218; Forbes pp 81, 88 and 128–30; Morse iv p 188; Loines pp 339–40 and 343; Lothrop; Forest Hills.

| 164. | NAPIER, WILLIAM JOHN | *British* |

9th Baron Napier of Merchistoun

LORD NAPIER, the first Superintendent of British Trade in China following the lapse of the Company's monopoly in 1833, died at Macao in the morning of Saturday, 11 October 1834. He had expressed the wish that his grave should adjoin that of his friend, the late Dr Morrison, and was accordingly laid to rest in the Old Cemetery.

The tombs of Morrison (141), buried in 1834, and his wife Mary (142), buried in 1821, are only 30 cm apart. In 1834, the only lots nearby and vacant were those to the east and the west of the Morrison graves; Napier's lot can only have been one of these. The east lot is now occupied by Eliza Wedderburn, buried in 1838 (145), and the west by the Speers, mother and child buried in 1847 (140). There was one other unoccupied lot left in

the immediate neighbourhood at the time of his death, and that was assigned for the burial of John Robert Morrison in 1843 (143). It is not certain that his wish was put into effect nor, if it was, whether his first resting place was later taken either by 143 or by 140, or was elsewhere and not even close to Morrison's.

Two memorials to him exist. One is with his family in the Ettrick church in Scotland, a marble tablet let into the wall of its graveyard; the other is a marble column, bought by public subscription raised in Canton and Macao in the year of his death, now in the Colonial Cemetery at Hong Kong. The inscription in Ettrick deepens the uncertainties, for it states not only that his remains are there, but that 'it was his desire that wherever he might die he should be buried here'.

At sea from 1803, his service in the navy included action in the Battle of Trafalgar, in several engagements of which he was wounded or taken prisoner, and was finally promoted to post-captain. When peace came in 1815, he retired from the service at the age of 29, and 'set a stout heart to a steep brae ... to cultivate the rural arts of peace', devoting himself to his father's estates to such effect that in 1818 he was elected Fellow of the Royal Society of Edinburgh for his work in agriculture. He succeeded to the peerage in 1823, and briefly represented the Scottish peers in the House of Lords. The next year he renewed his active service in the navy, and returned home finally in 1826.

Napier's appointment to China at the end of 1833 was based in Palmerston's mistaken conviction that the Chinese would be pleased to co-operate with a man of hereditary rank, one who might be seen to be a direct representative of the Crown. The Chinese were to misunderstand the prime minister's choice of a naval officer. However highly placed in his own country, no foreigner would be accepted as the equal of mandarins unless he came bearing tribute to the Emperor; and officers of the forces were treated in China as markedly inferior to mandarins – 'the Celestial Empire appoints officers: civil ones to rule the people, military ones to intimidate the wicked. The petty affairs of commerce are to be directed by the merchants themselves; the officers having nothing to hear on the subject.' And that was that.

Among the appointments Napier made to the commission when he arrived in Macao were those of Dr Robert Morrison (141) as its Chinese secretary and interpreter and Dr T.R. Colledge (see 94, 95, 96) as its physician. To his chagrin, the ideograms given to him by the Chinese to denote his name, as transliterated into Cantonese speech, turned out to mean 'laboriously vile', and in official Mandarin communications he was called the 'barbarian eye'.

With the intention of presenting a letter to the Viceroy in the terms of his London brief, but too impatient to wait for the 'chops' which the Chinese authorities required before foreigners might move upriver, and despite prudent advice from his staff and the British merchants in Macao, he and his entourage moved to Canton near the end of July 1834, in the very middle of the prohibited season. The Viceroy had in the meantime despatched an official to prevent Napier from leaving Macao, but their ships had crossed, unnoticed, on the river. Since his letter was not even in the obligatory form of a petition, and there was no machinery for communicating with barbarian officials simply by letter, the Viceroy refused to receive it and put the case to Peking in a memorial. It was in the middle of this impasse that Morrison died.

Discussion with the British merchants revealed a stiffened resistance: to which the reply of the Chinese authorities was first to stop all British trade and imprison some of the Chinese Hong merchants for daring to permit Napier's journey to Canton, and then to forbid Chinese residents from having further dealings with the British, including working for them and selling them provisions. Napier sent for a protective naval reinforcement, further incensing the authorities. His unceasing but fruitless efforts to move ahead with his mission put his health under severe strain and, when he fell sick from sheer exhaustion, he shifted temporarily into the more comfortable, private quarters of James Innes (137) and reluctantly decided to return to Macao, from where he might be more successful in opening negotiations. Through the good offices of two of the Hong merchants, Dr Colledge obtained the Viceroy's agreement that Napier might leave Canton, after what Gideon Nye dismissively dubbed 'the Napier fizzle'. Even with this agreement, Chinese obduracy and an organized rancour brought unnecessary delays in the course of the short voyage. Napier's fever worsened so much while he was on board, that his strength gave out only a fortnight after reaching Macao and, as the press reported, he 'expired of a lingering illness brought on by the arduous performance of his duties at Canton, aggravated by the treatment he received from the Chinese government when on his passage, in a sick state, to Macao'.

His funeral procession to the Old Cemetery was of great length, preceded by a Portuguese guard of honour and the Macao judiciary. The coffin was carried by five British naval captains and the Governor of Macao, Captain Bernardo de Souza d'Andrea, and followed by full contingents of the army and the navy, and by British and Portuguese mourners. Almost the whole of Macao's population turned out to watch. The service was directed by the Rev G.H. Vachell, to be followed by a memorial service some two weeks later in the Company's former Chapel where Napier was accustomed to worship, conducted by Rev E.C. Bridgman, his American friend.

Lady Napier, who during his absence in Canton had been 'insulted in her own house by the petty and obtrusive annoyances of the Chinese officer', left Macao with her family on 10 December 1834. A contemporary wrote of Napier's burial 'in the Protestant burial ground, from whence his remains were disinterred to be taken to England on Lady Napier's return'. The interval before she left was too short, however, for engaging in negotiation and disinterment herself, and the process was com-

pleted by James Matheson in March 1835. Napier's body left for Scotland in the charge of Captain Dalrymple on board the Company's ship *Orwell*. Matheson sailed with the ship, reporting to William Jardine in a letter posted en route at Anjer, that 'His Lordship's remains repose on the poop under cover of green canvas, there being no room in the Tween Decks'.

A testimonial fund was opened for the erection of a memorial at Canton, with Fox, Rawson & Co of Canton as treasurer; of the $2,200 collected in Canton, Lintin, and Macao, $500 was to be spent on a monument, the rest 'in founding some be-nevolent and useful institution in China to be connected with the name of Napier'. James Matheson made arrangements for the monument to be designed and sculptured in England as soon as he arrived, and he reported to the widow from Macao in June 1839 that, though it had arrived, its erection (probably at Canton) was delayed, and it had been deposited temporarily in the Macao Chinese Custom House. Wells Williams stated in 1857 that 'the sculpture was received in China but never put up'. But that was not the end of it.

It was to be over a century later, in 1953, that a memorial column was found in Hong Kong by a ship's captain, while rooting about in an old marble-grinding shop, lying next in line to be pulverized for construction works: the column bore a long inscription in English, and proved to be Napier's. Its top was truncated, probably for a bust, which was missing. Bought from the finder by the

Government for $100, it was put into store to await the building of the new Hong Kong City Hall, where it might repose in a place of honour. A news report of the find suggested that the monument was probably erected in the old cemetery, under the wall of Canton. It has now found a place, however, in the Colonial Cemetery in Hong Kong, where it commemorates a life 'sacrificed to the zeal with which he endeavoured to discharge the arduous duties of the situation ... erected by the British community in China'.

OTHER OBSERVERS: Not recorded by other observers.
REFER TO: Canton R of 19/8, 20/9, 21 and 28/10, and 2 and 16/12/1834; FInd of 23/4 and 21/5/1835; FC&HKG of 1/8/1848; CM of 8/8/1950; Ch Rep xi p 27; CO 129/28 for December 1847 and March 1849, and 129/30 for August–December 1849; Blackwood's xvii; Williams ii, pp 465 and 481; Fairbank; Williamson; Napier.

165.   HENRY DAVIES MARGESSON   *British*

FOUNDER OF THE firm of Margesson & Co, which operated for many years in south China, Henry Margesson was a trading resident of long and senior standing in Macao. He was eldest of the five children of the Rev William Margesson, rector of Whetlington – not of Ockley, the place he now lies buried along with his wife. Another member of the firm is buried in the New Protestant Cemetery. Margesson died when the steamer *Hayomaro*, origi-nally constructed to be a blockade runner in the

American Civil War, struck a rock while speeding at 14 knots in a smooth sea near Yokohama, cap-sized with her bottom torn out, and sank in deep water in seven minutes. While passengers, Margesson among them, were being lowered over the side of the sinking vessel in a boat, one of its falls slipped through the davit block and the boat shot perpendicularly into the sea. The Europeans on board with Margesson were a Hungarian pianist sailing from Yokohama after a concert, a journalist of the *Hiogo News*, two Germans, and two of the survivors, the Count de Mouton from Manila and a Mr Cream; the Captain and the second engineer went down with the ship; eight Japanese passengers and some of the crew were drowned.

Margesson's memorial, the tablet on the wall left of the east window inside the chapel, is in form, size, and design the exact twin of 166 on the right of the east window, and both were executed for the old chapel by Gaffin & Co, monumental masons of London. Incised on white marble tablets 76 cm wide, 61 cm high

IN MEMORY
OF
HENRY DAVIES MARGESSON,
SON OF THE REVᴰ WILLIAM MARGESSON,
OF OCKLEY, SURREY,
BORN ON THE 1ˢᵀ OF SEPTEMBER 1823;
WHO WAS DROWNED
BY THE LOSS OF THE STEAMER "HAYOMARO"
NEAR YOKOHAMA, JAPAN, ON THE 17ᵀᴴ JUNE 1869,
AFTER A RESIDENCE OF 23 YEARS IN CHINA,
AND ON THE EVE OF HIS RETURN FOR EUROPE.

"AND THE SEA GAVE UP THE DEAD
WHICH WERE IN IT."   REV. XX. 13.

"I KNOW THAT HE SHALL RISE AGAIN, IN THE
RESURRECTION AT THE LAST DAY."   S. JOHN. XI. 24.

and 2 cm thick, they are both mounted on rectangular bases of black marble, 13 cm larger in width and height, so that the inscription tablets show black borders.

Each is surrounded by a frame locally made in moulded plaster. Of high-class workmanship, the lettering of the inscription is leaded, and each leaded letter preserved under black paint.

REFER TO: Collins; Gould; Times of 28/7 and 14/8/1869 (quoting the *Japan Times*).

---

166. JAMES BRIDGES ENDICOTT *American*

James Endicott's daughters 'Lily' (Fidelia) and Rosalie are buried in the graveyard attached to the chapel (33 and 34), as are many of his friends and his uncle, Captain Henry Bridges (108), from whose family he derived his middle name. Endicott was born in Danvers, Mass., and is a direct lineal descendant of John Endicott who left England in 1628 and became the founder and first governor of

the State of Massachusetts. James Endicott died of typhoid in 1870, after living for 35 years in Macao, Canton and Hong Kong, and lies buried in the Colonial Cemetery in Happy Valley, Hong Kong.

The other tablet inside the chapel, Endicott's memorial in Macao, is also set on the wall, but to the right of the east window, and is in size and design the twin of 165 to its left. Both were executed

† SACRED
TO THE MEMORY OF
JAMES B. ENDICOTT,
WHO RESIDED MANY YEARS IN THIS CITY.
HE WAS BORN AT
DANVERS, MASS: U.S.A., AUGUST 6TH 1814,
ARRIVING IN CHINA IN 1833, WHERE HE LIVED 35 YEARS,
AND DIED AFTER A SHORT ILLNESS, NOVEMBER 5TH 1870,
HE IS BURIED IN THE "HAPPY VALLEY" HONGKONG,
WHERE HIS DEATH OCCURRED.
TWO OF HIS CHILDREN, LILLY AND ROSALIE, ARE SLEEPING
IN THE CEMETERY ADJOINING THIS CHURCH.

HE WAS AN AFFECTIONATE FATHER,
A FAITHFUL HUSBAND AND WARMHEARTED FRIEND,
AND A GENEROUS HELPER OF ALL WHO LABOURED TO EXTEND
THE KINGDOM OF OUR LORD AND SAVIOUR JESUS CHRIST

GIVEN TO HOSPITALITY.
ROM. XII.13

by the same craftsmen in London, as was his memorial in the Hong Kong Colonial Cemetery at Happy Valley. The brief biblical quotation at the end of the inscription is from The Epistle to the Romans 12.13.

REFER TO: Gould.

James Endicott

10

The Stones in the Wall

TWENTY-THREE memorials are set into the wall dividing the upper terrace from the lower. All but one bear dates in the late 18th century and before the East India Company had acquired the grave-yard for burials and had ceased burying Company associates in the garden next door. Those here, numbered from 167 to 177 and from 179 to 189, were removed from their original resting places in the Meesenberg Hill beyond the walls of Catholic Macao, at a time when the hill was being levelled to provide fill for sea-front reclamation. Several others (41, 42, 43, 44, 58, 90 and 155) had already been removed from the hills to the Old Cemetery at the time the Company acquired it.

Though they are now set upright in the terrace wall, not all are headstones: some had been the table-tops of tombs. Samuel Proctor (189) was one, for instance, who had once lain beneath his stone ('Under this lieth the body'). It was long after the recordings of memorials in the Old Protestant Cemetery were completed that Lindsay and May Ride

discovered them, piled up unceremoniously in the New Protestant Cemetery. In 1971 they undertook to have them removed once again and more safely re-sited, for some future historian to investigate.

When arranging for their removal to the Old Cemetery, the Rides secured funds from the Trustees to have the retaining wall rebuilt, the lower terrace properly drained, and the stones set into place along the new wall. None of them was in place, therefore, when the various numberings and recordings were done; the records, including the Ride manuscripts, lack entries of any kind. In the following pages they bear the numbers given to them in 1985 by Monsignor Teixeira.

Teixeira's number 178 is the memorial of Sir Lindsay Ride. In order to accommodate his tablet in the place considered appropriate, the re-sited stone of Samuel Proctor, who had died in January 1792, was taken from the middle of the terrace wall and removed yet again, to a space far to the right which was vacant (now numbered 189).

167–174

167. ALEXANDER McNEILL   *British*
Date of death: 21 July 1777
Age at death: 40 years
Sex: Male
Previous number (New Protestant Cemetery): 163

168. J.A. BULLER   *British*
Date of death: 1773
Age at death: Adult
Sex: Male
Previous number (New Protestant Cemetery): A

169. ADOLPH FERDINAND MOURIER
Swedish
Date of death: 1776
Age at death: 10 months
Sex: Male
Previous number (New Protestant Cemetery): 165

170. AUGUSTA BARCLAY   *British*
Date of death: 30 September 1780
Age at death: 9 months
Sex: Female
Previous number (New Protestant Cemetery): B

171. WILHELM MEESEBERG   *German*
Date of death: 6 June 1767
Age at death: 35 years
Sex: Male
Previous number (New Protestant Cemetery): 167

172. J.D. SCHRODER   *Swedish*
Date of death: 6 June 1775
Age at death: Adult
Sex: Male
Previous number (New Protestant Cemetery): 168

176–179

173. EGBERT KARNEBECK   *Dutch*

Date of death: 21 July 1785

Age at death: 40 years

Sex: Male

Previous number (New Protestant Cemetery): 169

174. PIETER KINTSIUS   *Dutch*

Date of death: 25 June 1786

Age at death: 55 years

Sex: Male

Previous number (New Protestant Cemetery): 170

175. JOHN JORDAN   *British*

Date of death: 28 August 1786

Age at death: 20 years

Sex: Male

Previous number (New Protestant Cemetery): 171

176. DANIEL WALKER   *British*

Date of death: 27 June 1786

Age at death: 47 years

Sex: Male

Previous number (New Protestant Cemetery): 172

177. DANIEL REID   *American*

Date of death: 24 November 1797

Age at death: 34 years

Sex: Male

Previous number (New Protestant Cemetery): 179

178.   SIR LINDSAY TASMAN RIDE   *Australian*

In memory of
LINDSAY TASMAN RIDE
Knight, Scholar, Soldier, Musician, Sportsman
Benefactor and Friend
Born 10th October 1898 Victoria Australia
Died 17th October 1977 Hong Kong

*His ashes lie in this quiet garden he
did so much to make more beautiful
His eager invincible spirit lives in God.*

*One who never turned his back but
marched breast forward – Never
doubted clouds would break – Never
dreamed though right were worsted
wrong would triumph. Held we fall
to rise, are baffled to fight better,
Sleep to wake.*

O Melhor Guia do Futuro E O Passado
Inscription

SIR LINDSAY RIDE, CBE (mil), ED, MA, DM (Oxon), Hon LLD (London, Toronto and Hong Kong), Hon RAM, author with his wife May of the manuscripts from which this published edition of *An East India Company Cemetery* is derived, died of heart failure while in a coma, at the advanced age of 79 following a protracted and wasting illness, before they were able to complete a final version of the work.

A geneticist, he occupied the Chair of Physiology in the University of Hong Kong from the age of 30, after an education in Australia and, as a Rhodes Scholar, at New College, Oxford. His *Genetics and the Clinician* was published in 1939, but did not survive the air raids on London, in which the entire edition was destroyed. A member of the Hong Kong Volunteer Defence Force, of which in later years he became honorary colonel, he was taken prisoner in 1941 on the surrender of the colony to the Japanese. He escaped to seek refuge in Free China, where he organized the British Army Aid Group, with the single object of helping to pass through the Japanese-held territories in China, those who had escaped from the prisoner-of-war and internment camps in Hong Kong. Returning to his Chair after the war, he was appointed the University's fifth Vice-Chancellor in 1949 and, when he retired in 1964, was the longest-serving of its principals.

Prominent in Hong Kong musical life as a choral conductor, he made the Vice-Chancellor's Lodge a mecca for visiting musicians, as well as for scholars. This brought him election to the small band of honorary Royal Academicians of Music and, at the end of the University's golden year of celebrations, he was knighted in 1962 for his services to education and the arts.

As a Presbyterian and son and grandson of Presbyterian ministers, one of his chief interests lay in the lives and works of Protestant missionaries in the Far East. He published a monograph on Robert Morrison, and the biographical introduction to a 1970 reprint of James Legge's five-volume translation of *The Chinese Classics*. Macao was an abiding interest common to both himself and his wife, and it was this and his study of Morrison that led them to start together their survey of the Old Protestant Cemetery there. His wife May, née Witchell, was his second; she comes from an old, established Hong Kong family.

The Ride tablet, set into the wall of the lower terrace, is a very dark grey stone fom China. Rectangular with a gently arched top, its frame is of granite terrazzo, cast and polished on the site. It is some 114 cm high and 76 cm wide and, like some of its neighbours, is placed mid-height on the wall.

The texts of the inscription were from suggestions of two of his friends: the English quotation from Browning's *Asolando* (the 'Epilogue') was proposed by the Rev Cyril Clarke; Ride had himself heard and liked the final line in Portuguese once quoted by the Macao historian Monsignor Manuel Teixeira, SJ. The architect Dr S.E.T. Cusdin, another friend who was the Rides' architectural consultant when preparing the cemetery manuscripts, designed the tablet and the lettering of its inscription 'to comply with the highest tradition of the Trajan Column in Rome'. The Hong Kong contractor Fook Lee offered both the stone and his sculptor to cut it, 'as his contribution to Sir Lindsay'; Ho Sai-chiu, OBE, JP, another friend and later a member of the Legislative Council of Hong Kong, directed the work with the approval of the present Trustees of the church and graveyard, the Hongkong and Shanghai Bank.

REFER TO: Cusdin; obituaries, including Mellor.

269

184–188

179. WILLIAM HUBBART   *British*
Date of death: 29 March 1787
Age at death: 24 years
Sex: Male
Previous number (New Protestant Cemetery): 181

180. HOWARD   *British*
{first name unknown}
Date of death: 8 October 1810
Age at death: Adult
Sex: Male
Previous number (New Protestant Cemetery): 190

181. F.W. SCHNITGERS   *German*
Date of death: 30 May 1807
Age at death: 34 years
Sex: Male
Previous number (New Protestant Cemetery): 191

182. ANDREW WILHELM BOSMA   *Dutch*
Date of death: 15 January 1795
Age at death: 3 years
Sex: Male
Previous number (New Protestant Cemetery): 192

183. MARY LOUISE WADE   *British*
Date of death: 23 June 1858
Age at death: 10 months
Sex: Female
Previous number (New Protestant Cemetery): E

184. WILLIAM S. BRABAN   *British*
Date of death: 28 June 1862
Age at death: 29 years
Sex: Male
Previous number (New Protestant Cemetery): D

185. WILLIAM STUCKEY *British*

Date of death: 1861
Age at death: 19 years
Sex: Male
Previous number (New Protestant Cemetery): 201

186. THOMAS PORTER *British*

Date of death: 23 April 1864
Age at death: 22 years
Sex: Male
Previous number (New Protestant Cemetery): 217

187. EDWARD RUSSELL *British*

Date of death: 24 April 1861
Age at death: Adult
Sex: Male
Previous number (New Protestant Cemetery): G

188. THOMAS PENNINGTON *British*

Date of death: 1 January 1861
Age at death: Adult
Sex: Male
Previous number (New Protestant Cemetery): C

189. SAMUEL PROCTOR *American*

Date of death: 25 November 1797
Age at death: 34 years
Sex: Male
Previous number (New Protestant Cemetery): 180

Chronology

1557   The Portuguese settlement at Macao is permanently established.

1599   London merchants trading in the East Indies are granted a monopoly of English trade to the East by charter.

1602   The Dutch East India Company is established by charter.

1644   China's Ming rule is overthrown by the Manchus, heralding the advent of the Ta Ch'ing (or Manchu) Dynasty, which remains in power until Sun Yat-sen's revolutionary forces proclaim a Republic in 1912.

1700   Regular trading between Britain and China opens.

1709   The group of merchants operating the trading monopoly granted in 1599 becomes known as the English East India Company.

1720   The Chinese commissioner of customs in Canton (the Hoppo) appoints the Co-Hong, a group of Chinese merchants given the monopoly of the trade with foreigners.

1729   The first Dutch ships are allowed to trade from Canton. The Emperor Yung Cheng proscribes the import of opium into China.

1757   Foreign maritime trade is restricted to Canton, and remains so until 1842.

1760   All foreign trade is centralized in Canton.

1771   The Hoppo disbands his Canton Co-Hong.

1773   The English East India Company appoints a Select Committee of Supercargoes to control from Canton and Macao the monopoly of British trade with China.

1784   The British government appoints a Commission for the Affairs of India to assume control of the English East India Company's properties there. The first trading ship from the newly independent United States of America reaches Macao.

1793   Earl Macartney is sent on an embassy to Peking with the purpose of opening other ports on the China coast to British maritime commerce; but without success. The Hoppo revives his Co-Hong in Canton.

1800   Despite imperial prohibition, the illicit annual trade in opium mounts to 5,000 chests.

1807   Dr Robert Morrison, the first Protestant missionary to China, arrives in Macao, later to translate the Bible into Chinese, and to become author of the first Chinese-English dictionary.

1809   The English East India Company officially prohibits its officers from trading in opium.

1813   The British government reviews the East India Company's charter, redefines the status of its churches, forms a bishopric in India, and abolishes the Indian trade monopoly. Letters-patent for this.

1814   The East India Company is empowered to acquire and maintain church property out of its Indian revenue.

1816   Lord Amherst is sent as British ambassador to Peking, but is not received at court.

1820   The Company appoints its first resident chaplain for duty in Macao and Canton.

1821   Trading conditions at Canton are made intolerable by official arbitrariness and corruption and limits placed on movement, with all appeal to Peking denied. The contraband trade in Indian opium is moved from Canton and Macao to Lintin Island. The East India Company purchases a site for a Protestant graveyard in Macao.

1830   The East India Company purchases an adjoining site, with a building used thereafter as a mortuary chapel.

1834   The East India Company's monopoly of British trade with China is not renewed, removing one of the main means of commercial regulation in Canton. Its property in Macao reverts to the government in England. A temporary hiatus in trading follows the arrival in Macao of Lord Napier in July as the first superintendent of British trade in China. Napier dies in November and is succeeded by Captain Charles Elliot.

1836   Proposals in Peking to legalize the importing of opium, then amounting to about 30,000 chests annually, and worry lest the drain on *sycee* to pay for it should prove intolerable, create a policy vacuum until

1839   Lin Tse-hsü is despatched to Canton (3/10/1839) as Imperial Opium Commissioner, forces the surrender of opium stocks, and sets fire to them. Shows of foreign strength follow.

1840   The British occupy Chusan and the forts in the Canton River.

1841   Kishen (Ch'i-shan) settles terms with Captain Elliot at Chuenpi, repudiated by the British and the Chinese governments.

1841   War starts, the British occupy Chinkiang
−2   on the Grand Canal and several of the coastal

ports, and Elliot's successor, Sir Henry Pottinger, dictates the terms of the Treaty of Nanking (29/8/1842), which put an end to the Canton monopoly of the China trade, cede Hong Kong to Britain, and open up the Treaty Ports of Amoy, Canton, Foochow, Ningpo and Shanghai for foreign consular activity and international commerce.

1843   The treaty is widened so as to accord a favoured status to Britain and settle the detail of a new trading system (8/10/1843). There is no cease to the opium trade. The English East India Company's mortuary chapel in Macao starts functioning as a Protestant Church.

1844   Protestantism is tolerated. The prohibition against foreign study of Chinese is removed. Through the efforts of US ambassador Caleb Cushing, the Americans secure extraterritorial rights, later extended to other nations.

1846   Macao ceases to be ruled from Goa and assumes the status of a Portuguese colony, responsible direct to Lisbon.

1846   With the opposition in Canton to the
−9   appearance of foreigners in the streets, Anglo-Chinese hostility grows.

1849   Macao ceases its an annual tribute to Peking from customs revenue.

1850   Taxes upon farmers in China and the loss of
−64   crops through natural disasters bring unrest, and with it the Taiping Rebellion.

1854   Following the seizure of Shanghai by the rebels (7/9/1853), a foreign-controlled customs inspectorate is formed (12/7/1854). Commodore Matthew C. Perry leads an American expedition to Japan to settle a commercial-diplomatic treaty.

1856 An incident involving the lorcha *Arrow* inflates Anglo-Chinese hostilities at Canton.

1857 The Portuguese authorities decide that no further burials shall take place within the city's limits and the Protestant burial ground in Macao is formally closed.

1857 The Anglo-French expropriation of Canton
−8 and threats in the north compel the Chinese government to conclude Treaties of Tientsin (June) with Britain, France, America and Russia. Under their terms, trade and religious missions are permitted in the interior of China and legations in Peking; opium imports are legalized; a maritime customs service is formed under a foreign inspector-general; and 11 more ports are opened to foreign trade.

1858 Land is purchased for a New Protestant Cemetery outside the Macao city walls, the former site becomes known as the Old Protestant Cemetery. American traders are officially prohibited from trading in opium.

1859 British officials are refused a demand that foreign diplomats be admitted to Peking.

1860 As a result, a large force of British and French troops occupy the capital (12/10/1860), upon which the Chinese grant further concessions.

1862 China confirms the perpetuity of the Portuguese occupation of Macao.

1870 The Old Protestant Cemetery in Macao is transferred to the care of the New Cemetery trustees.

1887 Macao is seceded to Portugal (1/12/1887) and becomes a province.

1898 Britain secures a 99-year lease of the New Territories in Hong Kong and, with France, Germany, Russia and Japan, other concessions from China.

Sources

LISTINGS OF MEMORIALS
HSPH H.S.P. Hopkinson, 1939 (see below)
JMB J.M. Braga, 1940 (see below)
OL Official List
PCL Protestant Church List
MT M. Teixeira (1985) (see below)

PERIODICALS AND NEWSPAPERS
ACK Anglo-Chinese Kalendar (Canton)
AmJNB American Journal of National Biography
Bengal P&P Bengal Past and Present (Calcutta)
Bengal Obit The Bengal Obituary (Calcutta)
Blackwood's Blackwood's Edinburgh Magazine
Canton P The Canton Press
Canton R The Canton Register
CelEmp The Celestial Empire (Shanghai)
Ch Courier The Chinese Courier
Ch Rep The Chinese Repository (Canton)
China J The China Journal (Shanghai)
China R The China Register (Shanghai)
CM The China Mail (Hong Kong)
Dixson HKG Dixson's Hong Kong Gazette/Recorder
Dixson HKSL Dixson's Hong Kong Shipping List
Dundee D Dundee Directory
Dundee P&CA Dundee, Perth, and Cupar Advertiser
EIK/AR East India Kalendar; or Asiatic Register (London)
EIR&D East India Register and Directory (G.H. Brown and F. Clark)
EIR&AL East India Register and Army List
FC&HKG The Friend of China and Hong Kong Gazette (Hong Kong)
FInd The Friend of India (Serampore)
Genealy Mag The Genealogists' Magazine (London)
Gent Mag The Gentleman's Magazine and Historical Chronicle (London)
HKA&D The Hong Kong Advertiser and Directory
HKR The Hong Kong Register
Ind M The Indian Mail
JAS Journal of the Royal Asiatic Society (London)
JASHK Journal of the Hong Kong Branch, Royal Asiatic Society
NSWG New South Wales Gazette
PT Times The Peking and Tientsin Times
Salem G The Salem Gazette
SFP&MA The Singapore Free Press and Mercantile Advertiser
Sydney MH The Sydney Morning Herald
Times The Times (London)

OTHERS
Alexander C. Alexander: Register of Commissioned and Warrant Officers of the Navy of the United States including Officers of the Marine Corps (Washington, 1845, 1848)
Augur Helen Augur: Tall Ships to Cathay (Doubleday, New York 1951)

Bakker Yvonne Bakker of Soest, Holland, great-granddaughter of 114: Personal communication (1968)

Ball 1903 John Dyer Ball: Things Chinese (Shanghai 1903)

Ball 1905 John Dyer Ball: Macao: the Holy City: the gem of the orient earth (China Baptist Publication Society, Canton 1905)

Ballot H.W. Ballot: University College London 1826–1926 (University of London Press 1929)

Bapt R MSS Baptismal Records in the Guildhall Library, London

Bard Dr Solomon Bard: Traders of Hong Kong: some foreign merchant houses, 1841–1899 (UrbanCouncil, Hong Kong 1993)

Barnstable Epi Barnstable, Mass., Epitaphs 1683–1895 (New England Historic Genealogical Society, Boston USA)

Barnstable Marr Barnstable, Mass., Marriages 1638–1874 (New England Historic Genealogical Society, Boston USA)

Bateson Charles Bateson: The Convict Ships, 1787–1868 (Brown, Son, and Ferguson, Glasgow 1959)

Bennett George Bennett: Wanderings in New South Wales, Batavia, Pedir Coast, Singapore, and China, in 2 vols. (R. Bentley, London 1834)

Blake Clagette Blake: Charles Elliot, R.N., 1801–1875. A servant of Britain overseas (Cleaver Hume, London 1960)

Bonnant Dr George Bonnant: Personal communication (105)

Bovill E. Bovill: 'George Chinnery (1774–1852)' in Notes and Queries pp 268–9 (June 1954)

Braga J.M. Braga: Tombstones in the English Cemeteries at Macao (Macao Economic Services Department 1940)

Braga 1949 J.M. Braga: The Western Pioneers and their Discovery of Macao (Impresa Nacional, Macao 1949)

Braga Jack Jack Braga: Personal communication: Plowden family (158)

Braudel Fernand Braudel: Les jeux de l'échange (Librairie Armand Colin, Paris 1979)

Buckley C.B. Buckley: An Anecdotal History of Old Times in Singapore (Fraser and Neave, Singapore 1902)

Burgess Frederick Bevan Burgess: English Churchyard Memorials (Lutterworth, London 1963)

Burial R MSS Burial Records in the Guildhall Library, London

Burke 1976 Burke's Irish Family Records (London 1976)

Burke 1980 Burke's Peerage and Baronetage (London 1980)

Burt Nathaniel Burt: The Perennial Philadelphian: the anatomy of an American aristocracy (Little, Brown & Co, Boston and Toronto 1963)

Cator Dr Fritz Cator, former Netherlands Consul-General in Hong Kong: Personal communication (1958): international nature of the cemetery trusteeship

Chatterton Edward Keble Chatterton: The Old East Indiamen (John Lane, London 1933)

China M The China Mission Handbook (1896)

Clark Mrs Norman Clark: Personal communication: Plowden family (161)

Clodd Harold Parker Clodd: Malaya's First British Pioneer. The life of Francis Light (Luzac, London 1948)

CMH The China Mission Handbook (American Presbyterian Press, Shanghai 1896)

CO 129 (etc) Colonial Office Papers

Coates 1966 Austin Coates: Prelude to Hong Kong (Routledge and Kegan Paul, London 1966)

Coates 1978 Austin Coates: A Macao Narrative (Heinemann, Hong Kong 1978)

Collins Rev M.A.R. Collins: Personal communication: church records (165)

ConfM Conference of Missions, report (Liverpool 1860)

Conner Dr Patrick Conner: George Chinnery, 1774–1852: Artist of India and the China coast (Antique Collectors' Club, Woodbridge 1993)

COPR Colonial Office Personal Records

Cotton Julius James Cotton: 'George Chinnery, Artist, 1774–1852' from Bengal Past and Present xxxvii (reprint, Calcutta 1924)

Crawford 1914 Dirom Grey Crawford: A History of the Indian Medical Service, 1600–1913, in 2 vols. (W. Thacker, London 1914)

Crawford 1930 Dirom Grey Crawford: Roll of the Indian Medical Service, 1615–1930 (W. Thacker, London 1930)

Cree Michael Levien (ed): The Cree Journals (Webber and Bower, Exeter 1981)

Cunynghame Sir Arthur Augustus Thurlow Cunynghame: An Aide-de-Camp's Recollections of Service in China, in 2 vols. (Otley, London 1844)

Cusdin Dr S.E.T. Cusdin: Personal communication (1992): (178)

Cutler Carl C. Cutler: Greyhounds of the Sea (Halcyon House, New York 1930)

DAB Dictionary of American Biography

D'Aquino Gus d'Aquino: Personal communication: English East India Company land purchase in Macao

Davies Evan Davies: Memoir of the Rev. Samuel Dyer, Sixteen Years Missionary to the Chinese (J. Snow, London 1846)

Davis Professor S.G. Davis, University of Hong Kong: Personal communication: 'Canton marble' (140)

Dean Rev Dr William Dean: The China Mission... With Biographical Sketches (Sheldon & Co, New York 1859)

Dermigny Louis Dermigny: La Chine et l'Occident. Le commerce à Canton au XVIII siècle, 1719–1833, in 4 vols. (Paris 1964)

DNB Sir Stephen Leslie and Sir Sidney Lee: Dictionary of National Biography, in 63 vols (Smith, Elder, London 1885–1904)

Dodge Ernest Stanley Dodge: New England and the South Seas (Harvard University Press, Boston 1965)

Downing Charles Toogood Downing: The Fan-Qui in China, in 1836–7, 3 vols. in 1 (H. Colburn, London 1838)

Drake Professor F.S. Drake, University of Hong Kong: translations from Chinese (36, 141 and 143)

Drinker Henry S. Drinker: Personal communication (1964): and permission to quote from the MSS diary of Sandwith Drinker (39)

Dutch Archives Archives of the Dutch Factory in China (The Hague)

Eitel E.J. Eitel: Europe in China: the history of Hong Kong (Kelly and Walsh, Hong Kong 1895)

Eller Rear Admiral Eller, US Navy ret: Personal communications (1950s): Waldron's appointment to Hong Kong (75)

Ellis Sir Henry Ellis: Journal of the Proceedings of the Late Embassy to China (J. Murray, London 1817)

Endacott George Beer Endacott: A History of Hong Kong (OUP, London 1958)

Endacott George Beer Endacott and Dorothy E.

She: The Diocese of Hong Kong. A hundred years of church history 1849–1948 (Kelly & Walsh, Hong Kong 1949)

Fairbank John King Fairbank: Trade and Diplomacy on the China Coast. The opening of the treaty ports, 1842–1854, in 2 vols. (Harvard University Press, Cambridge, Mass. 1953)

Fielding K.J. Fielding: 'The settlement of Penang' in The Journal of the Malacca Branch of the Royal Asiatic Society i, p 37 (March 1955)

Fisher David Austin Fisher: St Michael's Church, Withington (Withington 1951)

Forbes Robert Bennet Forbes: Personal Reminiscences (Little, Brown & Co, Boston 1892)

Forest Hills Secretary, Forests Hills Cemetery, Boston, Mass., USA: Personal communication: access to and permission to use information from the files, on the Forbes brothers (163)

Frost John Frost: American Naval Biography (Butler, Philadelphia 1844)

Gallagher Louis Joseph Gallagher (tr): China in the Sixteenth Century: the journals of Matthew Ricci: 1583–1610 [Random House, New York 1953]

Galloway Rev John Galloway: Personal communication (1958): New Protestant Cemetery

Gannier Rev Keppel Gannier: 'Early days in Penang' in The Journal of the Malacca Branch of the Royal Asiatic Society i (1923)

Gould F.W. Gould, National Association of Monumental Masons, London: Personal communication (165, 166)

Green Professor A.W.T. Green of the University of Hong Kong: translations from the Latin (43 and 137)

Greenberg Michael Greenberg: British Trade and the Opening of China, 1800–1842 (Cambridge University Press, 1951)

Gregory Rear-Admiral G.D.A. Gregory, RN: Personal communication: Churchill (133)

Gunnis Rupert Gunnis: Dictionary of British Sculptors 1660–1851 (Odham's, London 1958)

Hardy Charles Hardy: A Register of Ships employed in the service of the Hon. the United East India Company. Revised, with considerable additions (Black, Parry, and Kingsbury, London 1811, 1835)

Hawks Francis L. Hawks: Narrative of the Expedition of an American Squadron to the China Seas and Japan (Appleton, New York 1856)

Hawks Wallach Francis L. Hawks: Narrative of the Expedition of an American Squadron to the China Seas and Japan, abridged and ed. by Sidney Wallach (as reissued by Macdonald, London 1954)

Heard The MSS Heard Papers in the Baker Library, Cambridge, Mass. USA

Hickey William Hickey (ed Peter Quennell): Memoirs of William Hickey (Hutchinson, London 1960)

HKBlBk Hong Kong Blue Book (Colonial Office papers, 129)

Hodson Major Vernon Charles Paget Hodson: List of the Officers of the Bengal Army, 1758–1834, in 4 parts (parts 1 and 2 Constable; parts 3 and 4 Phillimore; London 1927–47)

Hopkinson Captain H.S.P. Hopkinson, RN: 'Macao burials' in The Genealogists' Magazine viii no. 6, pp 325–30 (London, June 1939)

Hunter 1839 William C. Hunter: Journal of Occurrences at Canton (1839)

Hunter 1882 The Fan Kwae at Canton, before Treaty days, 1825–1844 (Kegan Paul, Trench, London 1882)

Hunter 1911 Bits of Old China (Kelly and Walsh, Shanghai 1911)

Hutcheon Robin Hutcheon: Chinnery, the Man and the Legend (South China Morning Post, Hong Kong 1975)

Ipland Dr J.H. Ipland (traced through Michael and Jacob Jebsen): Personal communication about his grandfather (20)

Keay John Keay: The Honourable Company. A history of the English East India Company (Harper Collins, London 1991)

Kinsman William A. Kinsman: Personal communication and family records at Newburyport, Mass., USA (112)

Kyshe James William Norton Kyshe: The History of the Laws and Courts of Hong Kong, in 2 vols. (Unwin, London 1898)

Leach Fayette Phelps Leach: Lawrence Leach of Salem, Massachusetts, and some of his Descendants, in 3 vols. (privately printed, USA 1924–6)

Lennox Captain W.C. Lennox: 'Journal of a voyage through the Straits of Malacca', in The Journal of the Singapore Branch of the Royal Asiatic Society vii (June 1881)

Liddell Mrs John Liddell: Personal communication

Ljungstedt Anders Ljungstedt: An Historical Sketch of the Portuguese Settlements in China (J. Monroe, Boston 1836)

Loines Elma Loines: The China Trade Post-bag of the Seth Low family of Salem and New York, 1829–1873 (Falmouth House, Manchester, Me., USA 1953)

Loomis Captain F. Kent Loomis, US Navy ret: Personal communications (3 to 7, 38, 64, 65, 68, 76, 77, 89 and 147)

Lothrop Francis Bacon Lothrop: Personal communications (1960): family detail (59 and 163)

Mackenzie Alexander Mackenzie: 'Introduction' to Ezra Hoyt Byington: The Puritan in England and New England (Robert Bros., Boston 1896)

Makepeace Walter Makepeace, etc (eds): One Hundred Years of Singapore, in 2 vols. (John Murray, London 1921)

Marriage R MSS Marriage Records in the Guild hall Library, London

MacLeod John MacLeod: Voyage of His Majesty's Ship Alceste, along the coast of Corea, to the island of Lew Chew (John Murray, London 1818)

Mellor Bernard Mellor: Obituaries in the South China Morning Post, Hong Kong, of 19/10/1977 and in the University of Hong Kong Gazette xxv no. 3 of 1/12/1977 (178)

Molony James Molony: MSS Memoirs (made available by the family)

Monroe Rebecca Kinsman Monroe: The Daily Life of Mrs Nathaniel Kinsman in China, 1846, and Letters of Rebecca Chase Kinsman (Essex Institute Historical Collections, USA)

Monroe Mary Mary Kinsman Monroe: Nathaniel Kinsman, Merchant of Salem, in the China Trade (Essex Institute Historical Collections, USA)

Montalto C.A. Montalto de Jesus: Historic Macao (Kelly and Walsh, Hong Kong 1902)

Morison Admiral Samuel Eliot Morison: The Maritime History of Massachusetts, 1783–1860 (Houghton, Miflin, Boston and New York 1921)

Morrison Eliza Morrison (comp): Memoirs of the Life and Labours of Robert Morrison; compiled by his widow, in 2 vols. (Longman, London 1839)

Morse Hosea Ballou Morse: The Chronicles of the

East India Company Trading to China 1635–1834, in 5 vols. (Clarendon Press, London 1926-9)

Napier Francis Nigel Napier, 14th Baron Napier and 5th Baron Ettrick: Personal communication: family records (164)

Neal David Augustus Neal: MSS Autobiography 1793–1860 (Baker Library, Cambridge, Mass., USA)

Nederlands Nederlands patriciaat [14e Jaargang]: (25, 99 and 106)

Neuchâtel Archives de l'Etat, Neuchâtel, Switzerland

Nye YH Dr Y.H. Nye of Macao: Personal communication: the Nye family

Nye Morning Gideon Nye: The Morning of my Life in China (Canton 1873)

Nye Peking Gideon Nye: Peking the Goal – the Sole Hope of Peace (Canton 1873)

Nye Friends Gideon Nye: MSS notes: 'Necrology – Deaths of my Contemporaries and Friends' (New Bedford Museum, USA)

Osselen J.R. Van Osselen of the Royal Inter-Ocean Lines, Hong Kong: translation from the Dutch (43)

Parkinson Cyril Northcote Parkinson: Trade in the Eastern Seas, 1793–1813 (Cambridge University Press 1937)

Peabody Peabody Museum Records, Salem, Mass., USA

Pearsall The National Maritime Museum at Greenwich, London: Personal communication

Pierce William Macbeth Pierce: Old Hancock County Families (Ellsworth, Me., USA 1933)

Philips Sir Cyril Henry Philips: The East India Company 1784–1834 (Manchester University Press 1961)

Planchet 1926 J.-M. Planchet (ed): Evariste Régis Huc: L'Empire Chinois, in 2 vols. (Peking 1926)

Planchet 1928 J.-M. Planchet: Le Cimitière et les Oeuvres Catholiques de Chala 1610–1927 (Peking 1928)

Poest A. van der Poest-Clement, National Archives, The Hague: Personal communication (1960): (45 and 99)

PT Times 1927 A British Resident in Peking: 'British memorials in Peking', supplement, Peking and Tientsin Times (15 August 1927)

RCoArchers History of the Royal Company of Archers (1875)

Redgrave Samuel Redgrave: A Dictionary of Artists of the English School (London, revised 1878)

Ride Lindsay Ride: Morrison, the Scholar and the Man (Hong Kong University Press 1957)

Rogers Rev Charles Rogers: Christian Heroes in the Army and Navy, 4th ed (Low, Marston, Searle, and Rivington, London 1889)

Ruschenberger William Samuel Waithman Ruschenberger: Narrative of a Voyage Round the World during the years 1835, 36, and 37: including a narrative of an Embassy to the sultan of Muscat and the king of Siam, in 2 vols. (R. Bentley, London 1838)

Salem VR Salem Vital Records (Salem, Mass., USA)

Scott Keith Stanley Malcolm Scott: Scott, 1118–1923: being a collection of 'Scott' pedigrees (Burke, London 1923)

Schoyer Preston Schoyer: Personal communication: Speer family (140)

Seth Hennessy Seth: Personal communication:

family records (8)

Shipping NSW archives office, Australia: Shipping Reports

Sleight Harry Dering Sleight: Sag Harbor in earlier days (privately published, Sag Harbor, NY, USA 1930)

Spencer Alfred Spencer (ed): Memoirs of William Hickey, (1749–1809), in 4 vols. (Hurst and Blackett, London 1913)

Stackpole Edouard A. Stackpole: The Sea-Hunters; the New England whalemen during two centuries, 1635–1835 (Lippincott, Philadelphia, Penna., USA 1953)

Staunton 1823 Sir George Thomas Staunton, Bt: Miscellaneous Notices Relating to China, and our Commercial Intercourse with that Country. Part the second (privately printed, Havant 1823)

Staunton 1833 Sir George Thomas Staunton, Bt: 'Penal laws of China' in the Chinese Repository ii, No. 3 (July 1833)

Stickney Lucy W. Stickney: The Kinsman Family. Genealogical record of the descendants of Robert Kinsman, of Ipswich, Mass. from 1634 to 1875 (Mudge, Boston, Mass., USA 1876)

Swift Swift: Barnstable Families (New England Historic Genealogical Society, Boston, Mass., USA 1888)

Tarbox George E. and Ruth Tarbox: Personal communications (1964): family records (76)

Taylor Fitch Waterman Taylor: The Flag-Ship; or, A Voyage Round the World, in the United States frigate Columbia, in 2 vols. (Appleton, New York, USA 1840)

Teixeira Monsignor Manuel Teixeira, SJ (translated in part from the Portuguese by Justina Wells): The Protestant Cemeteries of Macau (Serviços de Turismo de Macau 1985)

Thornton Captain Edward Thornton, RN: A Summary of the History of the East India Company (James Ridgway, London 1833)

US Navy Division of Naval History, Navy Department, Washington, DC: Personal communications: American service records; and (1994) Lieut.Cmdr. Richard Silveira, Chaplain, USN in Hong Kong

Waley Arthur David Waley: The Opium War through Chinese Eyes (Allen and Unwin, London 1958)

Wentworth John Wentworth: The Wentworth Genealogy: English and American, in 2 vols. (Mudge, Boston 1870)

Wilkinson Dr Paul B. Wilkinson: Personal communication: funding of the post-war restoration of the Protestant Chapel

Williams Samuel Wells Williams: The Middle Kingdom, in 2 vols. revised (C. Scribner's sons, New York, USA 1883)

Williamson Captain A.R. Williamson: Personal communications: 55, 57, 83, 104, property in China (120); and shipping (127), 164

Winstedt Sir Richard Olaf Winstedt: A History of Malaya (Marican, Singapore 1962)

Wood Winifred A. Wood: A Brief History of Hong Kong (South China Morning Post, Hong Kong 1940)

Woodberry G.R. and Mrs Charles D. Woodberry: Personal communications (1956): family records (19)

Wylie Alexander Wylie: Memorials of Protestant Missionaries to the Chinese (American Presbyterian Mission, Shanghai 1867)

Wylie Preface Alexander Wylie: Preface to Hymns (American Presbyterian Mission, Shanghai 1867)

List of names

Index

The memorial entries of Section II are printed in bold capital letters. Page references to selected illustrations are printed in italics.